MALATI AND MADHAVA

MALATI AND MADHAVA

OR

THE STOLEN MARRIAGE

A DRAMA,

TRANSLATED FROM THE ORIGINAL

SANSKRIT

H. H. WILSON.

GYAN

Published by

Gyan Publishing House
5, Ansari Road
Daryaganj, New Delhi-110002
Phone: 011-47034999, 9811692060
E-mail: books@gyanbooks.com

Distribution Network
gyanbooks.com
India, USA, Canada, UK, Australia, France

ISBN : 978-81-212-9508-6 (PB)
First Published, 1901

2nd Impression 2023

Printed at: Gyan Press, Delhi.

MALATI AND MADHAVA
Translator: H. H. WILSON

MALATI AND MADHAVA;

OR

THE STOLEN MARRIAGE.

A DRAMA,

TRANSLATED FROM THE ORIGINAL SANSKRIT.

BY

H. H. WILSON.

1901.

INTRODUCTOIN.

MALATI and MADHAVA; or, the loves of the Youth Madhava and the maiden Malati has been already introduced to the knowledge of European readers, as an outline of the plot and a translation of part of the fifth Act were published by Mr. Colebrook in his Essay on Sanskrit and Prakrit Prosody. The specimens then given were calculated to convey a favourable impression of the merits of the drama, which the perusal of the entire piece will probably confirm.

The story of "Malati and Madhava" is one of pure invention, and the piece belongs to the class of compositions termed Prakarana. It is referred to as an example of the class by all the works on Rhetoric, the oldest of which it consequently precedes. The history of the drama, however, or more correctly of its author, is attended with more certainty than most of the topics of the literary history of the Hindus.

By the introductions to "Malati and Madhava," and the other dramas of the same writer, the "Uttara-Rama-Charitra" and the "Vira-Charitra," we are made fully acquainted with his origin and family. It appears from these accounts that Bhavabhuti, also named Srikantha, or he in whose throat eloquence resides, was the son of a native of the South of India, a Brahman of Berar or Beder, and a member of the tribe of Brahmans who pretend to trace their descent from the sage Kasyapa, of whom it is said that some are still to be found in the vicinity of Condavir. The site of Bhavabhuti's birth-place is fully corroborated by the peculiar talent he displays in describing nature in her magnificience, a talent very unusual in Hindu bards, who delight to portray her minuter beauties, and one which he no doubt derived from his early familiarity with the eternal mountains and forests of Gondwana.

It appears, however, that the place of Bhavbhuti's nativity was not the scene of his literary triumphs and that these were attained under the patronage of the princes of Hindustan. The precision with which he delineates the topographical features of Ujjayini and its vicinity, leaves little doubt of his having spent some time at that city, for accuracy in this respect could have been obtained at any time in India only by actual observation. The "Bhoja-Pravandha" indeed, includes Bhavabhuti amongst the writers at the court of Bhoja at Dhar, but, as intimated elsewhere, this work can only be received as an authority for the priority of the writers described in it to the date of its own composition ; the grouping, whether as regards place or time, being altogether fanciful. A preferable authority, the text of the "Dasa-Rupaka," refers Bhavabhuti to some period anterior to Munja, predecessor of Bhoja, by its alluding clearly to Malati and Madhava, and from it therefore we gather that the play was composed before the eleventh century. How long anterior to that date we have also evidence to substantiate, and from the history of Cashmir we learn that Bhavabhuti flourished in the eighth century, being patronised by Yosovarman, the sovereign of Kanoj, who reigned about A. D. 720.

The date thus given to the compositions of Bhavabhuti is quite in harmony with their internal evidence. The manners are purely Hindu without any foreign admixture. The appearance of women of rank in public, and their exemption from any personal restraint in their own habitations, are very incompatible with the presence of Mohammedan rulers. The licensed existence of Bauddha ascetics, their access to the great, and their employment as teachers of science, are other peculiarities characteristic of an early date, whilst the worship of Siva in his terrific forms, and the prevalence of the practices of the Yoga, are indications of a similar tendency. The Linga worship of Siva, we know, was every where the predominant form of the Hindu faith when the Mohamedans first invaded India. With respect to the Yogins; by whom mystical rites were mostly cultivated, it may be observed that there are many reasons for giving them a remote date: the excavations at Elephanta and Ellora appear to be their work; the sect is now almost extinct in Hindustan; and the "Kasi-Khanda," a work probably of seven or eight centuries remote, states that the Yoga cannot be practised in the present age. Mysticism, in fact, gave way first to the philosophy of Sankara Acharya in the seventh or eighth century, and was finally expelled by the new doctrine of Bhakti, or faith, which was introduced by Ramanuja and the Vaishnavas in the eleventh century, and has since continued to be the ruling dogma of every sect of Hindus.

The style of "Malati and Madhava" may also be referred to the period at which we may conclude that it was written. It is free from the verbal quibbling and extravagance of combination which the compositions of the time of Bhoja offer, but it comes very near to them: although classical, it is highly laboured; although forcible, it is diffuse, and is not unfrequently obscure. It abounds in the most complicated prosody, and is cited by Mr. Colebrooke for a specimen of the measure called dandaka, or a verse of fifty-four syllables, and a stanza consequently containing two hundred and sixteen. The author is also fond of an unreasonable display of learning, and occasionally substitutes the phraseology of logic or metaphysics for the language of poetry and nature. At the same time, the beauties predominate over the defects, and the language of the drama is in general of extraordinary beauty and power. The blemishes of the composition have materially affected the translation; and while it is very probable that the obscurity of some passages has led to an inexact interpretation of their import, the prosaic prolixity of others has involved the necessity of considerable compression and occasional omissions. The latter, when of any importance, will be particularised as they occur.

"Malati and Madhava" divides with "Sakuntala" the honour of being still occasionally, although not very commonly read by the Pandits; copies of it, therefore, are not very scarce. That used for the present translation was transcribed from Mr. Colebrooke's, as being singularly free from errors. It had the advantage also of being illustrated by two excellent commentaries. The most copious of these is the work of Jagaddhara, the son of Ratnadhara, described as a learned teacher, the prince of Pandits and poets, and administrator of law; the other is by a royal hand, the Rajadhiraja Malanka. We have no further particulars of these commentators, except that the first is known to have been a Maithila Brahman, and not very ancient.

DRAMATIS PERSONÆ.

MEN.

Madhava.—The son of Devarata, studying at Padmavati in love with Malati.

Makaranda.—His friend, in love with Madayantika.

Kalahamsa.—Madhava's servant.

Aghoraghanta.—Priest of Chamunda, a terrific goddess.

A messenger.

WOMEN.

Malati.—The daughter of the Minister of State Bhurivasu, in love with Madhava.

Madayantika.—The sister of Nandana and friend of Malati, in love with Makaranda.

Kamandaki.—Priestess of Buddha, nurse of Malati, and preceptress of Madhava.

Kapala-Kundala.—Priestess of Chamunda.

Saudamini.—Disciple of Kamandaki, and possessor of magical powers.

Lavangika.—Foster-sister of Malati.

Mandarika.—Attendant of Kamandaki, beloved by Kalahamsa.

Buddharakshita
Avalokita } Disciples of Kamandaki.

Female Attendants.

PERSONS SPOKEN OF.

The Sovereign of Padmavati.

Nandana.—His favourite, the brother of Madayantika.

Bhurivasu.—His minister, the father of Malati.

Devarata.—The father of Madhava, and Minister at Kundinapura.

SCENE.—Ujjayini (Ougein), designated mos usually as *Padmavati*, and its vicinity

TIME.—A few days.

PRELUDE.

BENEDICTION.

MAY the trepidations of Vinayaka's countenance, attended by the cry of terror, long preserve you! those trepidations which at the dance of Sulapani proceeded from the entrance into his nostrils of the Lord of serpents with contracted hood, frightened at the cry of Kumara's peacocks, upon hearing the sound of the tabor struck by the delighted Nandi, and whence the regions were filled with the buzzing of bees flying away from his temples.

May the tresses interwoven with a circular garland of serpents for flowers, where the waters of the Mandakini are flowing over the lower chaplet of skulls worn in the crest, luminous with the light of the eye of the forehead, sparking like lightning, and of which the young moon is confounded with the point of the Ketaka flower, preserve thee!

Enter MANAGER.

Enough! what need of prolixity. (*Looking to the East.*) Ha! the celestial luminary, enlightening all the divisions of the world, is completely risen. I salute him. (*Bowing.*) Oh thou. the universal form, who art the vessel of all auspicious light, be propitious to me, and enable me to support the burthen of the drama; remove from me, Lord of the world, thus prostrate, every sin, and augment all that is favourable to success. (*Looking off the stage.*) Ho! Marisha! the auspicious preparations are complete; from all quarters persons of distinction have come to celebrate the festival of Kalapriyanatha, and I have been commanded by these wise and learned auditors to represent to them some new dramatic tale. How now! are the actors lazy?

Enter ACTOR.

Actor.—We are not informed, sir, of the kind of piece required by the audience.

Man.—Say, Marisha, what are those qualities which the virtuous, the wise, the venerable, the learned, and the Brahmans require in a drama?

Actor.—Profound exposition of the various passions, pleasing interchange of mutual affection, loftiness of character, delicate expression of desire, a surprising story, and elegant language.

Man.—Then I recollect one.

Actor.—What is it, sir?

Man.—There is in the South, and in the province of Vidarbha, a city named Padmanagara, where dwelt certain Brahmans of the family of Kasyapa, and followers of the Tittiri portion of the Vedas according to the teacher Charana; taking precedence at festivals, maintaining the five fires, observers of religious obligations, drinkers of the Soma juice, possessing names of note, and learned in the Vedas. These Brahmans constantly reverenced the study of holy writ, for the knowledge of truth; wealth, for the celebration of religious rites; wives, for the propagation of offspring; and life, for the practice of devotion.

Of this' family, the grandson of one whose well-selected name Bhatta-Gopala, and the son of the pure in famè Nilakantha, whose auspicious appellation was Bhavabhuti, surnamed Srikantha, and whose mother was Jatukarni, a poet familiar through friendship with actors, has given us a drama composed by him, replete with all qualities. To which indeed this sentence is applicable. "How little do they know who speak of us with censure! This entertainment is not for them. Possibly some one exists, or will exist, of similar tastes with myself; for time is boundless, and the world is wide;".

Again, what avails it to boast a knowledge of the Yoga, of the Sankhya, of the Upanishads, or of the Vedas? no benefit accrues from them in a dramatic composition, Fertility of imagination, melody of expression, and richness of meaning, are the indications of learning and of genius. Such a drama has been entrusted to us by the friendly and venerable Bhavabhuti, entitled Malati and Madhava, one written by himself. Let all the áctors, prepared to represent this with their best abilities in the presence of the divine Kalapriyanatha, appear before me in the parts I have assigned them.

Actor.—(*After a pause.*) Your orders shall be obeyed; but it is necessary to exhibit it with becoming decorations, and first, our chief actor in the costume of Kamandaki, an old female Saugata beggar, is to appear, together with Avalokita, one of her disciples, for whose character I am cast.

Man.—Very well; what more ?

Actor.—Then the semblance of Madhava, the hero of the fiction, and lover of Malati, is to be assumed; how is this to be effected ?

Man.—That is described after Makaranda and Kalahamsa enter.

Actor.—We are ready then to exhibit our performance in the presence of the assembly.

Man.—Very well; I take the character of Kamandaki.

Actor.—I am avalokita.

[*Exeunt.*

END OF THE PRELUDE.

MALATI AND MADHAVA.

ACT I.

SCENE I.—KAMANDAKI'S HOUSE.

Enter KAMANDAKI *and* AVALOKITA.

Kam.—Daughter, Avalokita.

Ava.—Mistress, your commands?

Kam.—I have a task in hand: connubial rites
Must join the amiable progeny
Of Bhurivasu and of Devarata,
Long cherished friends: fair Malati the maid,
And Madhava the youth. Auspicious signs
Forerun a happy fate, and even now
My throbbing eye-ball tells propitious destiny
Shall crown my schemes.

Ava.—In truth an anxious care
This business proves; and much it moves my wonder,

How it should happen, one in rank and power.
High raised, as Bhurivasu, should require,
To wed his child, the services of one
Arrayed in tattered weeds, whose humble food
Is the scant dole of charity, and whose thoughts
Disdain the obstacles that worldly troubles
Oppose to sanctity and final bliss.

Kam.—Thou errest, daughter. That the minister
Appoints me to such duty, is the fruit
Of his regard and confidence, and with prayers
And penances, and life, I am prepared
All that my friend ordains me to fulfil.
Recall you not, when from far distant realms
Assembling students crowded to our school
To gather science? Then, before my friend,
Saudamini and me, it was convened
By these two statesmen—at that time associate
In amity and study—that their children,
When ripe in years, in love should be united.
Hence Devarata, Vidarbha's king,
The pious councillor, sends from the capital,
Kundinapur, to study in our schools,
His son the blooming Madhava, a youth
Of more than common merit, to acquit
The troth erst plighted, thus by him recalled
To the remembrance of his ancient friend.

Ava.—But why this mystery? Why should not wed
The youth and maiden as their state bocomes
them?
And why to you their stolen loves entrusted

Kam.—The favourite of the sovereign, Nandana,
Sues him for Malati, The king demands
The maiden of her father. To evade
His anger if the suit should be rejected,
Is this ingenious device adopted.

Ava.—Yet why thus strange to Madhava? his name
Seems even to the minister unknown.
Small proof of his regard.

Kam.—A mere pretext. He knows youth indiscreet,
And fears to trust the lovers with his counsels.
Let the world deem their union was the work
Of mutual passion only; so the king
And Nandana are foiled, nor we to blame.
A wise man veils his projects from the world;
Silent effects his schemes; whilst all his acts
Bespeak indifference, and his cheerful man-
ners.
Show to suspicion's eye a heart at ease.

Ava.—I comprehend your plans—'its for this cause,
That by our orders I so often Madhava
Have sent on various pleas along the road
By Bhurivasu's palace.

Kam.—True; and as I learn,
The princess from her casement has beheld

The youth—he graceful as the god of love,
Herself love's blooming bride—nor seen in vain.
Her waning form too faithfully betrays
The lurking care she now first learns to suffer.

Ava.—To soothe that care, then, has her skill portrayed
The lineaments of Madhava, to-day
Left by her foster-sister with Mandarika.

Kam.—In sooth not ill devised. Lavangika
Knows that the youth's attendant, Kalahamsa,
Doth love Mandarika, and shrewdly deems
That from her hands he will obtain the portrait
To show his master.

Aaa.—I have borne my part;
And to the garden of love's god directed
The steps of Madhava at early dawn.
It is the festival of Madana. The princess
And damsel train will to his groves proceed,
And thus the youthful pair to-day will meet.

Kam.—Thanks, daughter, for your kindly zeal to aid
The object of my wishes. But now inform me,
If you have tidings of Saudamini,
Mine ancient pupil?

Ava.—I learn that upon mount Sri-Parvata
She now resides, where, won by desp'rate penance,
Power more than earthly waits upon her will.

Kam.—Whence is this information?

Ava.—The formidable deity *Chamunda*
Is worshipped near the city cemetery.
Kam.—She whom her miscreant votaries aver
Delights in living sacrifice?
Ava.—The same.
From one of these, Kapala-Kundala,
I learnt the news, as I encountered her
By chance at eve. She is the pupil
Of a skull-bearing seer, Aghoraghanta,
A wandering mendicant, but dwelling now
Amidst the neighbouring forest. He has late,
Come from *Sri-Parvata.*
Kam.—'Tis like Saudamini.
Ava.—Of her enough.
More pleasing themes attend, for Makaranda,
The early friend of Madhava, adores
The lady Madayantika, the sister
Of the king's favourite, and to secure
His happiness will yield to Madhava
Scarce less delight than to ensure his own.
Kam.—It has not been forgotten. Buddharakshita
Attends that charge.
Ava.—This, mistress, was well done.
Kam.—Come, daughter, let us forth, and having learnt
How Madhava has fared, repair to Malati,
I know her spirit lofty: we must proceed
With prudence if we would obtain success

May mighty *Brahma*, whose consummate skill
With sympathising merit has endowed
The graceful pair, perfect his high design.
May our devices prosper: may the youth
Obtain his wishes, and his love be crowned
With the fair maid's affection : as the lotus,
Buds in full beauty to the tender light
The moon autumnal sheds upon its leaves.

[*Exeunt.*

SCENE II.—A GARDEN.

Enter KALAHAMSA (*with a picture.*)

I wonder where my master is to be found: he may well think his person equal to that of love himself, since it has made an impression upon the heart of Malati. I feel rather weary, and shall take the liberty of reposing myself in this grove till I see my master and his friend.

[*Retires.*

Enter MAKARANDA.

I learn from Avalokita, my friend
Is in the grove of Madana, and thither
I go to seek him. Ha! he comes this way:
Yet something sure disturbs him, for his step
Has not its wonted nimbleness, his eyes
Are fixed on vacancy, his whole attire
Is disarrayed, and heaves his frequent sigh.
Has love been busy here, whose potent will,
By every lovely attribute administered,

Pervades the world, and on the form of youth,
Works sad and wondrous change?

Enter MADHAVA.

'Tis strange—'tis passing strange, my vagrant thoughts
No more return to me. Deserting shame,
Or self-respect, or fortitude, or judgment,
They dwell perverse upon one fond idea—
The lovely image of the moon-faced maid.
Wonder alone each faculty engrossed
As rapt I gazed upon her, and my heart,
As if immersed in heavenly nectar, glowed
Delusive ecstasy: too late I feel
I nursed a burning coal within my bosom.

Mak.—(*Coming forward.*) Madhava!
The sun is high, and darts his fiercest rays
Upon the aching brow: here let us enter,
And rest awhile beneath the garden's shades.

Madh.—Even as you please.

[*Exeunt.*

KALAHAMSA *advances.*

My master and his friend are undoubtedly the two greatest ornaments of this garden. Well; shall I now take him this picture of himself—the delight of the eyes of Malati and solace of her amorous pain; perhaps I had better let him repose himself awhile. It shall be so.

[*Exit.*

ANOTHER PART OF THE GARDEN.

Enter MADHAVA *and* MAKARANDA.

Mak.—Here, at the foot of this wide-spreading tree,
Amidst the fragrance that the breezes waft
Abroad from every bud, let us recline.
[*They lie down.*
To-day was one of peril, Madhava.
You could not sure behold the num'rouse concours.
Of all our city's beauty, bound to pay
Their annual homage at the shrine of love,
And scape unharmed. In sooth, to me it seems
The shaft has 'lighted, and has grazed thy heart.
Nay, never droop the lotus of thy face :
If struck, reveal thy heart: why shame to bear it ?
Who can resist the heart-born deity ?|
Creatures of passion, all confess his power,
And Gods themselves are impotent as we.

Madh.—I own my weakness—listen to its cause.
By Avalokita advised, I went
To *Kamadeva's* temple, where I strayed,
Till weary I reclined beside a fountain
That laves the deep roots of a stately tree,
Whose clustering blossoms wooed the wanton bees

To cull their sweet inebriating fragrance.
Lulled by their songs, and tempted by the shade,
I laid me down, and in pure idleness,
To while away the time, I gathered round me
The new fall'n blossoms, and assiduous wove
A flowery garland. Whilst I was thus employed.
There issued from the fane a beauteous maid.
Stately her gait—yet graceful as the banner
Love waves in triumph o'er a prostrate world.
Her train bespoke a princely rank—her garb
With youth's appropriate ornaments was graced—
Her form was beauty's shrine, or of that shrine
Radiant she moved the guardian deity.
To mould her charms, whatever nature offers
Fairest and best, had surely been assembled,
And love omnipotent was her creator.
Led by her maidens to recollect the flowers.
That thickly hung on my o'ershadowing tree,
She neared the spot. Ah! then too plain I noted
The signs of passion, for some happy youth,
Long entertained, the lovely maid revealed.
As slender as the lotus stalk her shape ;
Her pallid cheeks, like unstained ivory,
Rivalled the beauty of the spotless moon ;

And still her prompt compliance with the wishes
Of her attendant damsels showed herself
Indifferent to all. I scarce had gazed
Upon her, but my eye felt new delight,
As bathed with nectar, and she drew my heart
As pow'rfully as attracts the magnet gem
The unresisting ore, at once towards her.
That heart, though causeless be its sudden passion,
Is fixed on her for ever, chance what may,
And though my portion be henceforth despair.
The goddess destiny decrees at pleasure
The good or ill of all created beings.

Mak.—Nay, Madhava, this cannot be, believe me,
Without some cause. Behold! all nature's sympathies
Spring not from outward form, but inward virtue.
The lotus buds not till to the sun has risen;
Nor melts the moon-gem till it feels the moon.
What then ensued?

Madh.—When her fair train beheld me, they exchanged
Expressive looks and smiles, and each to each,
As if they knew me, murmured—This is he!
The music of their tinkiling zones was stilled,

Repressed the silver echo of their anklets
Sharp clanging to their undulating motion.
Hushed was the melody their bracelets made,
Whilst their fair lotus palms, in sportive mood,
Were beating measure to their merriment.
Silent they stood, and with extended fingers,
As if they said, "The fates have favoured us,
Lady, behold *him* here!"

Mak.—(*To himself.*) This is indeed
A proof of preconceived regard.

Kal.—(*Advancing.*) What is all this about? some pleasing story of which woman is the object?

Mak.—Proceed, my friend.

Madh.—What words shall picture what those looks conveyed;
The lore of love those lotus eyes revealed?
What firmness could resist the honest warmth
Of nature's mute expressiveness, nor fall
Before those orbs, that now like opening buds,
Beneath the creeper of the tremulous brow
Expansive bloomed, and now retiring shrunk
But half-averted from the answering gaze,
Then dropped the veiling lashes o'er their brightness?
I felt their influence, and those looks of love,
Beaming with mild timidity, and moist
With sweet adandonment, bore off my heart—

Nay plucked it from my bosom by the roots
All pierced with wounds.
Incredulous of my happiness, I sought
To mark her passion, nor display my own,
Though every limb partook the fond emotion.
Thence I resumed my task, and wove my wreath,
Seeming intent, till she at length withdrew
Attended by her maidens and a guard
Of eunuchs armed with staves and javelins.
A stately elephant recieved the princess
And bore her towards the city. Whilst they moved,
As winds the lily on its slender stalk,
So turned her head towards the grove of *Kama*,
And from her delicate lids she shot retiring
Glances, with venom and ambrosia tipped.
My breast received the shafts. A mingled flame.
And deathly chillness, since atternate spread
Throughout my form, and doom me to such agony
Words cannot paint, the world has never witnessed.
Perception dimly pictures present objects,
And past perceptions fade from recollection!
Vain were the lunar ray or gelid stream

To cool my body's fever, whilst my mind
Whirls in perpetual round, and knows not rest.

Kal.—The object of this passion must assuredly be Malati.

Mak.—(*To himself.*) My friend is lost, my counsels were but vain:
And e'en the wish were idle, that the diety,
Self-born, should spare his years, nor with sad change
Soil his pure mind. The flow'ry bow is strung,
And ardent youth is reckless of the peril.
(*To Madhava.*) Know you the name and race of that fair lady ?

Madh.—Hear how I learnt them. Ere she had departed,
One of her train, apparently intent
On gathering flowers, privately approached me,
And borrowing from the garland I had woven
A covert for her meaning, thus addressed me—
"Well has been strung this string of blooming beauty,
And pleasing is it in our lady's sight,
Who in like excellence herself excels—
May then success reward such high desert,
And this bright produce of creative art
Bear richest fruit, exalted to that station
Its merit claims—suspended round the neck

Of Bhurivasu's daughter, Malati,
Whose foster-sister, and whose nearest friend,
Lavangika now stands before you."

Kal.—This is as we wish, and fortune favours the design of the flower-armed deity.

Mak.—Malati, the daughter of the minister,
A mark for elevated rank, her name
Is ever in the mouth of her preceptress;
And rumour adds, the king solicits her
In marriage for his favourite, Nandana.

Madh.—Requested by Lavangika I gave her
The flow'ry wreath. She took it with respect,
As 'twere a precious gift, and all the while
The eyes of Malati were fixed on her.
Bowing with reverence, she then retired.
And quickly disappeared amidst the throng.
The princess and the people left the grove
And I directed hitherward my steps.

Mak.—Your story, Madhava, most plainly shows,
That Malati's affection is your own;
And the soft cheek, whose pallid tint denoted
Love preconceived, is pale alone for you.
She must have seen you, though we know not where;
But maidens of her rank do not allow
Their eyes to rest on one to whom they have not
Already given their hearts: and then those looks

That passed among her maidens, plainly showed
The passion you had wakened in their mistress.
Then comes her foster-sister's clear enigma,
And tells intelligibly whose her heart.

Kal.—(*Advancing.*) Look at this picture.

Mak.—Madhava's counterfeit—whose work is this?

Kal.—Hers who has stolen his heart.

Mak.—What, Malati?

Kal.—The same.

Madh.—This gives me faith, dear friend, in your conjectures.

Mak.—But, Kalahamsa, how came you by this?

Kal.—Mandarika gave it to me. She had it from Lavangika.

Mak.—And what induced the princess to delineate
This picture? did Mandarika inform you?

Kal.—She painted it to amuse and relieve her distress.

Mak.—What say you, Madhava? this lovely maid,
The soft light of your eyes, assuredly
Regards you bound to her in love's alliance.
What should prevent your union? Fate and love
Combined seem labouring to effect it. Come,
Let me behold the wondrous form that works
Such change in yours,—you have the skill; portray her,

Madh.—To please you I will try. Bring me the pencil. (To *Kalahamsa.*)

(*Draws.*)

Hard is the task you have assigned me.—
A chilly tremor spreads through all my frame.
Damp dews distil from every opening pore,
And starting fast, my tears repeatedly
Dim the faint outline that my trembling hand,
Oh, how unworthily! attempts to picture:
Yet with what skill I have, 'tis done.

Mak.—(*Taking the drawing.*) Most excellent and worthy of your passion.

It may be said of her—(*Writes on the drawihg*)
"Whatever nature's loveliness displays
May seem to others beautiful and bright;
But since these charms have broke upon my gaze,
They form my life's sole exquisite delight."

Enter MANDARIKA *hastily.*

Man.—Ha! Kalahamsa, you are at last overtaken, Makaranda, Madhava, sirs, I salute you.

Mak.—Approach, Mandarika; what brings you hither

Man.—I followed Kalahamsa to recover a picture.

Kal.—(*Gives her the one Madhava has.*) Here it is, take it.

Man.—Malati's picture, I protest. How came this here? Who has painted it?

Kal.—He whom she delineated, and with much the same intention.

Mak.—He tells you truth ; and now do you be honest.
Inform us how, and where, first Malati
Saw Madhava ?

Man.—She was called to the lattice by Lavangika to look at him as he passed the palace.

Mak.—So I supposed. We frequently have passed
In that direction.

Man.—With your permission, I will communicate these events to my friend Lavangika.

Mak.—You have free leave

[*Exit Mandarika.*

Mak.—The monarch of a thousand beams now darts
His hottest rays ; 'tis noon, let us go home.

Madh.—Willingly—
The day's warm influence surely washes off
The careful labours of the morning toilet,
And steals those sandal marks, so neatly laid
In graceful lines across the flowery cheek.
Play o'er my limbs, ye soft refreshing breezes,
Whose previous homage has been paid to beauty,
And wrap in soft embrace my fair one's charms,
Diffusing o'er her form the honied fragrance
Shook from the jasmine's scarce-unfolded blossom.

Mak.—Alas ! the flowe'r armed and resistless, deity
Has sadly changed the person of my friend ;

Like the young elephant, when fever preys
On his yet tender frame. Our only hope
Is now Kamandaki.

Madh.—'Tis strange, most strange!
Where'er I turn, the same loved charms appear
On every side. Bright as the golden bud
Of the young lotus gleams her beauteous face,
Though oft averted from my fond regards.
Alas! my friend, this fascination spreads
O'er all my senses, and a feverish flame
Consumes my strength—my heart is all on fire,
My mind is tossed with doubt—and every faculty
In one fond thought absorbed, I cease to be
Myself, or conscious of the thing I am.

[*Exeunt.*

END OF THE FIRST ACT.

ACT II.

THE DWELLING OF MALATI.

Enter two FEMALE ATTENDANTS *meeting.*

First Att.—Hey, friend, I saw you just now near the music-room, in deep conversation with Avalokita: what were you two talking about?

Second Att.—The whole story of the grove of *Kama* has been carried to Kamandaki by Madhava's friend; and she being desirous of seeing Malati, sent Avalokita to her, who was telling me, that she had left Lavangika and the princess together.

First Att.—Why, Lavangika said she wanted to gather *bakula* flowers in the grove of *Madana,* and has not since returned: has she been heard of?

Second Att.—Yes, the princess saw her coming, on which she dismissed her attendants at the door of her apartments, but detained Lavangika.

First Att.—She had some very agreeable news to tell Malati, I suppose, of the youth Madhava.

Second Att.—It is a hopeless passion I am afraid, and to-day's interview will only add to her distress. To-morrow the king gives the princess to Nandana; her father has consented to the match.

First Att.—Consented!

Second Att.—Yes, he told the king that he was "lord over his own daughter." This passion of Malati and Madhava will only yield them misery as long as they live.

First Att.—Now, then, we shall see what Kamandaki can do, and whether she will put forth her power.

Second Att.—You talk idly. Come, let us depart.

[*Exeunt.*

Enter MALATI *and* LAVANGIKA.

Mal.—Proceed, my dear Lavangika, proceed.

Lav.—This flowry wreath then did he send by me.

Mal.—(*Taking it.*) 'Tis strung unevenly.

Lav.—The fault is yours.

Mal.—How should that be?

Lav.—Where, deem you, were his thoughts?
Who caused that dark-hued youth's deep agitation?

Mal.—Dearest Lavangika,
You ever speak me comfort.

Lav.—There might be better comfort. He himself,
Here in your presence—gazing raft upon you
With look intent, from eyes that tremulous glow,
Like the blown lotus shaken by the zephyr,
Forced, from the timid plea of weaving chaplets,
To dart upon you glances of delight,

From underneath the arching brow, that waves
In curve as graceful as the brow of *Kama*.

Mal.—How can I credit this? how should I know,
From such brief interview, if the graceful youth
Be true, or if he only seek to mock me?

Lav.—You have no need to fear in this, believe me.

Mal.—Well, well; complete your story.

Lav.—When I received the garland, I departed
And mingled with the crowd; thence to Mandarika
I hastened, to receive again the picture
That in the morning had been left with her.

Mal.—With her!—With what intent?

Lav.—She has a lover, Kalahamsaka,
A follower of Madhava, and I knew
To him the picture would be shown, and all
That thence ensued would be revealed to me.

Mal.—(*Apart.*) Then Madhava has seen it?
(*Aloud.*) What is your dearest wish, Lavangika?

Lav.—That he whose heart now pines in hopeless passion,
May soothe his sorrows with this bright resemblance
Of the fair cause of his distress.

(*Shows Malati the picture drawn by Madhava.*)

Mal.—(*Contemplating* it.) Yet still
My heart is ill at ease. I doubt me much
That this will prove a treach'rous comforter—
What have we here?

(*Reads Makaranda's lines.*)

Oh, Madhava! the graces of thy form,
Thy flattering tongue, and fascinating gaze,
Are all alike resistless—happy she
Who never has beheld them. On my heart
They, cruel, shed interminable anguish.
(*Weeps.*)

Lav.—Why, dearest friend, despond?

Mal.—What should I hope?

Lav.—Be sure of this, that he on whose account,
Like the young blossom from its slender stem
Plucked rude, you droop, and taste no more the fragrance
Of the sweet jasmine—he, too, has been taught,
By love's relentless god, how hard it is
To bear such agony.

Mal.—May happiness
Await his youth; for me, I dare not hope.
This is a day of strange and changeful feeling.
Love spreads through every vein like subtlest poison,
And like the fire that brightens in the breeze

Consumes this feeble frame—resistless fever
Preys on each fibre—fatal is its fury.
No one can bring me aid, nor tender mother
Nor father, nor Lavangika can save me.

Lav.—Such mutual passion may, in sooth, bestow
Delight when lovers meet; but when apart
Condemns them to affliction. From a brief
And passing gaze, thy life was brought in peril;
And now to-day his nearer presence sheds
A fiercer fever on thy delicate frame.
What now is to be said? We must admit,
The rarest and most difficult attainment
Of all on earth, is union with a lover,
Of equal excellence and like affection.

Mal.—Life is distasteful to me: leave me, friend:
And yet I wrong thy gentleness. Repeatedly
Recurring to the anguish of my heart,
I lose all fortitude, and in my grief
Become capricious and unjust—forgive me.
Let the full moon blaze in the nightly sky:
Let love rage on, death screens me from his fury.
What should exact my love and veneration?
My father, and my mother, and my race,
Of still unblemished honour—not my life:
No! nor the mortal who subdues my heart.

Lav.—(*Apart.*) What is to be done?

(An ATTENDANT *enters, but without advancing far.)*

Att.—The venerable Kamandaki.

Both.—What would she?

Att.—She seeks admission to the princess.

Both.—What should delay her?

(Attendant retires; MALATI *conceals the picture.)*

Lav.—*(Aside.)* In good time she comes.

Enter KAMANDAKI *and* AVALOKITA.

Kam.—*(Soliloquises.)*

So far, my friend, respected Bhurivasu,
So far is well: in either world, assent
Awaits thy answer to the king. He, of his own,
Is the undoubted lord. Fate is our friend,
In all that chanced to-day in *Kama's* grove,
And in the interchange of tender tokens,
The garland and the picture, all conspires.
To crown our sanguine wishes with success.
Best pledge of blissful union is the bond
Of mutual love; and well the sage has said,
"The marriage rite shall prosper, when the eye,
The tongue, and heart, unite the wedded pair."

Lav.—The lady Malati.

Kam.—*(Surveying her.)*

I view her with affliction, and delight.
Slender her frame, and delicate and pale,
Like the young plaintain, or the waning moon.

Soothing and pleasant is she to the eye,
Though thin and pallid be her cheek, and all
Declare the fires of love have triumphed here.
The hope of union with the youth engrosses
Her every thought. Loose and untied her zone,
Her soft lip quivers—starting drops suffuse
Her gentle lips—her bosom palpitates,
And her dark eye in soft abandonment
Moist, languid floats. Each look and gesture speaks
The fond desires that agitate her youth.
(*Approaches.*)

Lav.—(*To Malati.*) Behold!

Mal.—Priestess, I salute you. (*Bows.*)

Kam.—May you enjoy, dear lady, in due season,
The fruit of all your wishes.

Lav.—Pray, be seated.

Mal.—Is all propitious with the priestess?

Kam.—(*Sighing.*) All.

Love.—(*Aside.*) That sigh is but the prelude to our play;
I have my cue. (*Aloud.*) And yet, respected lady,
Methinks that sigh, that struggling makes its way
Through starting tears, is with your words at variance.
What can its import be?

Kam.—Behold these weeds :
Sorts such a garb with one you call your friend ?

Lav.—What follows ?

Kam:—I am grieved, like unmeet union
Should sentence youth and charms innumerable
Born to no profit, to a worthless bridegroom.

Lav.—You do not grieve alone ; the common voice
Condemns the minister's assent, and blames
His yielding Malati to be the bride
Of Nandana, because the king requests it.

Mal.—*(Aside.)* Alas ! I am an offering to the monarch
Presented by my father.

Kam.—'Tis most strange
How he could overlook the vast defects
Of such alliance. But how can those
Feel natural affection for their offspring,
Whose souls are sunk in schemes of policy ?
His only thought is clearly to secure
The friendship of the monarch's chosen friend
And boon companion, by his daughter's person.

Mal.—*(Apart.)* The king's regard is all in all with him ;
His Malati is nothing.

Lav.—'Tis as you say, dame ;
Or why should our young mistress thus be sacrificed,
To age and ugliness ?

Mal.—*(Apart.)* Ah, luckless wench!
A thunderbolt has struck me to the ground.

Lav.—To you she ever has been like daughter;
Save her, dear lady, from this living death.

Kam.—What can I aid? Fate and her sire alone
Exact obedience from a daughter. True,
Sakuntala, of *Kusika's* high race,
Bestowed her love on a self-chosen lord—
The king Dushyanta. A bright nymph of heaven.
Espoused a mortal monarch, *Pururavas*,
And the fair princess, *Vasavadatta*, scorned
The husband of her father's choice, and fled
With Prince *Udyana*. So poets tell.
But these were desperate acts, and must not be
Proposed for imitation. Let the minister
Complete his will—secure his master's favour
With the rich off'ring of his daughter's peace,
And yield this maiden to the sovereign's friend,
Like the pale moon, to *Rahu's* foul embrace.

Ava.—Mistress, time passes; it were well to think
Of Madhava, who needs your aid.

Kam.—'Tis well.
Permit me, princess, to depart.

Lav.—One moment. (*Aside to Malati.*)
Say, shall I ask the dame who is the youth,
And what his origin?

Mal.—Do so; I long to hear it.

Lav.—Inform us, pious dame, what youth is this
In whom you show such interest?

Kam.—The story though of import, needs no preface:—
The sovereign of *Vidarbha* boasts for minister
The sage and long-experienced Devarata,
Who bears the burthen of the state, and spreads
Throughout the world his piety and fame.
Such as himself your father knows him well,
For in their youth they were in study joined,
And trained to learning by the same preceptor;
And rarely in this world do we behold
Such characters as theirs; whose lofty rank
Is the abode of wisdom and of piety,
Of valour and of virtue; and whose fame
Spreads white and spotless through the universe.

Mal.—I have often heard my father speak of him.

Kam.—Bright as the rising moon, whose silver rays
First streaming o'er the eastern mountain, charm
The eyes of all mankind, a son from him
Has sprung, whose opening virtues early give
Occasion of rejoicing to the world.
Now, in his bloom, assiduous to collect
Ripe store of knowledge, has this youth been sent

From his paternal mansion to our city.
Here as he passes, many a lotus eye
Shoots from each casement soul-subduing glances,
But reckless he, along with Makaranda,
His friend and fellow of like years and worth,
Pursues his toils ;—his name is Madhava.

Mal.—(*Apart to Lavangika.*) Heard you, my friend ?

Lav.—In truth you have escaped
The perilous ocean, and the tree of heaven
Is now within your reach.

[*The conch is sounded without.*

Kam.—These echoing tones,
That through the deep recesses of the palace
Resounding spread, proclaim the eveniug hour.

[*They all rise.*

Mal.—(*Apart.*) Alas, my father ! thy ambition spurns
A daughter's happiness—yet in my grief,
Some hope I borrow from the youth's descent,
And trust we meet again.

Lav.—This is our way.

Kam.—*(Apart.)* So far so well. An unsuspected messenger,
I have discharged my duty. Malati
Is tutored to our wishes, and inspired
With hatred of the bride-groom—taught to question

Her father's love, reminded of examples
That vindicate the free choice of a husband.
Her admiration of her youthful lover
Is now approved by his illustrious birth
And my encomium of his high descent:
All this must strengthen and confirm her passion,
And now their union may be left to fate.
[*Exeunt.*

END OF THE SECOND ACT.

ACT III.

THE HOUSE OF KAMANDAKI.

Enter BUDDHARAKSHITA *and* AVALOKITA *meeting.*

Buddh.—Ho, Avalokita! where is our dame?

Ava. Do you not know! Disregarding the season for colecting alms, she is ever with the princess.

Buddh.—And where have you been?

Ava.—I have been to Madhava by her orders, to tell him to repair to the public garden of the temple of *Sankara*, and place himself in the grove of red *asoka* trees, that extends to the *Kantaki* bower.

Bnddh.—For what purpose?

Ava.—This is the fourteenth day of the dark fortnight. Persuading the princess that the god *Sankara* is to be propitiated with offerings of flowers gathered by one's self, the dame takes her and Lavangika thither, and whilst the former is collecting her oblation, she and Madhava will, as it were by accident, again encounter. But where are you going?

Buddh.—I am on my way to my friend Madayantika, to accompany her to the temple of *Sankara* also. I looked in to pay my respects to the priestess.

Ava.—And how speed yon in what you have in hand?

Buddh.—As our mistress could wish. I have won the entire confidence of Madayantika, and by expatiating on the suitableness and merit of Makaranda, have excited in her bosom the most lively affection for him and anxious wish to see him.

Ava.—This is well. Now to our several duties.

[*Exeunt.*

Scene II.—The Garden.

Enter Kamandaki.

Kam.—Poor girl! the lesson I have lately hinted
Has bowed her lofty spirit, and she seeks
To win me to her: mournfully she pines
When I am absent; brightens in my presence;
Whispers her secret thoughts to me; presents me
With costly gifts: when I depart she clings
Around my neck, and only lets me leave her
When I have vowed repeatedly return!
Then on my knee she sits, and bids me tell her
Again the stories of the nymphs that loved;
And questions o'er and o'er, with flimsy plea,
Their fate and conduct, then she silent pauses
As lost in meditation,—'tis enough:
To-day they meet. Daughter, this way; approach.

Enter MALATI *and* LAVANGIKA.

Mal.—(*Apart.*) Alas! my father loves his child no more,
But offers her a victim to ambition;
One hope alone sustains me.

Lav.—Taste, my friend,
The freshness of the breeze, that sweeps the blossoms,
And wafts around the *champaka's* perfume,
Breathing melodious with the buzz of bees
That cluster in the buds, and with the song
The *koil* warbles thick and hurried forth,
As on the flow'ry mango's top he sits,
And all inebriate with its nectar sings.
The garden gale comes wooingly to sip
The drops ambrosial from thy moonlike face.
Come on; those shades invite us.
[*They retire.*

Enter MADHAVA.

The pious dame is here—her presence fills
My heart with rapture. So the peafowl hails
The flash that heralds the approaching shower
Lavangika—the third—'tis she—
'Tis Malati! Ah me! a sudden chill
Pervades my heart and freezes every faculty,
To marble turned by her moon-beaming countenance,
Like mountains ice-bound by the gelid ray

Shot on their summits from the lunar gem.
How lovely she appears, as o'er her frame,
Like a fast-fading wreath, soft languor steals
And heightens every beauty. Now mine eyes
Are conscious of their being. As I gaze
My heart consumes, and love lights all his fires.

[*Approaches unobserved.*

Mal.—(*Advancing*,) Come, Lavangika, let us pluck flowers
From this delightfnl arbour.

Kam.—Nay, rest, my child;
Thy faltering tongue and languid frame evince
Fatigue: upon thy face the moist drops start,
And those bright eyes are shut—one might suspect,—
Thy form such soft abandonment betrays—
A lover's gaze were dwelling on thy beauties.
Come sit thee here; I have a tale to tell thee.

Mal.—You are obeyed.—*(Sits down by Kamandaki, who passes her hand under Malati's chin so as to hold up her face towards Madhava.)*

Kam.—There was a youth, named Madhava, who shared
With you an equal portion of my heart.

Lav.—So we have heard.

Kam.—He, from the luckless day
Of *Kama's* festival, has ceased to be
The master of himself, and though he told not
His sorrows to the moon or faithful friend,
His changing form, still lovely in decay,
Revealed the anguish he disdained to utter.
I hastened to his aid, and quickly guessed
The cause of his distress, when I was told
He had beheld this lovely countenance,—
The moon that swayed the heaving of his heart,
Like the deep waters of the tossing main.

Madh.(*Behind.*) How well she penetrates my secret!

Kam,—Reckless of life, his only pleasures now
Are tasks that feed and aggravate his flame.
He gazes on the mango buds ; he listens
Attentive to the *koil's* song ; he breasts
The breeze impregnate with the flowery fragrance ;
He hugs the lotus blossoms to his heart,
And basks beneath the deadly lunar beam—
This first fond passion preys upon my son,
And soon, I fear, cuts short his gentle being.

Mal.—(*To Lavangika.*)
Why does the dame alarm me thus with fear
Far life so dear to all: what can I say?

Lav.—(*To Kamandaki.*)
You are not terrified alone—like fears
Pervade us for the princess. She has often

Beheld the youth, as by the palace walls
His course has frequent chanced, since when she pines,
As droops the lotus on its slender stem
Beneath the scorching sun: her youthful sports
Delight no more; pensive apart she sits
Whole days, her cheek upon her hand reclined.
We fondly hoped those looks that were exchanged
In *Kama's* grove, when like the present god
The youthful Madhava appeared to grace
Love's festival, amidst his blooming votaries,
Would dissipate this melancholy mood,
And cheer her heart with hope, but passion since
Intenser rages in her tender heart,
And threatens her existence. Oh, befriend us!
If but a moment she could view the youth,
E'en that were such relief as earth receives
When, parched by sultry suns, she drinks revived
The bland and life-bestowing dews of heaven.
The hapless state of Malati affrights us,
Unfit to struggle with the sports of destiny.
Do thou exert thy powers, and then the pair,
Who claim alike thy pity and regard,
Redeemed from death, shall prosper in their loves,

Kam.—My heart is filled with sorrow and delight.
I pity her sad state, even whilst I joy
To find her justly conscious of desert.
Lav.—Behold these proofs, this picture of her lord!

(*Opening the garment over her breast.*)

And this decaying wreath, strung by his hands,
Dear as her life, thus cherished in her bosom.
Madh.—How enviable, dear garland, is thy fate,
Thus to be cherished like a friend, and waving
A graceful banner o'er that lovely bosom.

(*A noise behind.*)

"What ho! beware! in youthful strength and sport,
The tiger, in the temple's porch confined,
Has burst his iron cage, and roams at large,
With tail high waving like a banner, vast
And might limbed, he stalks along the groves.
Now in the midst of mangled forms his paw,
As pond'rous as the thunderbolt, has felled,
The monster stands, and in his maw engulfs,
Wide as a cave, the quivering flesh, or grinds,
The cracking bones with hard, sharp-pointed teeth;
From his deep throat he roars in thunder loud,

And men and beasts fly trembling from the echo;
Begrimed with blood and dust he follows fast,
And plies insatiate his death-dealing talons—
Look to your lives as best you may, avoid him."

Enter BUDDHARAKSHITA.

Buddh.—Alas, alas! my dear friend Madayantika!
Oh, save us, save us! Madayantika,
Our friend, the sister of the minister,
Is singled out and hunted by the tiger.

Mal.—Oh, horror!

Madh.—(*Rushing forward.*) Where is the savage!

Mal.—(*With delight, apart.*) He here!

Madh.—Now I am blessed indeed; her gaze surprised
Dwells greedily upon my presence, and enchains me
In flow'ry bonds, falls on my heart like balm.
And sheds a show'r of heavenly nectar o'er me.

Lav.—Can we not quit the garden?

Madh.—Follow me. (*Going.*)

Kam.—Beware, my son: though valiant, be not rash.

Mal.—(*Apart to Lavangika.*) I tremble now.

Madh.—A moment pause. I mark the savage spread
Dismay, his course is marked with carcases,
And all his steps sink deep in mire and gore.

Oh, horror! we are distant;—now he views
A maid—she flies, he follows.

All.—Madayantika!

Kam.—Behold, a youth advances— now he stoops
To grasp a fallen sword.

Madh.—He throws himself,
Brave youth, before the tiger: 'tis my friend!
'Tis Makaranda.

All.—Noble, valiant youth!

Madh.—Alas! the beast has wounded him.

Kam.—Joy, joy! the savage falls.

All.—What fate have we escaped!

Kam.—My generous son, he bleeds profusely:
Supported by the trembling maid, he rests
Upon his sword, along whose ruddy blade
The trickling torrent reddens to the ground.

Madh.—He faints; help, holy dame, preserve my friend.

Kam.—Fear not, fear not, but hasten to his succour.
[*Exeunt.*

END OF THE THIRD ACT.

ACT IV.

THE SAME SCENE.

MADHAVA *and* MAKARANDA *brought on by* MADAYANTIKA *and* LAVANGIKA *insensible.*

Maday.—(*To Kamandaki.*) Befriend him, pious dame; oh, save this youth!
Who to preserve my life has risked his own.

(*The others.*)—What should we do?

Kamandaki.—Sprinkle o'er their limbs.
The water of this ewer, and fan their faces
With your light robes.

(*They fan the youths and cast water from the Dame's kamandalu, or waterpot carried by an ascetic.*)

Mak.—*Sighs and looks up.*
Why thus alarmed, my friend?—I am well,
Quite well.

Maday.—(*With delight.*) Ah me! he is restored.

Malati.—(*Puts her hand to Madhava's forehead.*)
Lavangika.
How happy you, your friend again is conscious!

Madh.—(*Reviving.*) Rash youth, where are you? here to my heart.

(*They embrace; Kamandaki hangs o'er them.*)

Kam.—I revive. (*They all express delight.*)

Lav.—We all partake your joy!

Buddharakshita.—(*Apart to Madayantika.*) This is the youth.

Maday.—That, that is Madhava I know, and this
Is he you mean.

Buddh.—Have I not spoke him truly?

Maday.—Were his worth
Less than it shows, you had not so described him.
And Malati, as rumour runs, has fixed
Her heart upon his friend.

[*Turns to look at Makaranda.*

Kam.—(*Observing them apart.*)
Approving destiny has wrought to-day
The interview of yonder pair.
(*Aloud to Makaranda.*) Tell us, my son, by what propitious chance,
Conducted to this grove, you came to save
The life of this dear maid?

Mak.—I came to seek
My friend, directed to the grove of *Kama*
By Avalokita, and charged with news
I gathered in the city, which I feared
Would add to his affliction, when I saw
This noble maiden flying from the wrath
Of yon ferocious animal.

Kam.—(*Apart.*) 'Tis time
To pledge the faith of Malati, (*Aloud.*) My son,

(*To Madhava.*)

The joy your friend's escape must needs afford you.
Is fit occasion for you to present
Some token of regard to Malati.

Madh.—I willingly obey, and since to her
I owe my own recovery from the mist
The peril of my friend spread o'er my senses;
Here for returning consciousness, I pledge her,
A free-will offering each,—my heart, my life.

Lav.—I answer for my friend! she deems the gifts
Deserving her acceptance.

Mad.—(*Apart.*) On my word
The youth knows when to proffer what is sure
To meet with willing ears.

Maday.—(*Apart.*) But this news!
What should it be to render him unhappy?

Madh.—Now, Makaranda, tell us what you heard,
That threatened to afflict me?

Enter a MESSENGER.

Mess.—(*To Maday.*) Lady, the minister, your brother Nandana,
Desires your presence. It has pleased the king
In person to announce, that *Bhurivasu*
Consents this day to give him Malati:
He wills you therefore come and share his happiness.

Mak.—He brings you my intelligence.

[*Malati and Madhava express their despair.*

Maday.—(*Embracing Malati.*)
My dearest friend, this is indeed delightful.
One city saw owe birth ; our infant sports
And opening youth have ever found us friends :
And now you are my sister, and the pride
Of our illustrious house.

Kam.—In truth, my child.
Fate is propitious when she grants your brother
A bride like this.

Maday.—We rather thank your prayers.
My friend Lavangika, our every wish
Is gratified, now we obtain your princess.

Lav.—It may be : we have no concern with it.

Maday.—Come, wench (*to Buddharakshita*), let's hasten and get every thing
In order for the bridal.

[*They rise.*

Budd.—I attend you.

Lav.—(*Apart to Kam.*) This interchange of looks, from eyes that roll
Like the soft tremulous lotus, and express
The dear emotions and the new delights
That fill and agitate the heart, reveal
This couple conscious of the like desire.

Kam.—No doubt, they taste like pleasure from the look
So oft repeated, and the furtive glance
Tells a plain story ; sidelong and slow the eye
Glides to the angle of the drooping lids,

Half-closed by passion's birth; the brow is raised
In gentle curve, and the loose veiling lashes
Tremble in soft-abandonment: all speaks
The inward consciousness of new delight.

Maday.—(*To Buddh.*) Sure I shall see again this graceful youth,
The saviour of my life?

Buddh.—If fate so pleases.

[*Exeunt with Attendant.*

Madh.—(*Apart.*) Now let the thread of hope, long idly cherished,
Snap like the fibre of the lotus stem.
Come, boundless anguish, but by death relieved,
And frantic-grief, avowed despair possess
My every thought! be destiny appeased,
And love work all his vengeance. Adverse fate
Delights to aggravate my woes, and mocks me
With disappointment, after I have won—
No common prize—affection like my own.
I marked her as she heard her father's will:
Pale as the moon before the morning sun,
Her lovely countenance revealed her sorrows,
And added sharper poignancy to mine.

Kam.—(*Apart.*) I cannot bear their grief; and hope destroyed,
Life is a burthen (*Aloud.*) Madhava, my son,

Tell me, have you indulged the expectation,
The minister would give his daughter to you?

Madh.—*(Bashfully.)* No, never, never!

Kam.—Then were you ill apprised
Of past occurrences.

Mak.—We know this, dame,
That Malati already is betrothed.

Kam.—You know what you have heard; to all 'tis known,
That when the monarch for his favourite sued,
The minister replied, "Your majesty
Is master of your own—"

Mal.—So rumour goes.

Kam.—To-day we learn the king has given Malati
As if she were his own. But mark me, son;
The bond of human actions is good faith,
And promises control the acts of men:
In speech, the seeds of good and ill reside,
And all events are upon words dependent.
Do you not see in *Bhurivasu's* answer
A covert import lies?—for Malati
Is not the daughter of the sovereign;
Nor law nor social decency acknowledges
A monarch's will as the authority
To regulate a daughter's bridal compact.
Fie on it! It is not to be thought of—
And more, my son,—doubt you my vigilance?
Why, then, alarm the tender child with fears

Of such a fate I would not wish your foes ?—
Confide in me,—I will not spare my pains,
Nor life, if it be needed, to secure
Your union with the maiden.

Mak.—Well resolved.
There union is most suitable. Your heart,
Most holy dame, though from the world estranged,
Is softened still with pity and affection
Towards these thy children; and thy active love,
Howe'er opposed to pĕnance and devotion,
Shall like the will of destiny prevail.

Enter a MESSENGER.

The queen commands you, dame, with speed conduct
The lady Malati to the palace.

Kam.—Daughter, come.

(MADHAVA *and* MALATI *interchange looks and sighs.*)

Madh.—(*Apart.*) Out on the world's vicissitudes!
Fate, like a friend, first shows by blooming maid,
With tender passion like my own inspired;
Then with capricious fickleness afflicts
My heart with deeper anguish.

Mal.—(*Apart.*) Come what may,
This happiness is mine,—I have beheld him.

Lav.—This barbarous minister has taught my friend
To hate her being.

Mal.—(*Apart.*) Love of life has borne
Its fruits mature :—my father's cruely,
Stern as the offerer of human sacrifice,
And fate, alike relentless, have achieved
Their task. Ah me, unhappy ! to what friend,
To what kind refuge, can I now repair ?
[*Exit with Kamandaki and Lavangika.*

Madh.—I fear me much, the hope the dame encouraged
Sprang from the dread she entertained for her
Whom she has loved from birth. My luckless days
Will bear, I doubt, no fruit. What's to be done ;
(*Thinking.*)
Apply to horrid mysteries,—what else
Remains ? (*To Makaranda.*) How now, my friend methinks you grieve
For Madayantika.

Mak.—'Tis even so :
My mind recalls her timid wild embrace,
When fearful as the tender fawn, she clung,
With limbs diffusing nectar on my wounds,
Around me, heedless of her loose attire.

Madh.—She will be yours, for Buddharakshita.
Your friend, is hers ; and whom should she affect
But you, whom she embraced as her preserver

Snatched by your prowess from the monster's
fangs?
Nor did her looks proclaim you were a stranger.
The fond regard those lotus eyes expressed
Was clearly no new lesson.

Mak.—Let us hence.
Bathe where the *Sindhu* and the *Para* meet,
And then re-seek the town.

(*They rise and proceed.*)

This is the spot.
The union of the streams, whose favoured bank
Beholds our maidens, in the frequent bath,
Forego their robes, and with their tender
hands
Veiling imperfectly their charms, commit
Their lovely bosoms to the friendly wave.

[*Exeunt.*

END OF THE FOURTH ACT.

ACT V.

SCENE.—THE FIELD IN WHICH DEAD BODIES ARE BURNED IN THE VICINITY OF A TEMPLE.

Enter in the air in a heavenly car and in a hideous garb, KAPALAKUNDALA.

Glory to *Saktinath*, upon whose steps
The mighty goddesses attend, whom seek
Successfully alone the firm of thought.
He crowns the lofty aims of those who know
And hold his form, as the pervading spirit,
That, one with their own essence, makes his seat
The heart, the lotus centre of the sphere,
Six-fold, by ten nerves circled. Such am I.
Freed from all perishable bonds, I view
The eternal soul embodied as the God,
Forced by my spells to tread the mystic labyrinth,
And rise in splendour throned upon my heart.
Hence through the many channelled veins I draw.
The grosser elements of this mortal body,
And soar unwearied through the air, dividing
The water-shedding clouds. Upon my flight,

Horrific honours wait;—the hollow skulls,
That low descending from neck depend,
Emit fierce music as they clash together,
Or strike the trembling plates that gird
my loins.
Loose stream on every side my woven locks
In lengthening braids;—upon my pond'rous
staff,
The string of bells, light waving to and fro,
Jangles incessantly;—my banner floats
Upborne upon the wailing breeze, whose tone
Is deepened by the echoes it awakes
Amidst the caverns of each fleshless skull,
That hangs in dread array around my person.

(Alights and looks about.)

I scent the temple of *Karala*, near
The cemetery, and perfumed of old
By fetid odours from the funeral pile—
It is my present object—for to-day,
My wise preceptor, great Aghoraghanta,
Calls me to aid him in the powerful rite
That terminates his toils—to-day he offers
The promised gift, the gem of womankind,
A victim to the goddess. In this city
The damsel dwells, and I must make her
mine.

(*Looking out.*)

But who comes hitherward, of pleasing form,
With braided hair, and in one hand a sword?

The other—ha, it braves the world's restraints,
And soiled with blood, determinately grasps
A lump of human flesh ! And now I look,
I know the youth ; 'tis Madhava, the son
Of the old dame Kamandaki's dear friend.
What makes him vender of the flesh of man ?—
It matters not. Now to my work ; for see,
The hour of twilight hovers o'er the west ;
Along the skirts of the horizon steal
The winding glooms like dark *Tamala* blossoms ;
And earth's far bounds are lost, as if immersed
In nascent waters ; to the woods young night
Her own yet gentle shade imparts, as if
A wreath of smoke were wafted through the air,
And spread abroad in mist before the breeze.
[*Exit.*

Enter MADHAVA.

May those endearments yet be mine, that spring
From young affection and the dawn of passion,
Now first awakened in my Malati ;
Which for an instant only to imagine,
Inspires my heart with ecstasy unsullied
By all impure admixture. 'Twere enough

To be enfolded in her arms, to lean
My face upon her cheek, or to be prest
Against her firm and palpitating bosom,
Fragrant with perfume, and with pearls
adorned.
Yet this is too remote ; I will but ask
To see her face, the shrine of love once more,
Once more ! Ah no ! for ever in my view
She lives ; assiduous memory constant turns
To cherished hopes, and fed by hourly
thoughts,
One sole idea engrosses every sense,
Till all my inmost soul is Malati.

(A noise behind.)

Now wake the terrors of the place, beset
With crowding and malignant friends ; the
flames
From funeral pyres scarce lend their sullen
light,
Clogged with their fleshy prey, to dissipate
The fearful gloom thet hems them in. Pale
ghosts
Sport with foul goblins, and their dissonant
mirth
In shrill respondent shrieks is echoed round.
Well, be it so. I seek, and must adress them.
Demons of ill, and disembodied spirits,
Who haunt this spot, I bring you flesh for sale;

The flesh of man untouched by trenchant steel,
And worthy your acceptance. (*A great noise.*)
How the noise,
High, shrill, and indistinct, of chattering sprites
Communicative, fills the charnel ground!
Strange forms like foxes flit along the sky:
From the red hair of their lank bodies darts
The meteor blaze; or from their mouths, that stretch
From ear to ear thick-set with numerous fangs,
Or eyes, or beards, or brows, the radiance streams.
And now I see the goblin host: each stalks
On legs like palm-trees, a gaunt skeleton,
Whose fleshless bones are bound by starting sinews,
And scantly cased in black and shrivelled skin;
Like tall and withered trees by lightning scathed
They move, and as amidst their sapless trunks
The mighty serpent curls, so in each mouth
Wide yawning rolls the vast blood-dripping tongue.
They mark my coming, and the half-chewed morsel
Falls to the howling wolf,—and now they fly.

(*Pauses, and looking round.*)

Race, dastardly as hideous ! All is plunged
In utter gloom. (*Considering.*) The river flows before me,
The boundary of the funeral ground, that winds
Through mouldering bones its interrupted way.
Wild raves the torrent as it rushes past
And rends its crumbling banks ; the wailing owl
Hoots through its skirting groves, and to the sounds
The loud long moaning jackall yells reply.

(*Behind.*)

Ah, cruel father ! she you meant an offering
To the King's favour, now deserted dies.

Madh.—(*Alarmed.*) What voice was that so musical and wild,
That sounds like the affrighted osprey's cry ?
It bursts not unfamiliar to mine ear,
And penetrates my soul ;—my throbbing heart
Faint dies within me, and a lifeless chill
Steals along every limb !—my tottering steps
Can scarce sustain their load. What should this be ?
The dreadful sound came from *Karala's* fane,
Fit scene for deeds of horror. Be it so—
I must be satisfied. [*Rushes off.*

SCENE.—INSIDE OF THE TEMPLE OF CHAMUNDA.
AGHORAGHANTA, KAPALKUNDALA, *and*

MALATI *dressed as a victim.*

Mal.—Unpitying sire, thy haples daughter dies!
Mother beloved, remorseless fate consigns
Thy gentle heart to agony. Revered
And holy dame, who lived but for thy Malati,
Whose every thought was for her happiness,
Thy love will teach thee long and bitter anguish.
Ah, my dear friend, Lavangika, to thee
But in thy dreams I henceforth shall appear!

Madh.—(*Enters behind.*) My fears were true—'tis she! but still she lives.

Aghor.—(*Running round quickly as in worship.*)
Hail! hail! Chamunda, mighty goddess, hail!
I glorify thy sport, when in the dance
That fills the court of Shiva with delight,
Thy foot descending spurns the earthly globe.
Beneath the weight the broad-backed tortoise reels;
The egg of Brahma trembles at the shock;
And in a yawning chasm, that gapes like a hell,
The sevenfold main tumultuously rushes.
The elephant hide that robes thee, to thy steps
Swings to and fro;—the whirling talons rend
The cresent on thy brow;—from the torn orb
The trickling nectar falls, and every skull
That gems thy necklace laughs with horrid life.

Attendant spirits tremble and applaud;
The mountain falls before the powerful arms,
Around whose length the sable serpents twine
Their swelling forms, and knit terrific bands,
Whilst from the hood expanded frquent flash
Envenomed flames.
As rolls thy awful head,
The low'ring eye that glows amidst thy brow
A fiery circle designates, that wraps
The spheres within its terrible circumference:
Whilst by the banner on thy dreadful staff,
High waved, the stars are scattered from their orbits.
The three-eyed god exults in the embrace
Of his fair spouse, as *Gauri* sinks apalled
By the distracting cries of countless fiends
Who shout thy praise. Oh, may such dance afford
Whate'er we need—whate'er may yield us happiness!

Madh.—(*Behind.*) What luckless chance is this, that such a maid,
With crimson garb and garland like a victim
Adorned for sacrifice, should be the captive
Of impious wretches, like a timid fawn
Begirt by ravenous wolves: that she, the child
Of the all-powerful minister should lie
Thus in the jaws of death? Ah, cruel destiny,
How ruthless are thy purposes!

Kap.—Fair maid,
Think upon him whom thou in life hast loved,
For pitiless death is near thee.

Mal.—Ah, Madhava,
Lord of my heart! Oh may I after death
Live in thy memory! They do not die,
Whom love embalms in long and fond remembrance.

Kap.—Poor child, her heart is Madhava's.

Aghor.—(*Raising his sword.*) No matter—
Come what come may, we must delay no longer.
This offering vowed to thee, divine *Chamunda*,
Deign to accept.

Madh.—(*Rushes forward and snatches Malati up in his arms.*) Vile wretch, forbear!

Kap.—The term
Profane is thine.

Mal.—Oh, save me, save me! (*Embraces Madhava.*)

Madh.—Princess, do not fear.
A faithful friend, who in the hour of death
Finds courage to declare his love, is near thee—
Be of good courage—on this impious wretch,
The retribution of his crimes descends.

Aghor.—What sinful youth is this that interrupts
Our solemn rite?

Kap.—The lover of the maiden,
The pupil of Kamandaki, who treads
This precincts for unholy purposes,
And vends the flesh of man.

Madh.—Inform me, princess,
How has this chanced ?

Mal.—I know not, I reposed
At eve upon the terrace : when I woke
I found myself a prisoner.—But what led
Your steps to this retreat ?

Madh.—*(Ashamed.)* By passion urged,
Incited by the hope my life might be
Yet blest by this fair hand, I hither came
To invoke the unclean spirits of the dead.
Your cries I heard, and instant hurried here.

Mal.—And wert thou thus regardless of thyself,
And wandering here for me ?

Madh.—Blest was the chance
That snatched my love from the uplifted sword,
Like the pale moon from *Rahu's* rav'nous jaws.
My mind is yet with various passions tossed,
And terror, pity, wonder, joy, and rage,
By turns possess my soul.

Aghor.—Rash Brahman boy,
Thou seekest thy fate. The pitying stag defies

The tiger in the rescue of his doe,
And both are made the forest monarch's prey—
So shalt thou perish, who darest hope to save
The victim of my sacrifice. Thy blood,
As flies the severed head before my scymitar,
Shall stream an offering to the mighty mother
Of all created beings.

Madh.—Wretch accursed,
Impious and vile! Couldst thou raise thy sword
Against this delicate frame, that timid shrunk
Even from the flowers her fond companions cast
In sportive mood upon her—but my arm
Like Yama's mace now falls upon thy head.

Mal.—(*To Madaava.*) Lord of my life, refrain from violence:
His crime is baffled, let him be. Avoid
All needless peril.

Kap.—(*To Aghor.*) Holy sir, be firm;
Destroy the culprit.

Madh and Aghor.—(*To the women.*) Banish your alarms;
The villain dies. What other chance should wait
The issue of the contest, when the lion,
Whose talons 'light upon the elephant's brow,
As falls the thunderbolt upon the mountain,
Raises their might against the feeble deer.

(A noise behind.)

What, ho! ye who are now in search of Malati,
The venerable priestess whose commands
Are ever wise, enjoins ye to surround
The temple of *Karala*. This can be
The act of none but him who ministers
To the terrific goddess, and the princess
Can be an offering for no other shrine.

Kap.—We are surrounded!

Aghor.—Greater is the need
Of manly resolution.

Mal.—My dear father!
My venerable mistress!

Madh.—I will place
The princess out of peril with her friends,
Then swift return for vengeance.

(He carries Malati off and returns confronting Aghoraghanta.)

Now let the falchion piecemeal hew thy form,
Ring on thy bones, and cleave thy sinewy joints,
Sport in the yielding marrow, and divide,
Resistless in its fury, limb from limb.

[*Exeunt fighting.*

END OF THE FIFTH ACT.

ACT VI.

A PUBLIC PLACE.

Enter KAPALKUNDALA.

Alas! the cruel Madhava has slain
My venerable master in the cause
Of Malati. In vain, I strove to stay
His ruthless hand; he spurned my supplications.
What now remains?—vengenance? Yes, Madhava,
Thou yet shall feel my fury—no repose
Can the destroyer of the serpent brood
Expect to taste—the mother snake retains
Her wrath unmitigated, whets her fangs,
And hoards her venom, wakeful for revenge.

(*Without.*)

Ho, warriors! haste; be quick in preparation
Appointed by the elders. Let the Brahmans
Recite auspicious strains. Let all devise
Ingenious shows and fitting invocations,
Propitiating fate—for near at hand
The bridegroom train approaches. Till they come,
Obedient to the holy dames' injunctions,.

The matrons of her father's household send
The maiden to the temple of the deity
That guards our walls, to pray that nought molest,
No evil interrupt the happy rite.
Quick let a guard, in rich comparison
Arrayed, upon the brilliant train attend.

Kap.—'Tis well—I will keep vigilant watch ;
And in the bustle of this marriage feast,
I may perchance some fit occasion seize
To wreak my vengeange upon Madhava.
[*Exit.*

SCENE II.—INSIDE OF THE TEMPLE.

Enter KALAHAMSA.

I was ordered by my master, who is concealed within the shrine here with his friend Makaranda, to go and see whether the lady Malati leads the procession to this temple. I shall delight him.

Enter MADHAVA *and* MAKARANDA.

Madh.—How will this end ? from the first day I saw
The lovely maid, events succeeding add
Fresh fuel to my passion, and to-day
The crisis comes. Will the sage dame's device
Secure me bliss, or end in disappointment ?

Mak.—Fear not, my friend, her wisdom cannot fail.

Mal.—(*Approaches.*) My lord, you are favoured by fortune.

The lady Malati is on the road, at the head of the procession.

Madh.—Can it be true?

Mak.—Why should you doubting question?

They are at hand; for hark, a hollow murmur
Like that of rushing clouds, before the gate
Comes sudden on the ear, and now the drums
That peal in joy drown every other sound;
Here from the lattice we may see their march.

Kal.—Look, master, see how the white umbrellas float like trembling lotuses in the lake of the atmosphere. The numerous banners undulate like waves as they play before the wind of the Chowris, which hover about like swans; and now the elephants advance, their golden bells tinklinng as they stride; they are mounted by merry bevies of damsels, singing songs of rejoicing, uttered indistinctly as interupted by the betel that perfumes their mouths, and blazing like rays of light with glittering of jewels variegated tints, as if they were so many portions of the heavens decorated with fragments of Indra's bow.

Mak.—The state of *Bhurivasu* is, in sooth,

Most princely. As the countless jewels shoot
Their blaze into the sky, the heavens reflect
The countless hues, as if the peacock's plumage,
Or the mixed colours of the painted jay,
Played through the air, China's gorgeous silks

Vested the atmosphere, or *Indra's* bow.
Displayed throughout its many coloured radiance.

Kal.—The throng of attendants hastily forming a circle fall off to a respectful distance, and keep back the crowd with staves, covered with silver and gold. Her elephant, painted with vermilion, resembles the ruddy dawn, or with the starry garland on her brow, looks like the brilliant night. But she herself, the lovely object of all eyes, as pale and delicate as the new moon, advances from the ring.

Mak.—The beauteous damsel well becomes the grace
Of bridal honours. Her emaciate form
And pallid cheek, although they plainly show
Deep-rooted grief, heighten her loveliness,
Like some fair plant just budding into flower
And withered at the core. Behold! my friend,
The elephant kneels.

Mad.—And Malati descends,
And with the priestess and her faithful friend
Lavangika, comes hither.

[*They withdraw.*

SCENE III.—INSIDE OF THE TEMPLE.

Enter KAMANDAKI, MALATI, *and* LAVANGIKA.

Kam.—(*To herself.*) May fate assist the wishes of our hearts,
And may the just gods crown them with completion:
May I attain my aim, and this device,
That binds the children of my friends in love,
Secure their future happiness.

Mal.—(*Apart.*) Ah me!
What blest occasion will afford the means
Of death to free me from the world?—but no,
Death comes not to the wretch who prays his aid.

Lav.—(*Apart.*) This final parting from her love has plunged
My poor friend in despair.

Enter a FEMALE ATTENDANT *with a basket.*

Att.—(*To Kamandaki.*) His Excellency, dame, desires me to inform you, that his Majesty has sent this bridal dress and these ornaments, that Malati may put them on in presence of the deity.

Kam.—'Tis rightly judged—the place is most propitious.
Let us behold the gear!

Att.—This is the corset of white silk; this is the red muslin mantle—these are the ornaments; this the necklace—this is sandal, this the chaplet of flowers.

Kam.—(*Apart.*) It were a pleasant trick, and Madayantika
Will not be sorry to behold the youth.
(*Aloud.*) Inform the minister it shall be done
As he directs. (*Exit Servant.*) Daughter, Lavangika,
Attend the princess to the inner shrine.

Lav.—Where tarry you meanwhile?

Kam.—I would remain
Alone, and leisurely investigate
The value of these jewels. [*Exit.*

Mal.—(*Apart.*) Left with Lavangika alone!

Lav.—This is the door. Here let us enter.

(*They enter.—Scene changes to the interior of the Temple.*)

MADHAVA, MAKARANDA, *and* KALAHAMSA *discovered.*

Mak.—They come; let us conceal ourselves awhile,
Behind this pillar. [*They hide.*

Enter MALATI *and* LAVANGIKA.

Lav.—Here is the perfume for the person—here
The flowery garland. (*Offering them.*)

Mal.—What are they to me?

Lav.—Consider, my dear friend, you are sent here
By your respected mother to propitiate

The deity, and thus invoke good fortune
On the commencement of the marriage rite.

Mal.—Why thus distract a wretch whose heart is torn
With pangs intolerable, and whose mind
Is tortured by the wanton cruelty
Of unrelenting fate ?

Lav.—Alas ! what would you say !

Mal.—Whatever he whose fortunes are, like mine,
Blighted by unavailing hopes, might counsel.

Mak.—Heard you ?

Madh.—I heard—what little cheers my heart.

Mal.—(*Embracing Lavangika.*) My dearest friend, the sister of my soul,
Your hapless Malati, about to die
Unwedded, begs one proof of your affection.
From earliest infancy you have replied
Unvarying to my confidence—ah ! now,
Do not the first time disappoint my hopes—
Bear still my image in your heart, and see
The lotus lovely countenance of Madhava,
The shrine of each auspicious excellence.
(*Weeps.*)

Madh.—(*Behind.*) Delightful words that fortunately shed
Their nectar through my heart, and o'er my frame ;
Diffuse the powerful medicine that restores
The vigorous bloom of life's decaying flower.

Mal.—Then tell the brave preserver of my life,
He must not, if he ever prized my love,
When he shall here that I am dead, attempt
His days, but live to cherish my remembrance
Tell him, I hope he will not wholly lose
The recollection of this life's events;
Although the tenant of another world,
I here shall live in memory alone.
Do this, and all your Malati's desires
Your kindness will bestow.

Mak.—Alas, poor girl!

Madh.—The sad yet sweet tones of her fond despair
Awake contending sentiments—her grief
Excites both joy and pain, and fills my mind
With anguish and delight.

Lav.—I am overcome
With horror! let me hear no more, my friend,
Words of such evil omen.

Mal.—Ah, Lavangika,
You love the life of Malati alone—
Not Malati.

Lav.—What mean you?

Mal.—I have borne
Thus long a hateful life, sustained alone
By flattering promises I yet might wed
The lord of my election. This is past;
But 'tis my firm resolve to end my days,
Free from the stain of violated faith,

To the divinity whom I have served—
Then do not thou oppose me in my purposese.
(Falls at her feet.)

Mak.—Her love is boundless.
(Lavangika beckons to Madhava.)
Go, take her place.

Madh.—I tremble.

Mak.—'Tis a sign]
Of coming happiness!

Madh.—I go. *(Approaches gently and takes the station of Lavangika, who retrires.)*

Mal.—*(Kneeling.)* Speak your assent, my friend:

Madh.—Forego such desperate purpose, simple maid.
My heart, dear girl, will never bear thy loss.

Mal.—Behold me prostrate till you give consent!

Madh.—What can I say, desponding as thou art?
Do as thou wilt; but first this fond embracer.

Mal.—Now I am blest!

(Rises and throws herself into Madhava's arms.)

I have but half my friend;
For my fast-flowing tears obscure my sight.
Firm as the lotus cup, and smooth with down,
Thy form recalls a contact that allays
The fever of my grief: oh, bear its owner,
With hands thus elevated to your brow,
My farewell message. 'Tis long since these eyes

Have lost the sight of thy engaging countenance,
As brilliant as the broad bright beaming moon,
And lovelier than the full-blown lotus flower.
The sufferings of my frame, which not the rays
Of the mild lunar orb, nor the cool breath
Of Malaya could appease, have long distressed
My friendly train with bitterest affliction.
My heart, whose firmness, by incessant cares
Still growing more unbearable assailed,
Had sunk, was yet by hope sustained; but now
I hope no more. Let me still live, dear friend,
In your remembrance; and when I am gone,
May this the work of Madhava, preserved
Next to your heart, whene'er it meet your gaze,
Bring to your mind the Malati you loved.

(Goes to hang the garland round the neck of Madhava, and discovering her mistake starts back in alarm).

Madh.—*(Apart.)* The gentle pressure of her heaving bosom
Has spread delightful coolness through my frame,
As if combined upon my skin were strewed

Sandal and camphor—*saivala* and pearls—
The lotus fibre or the moonstone's dew.

Mal.—Lavangika betrays me!

Madh.—Gentle maid,
Your own experience only cannot teach you
What others have endured—but this belief,
Such days as you yave passed, such have I known,
Whose fevered flames have raged in every vein,
And anguish wrung conscious existence from me—
Thy love alone preserved my fleeting life.

Lav.—You are ensnared, my friend, as you deserved.

Kal.—This mutual confession is pleasant enough.

Mak.—Princess, you are merciful, it is true.
My friend has undergone so sad a time,
And yet exists—now may his hopes be crowned,
And with that plighted hand the golden thread
Shall gird, be happiness his future portion.

Lav.—How can you name the golden thread that girds
The bridal hand? Observe you not, her heart
Is agitated with the apprehension
Of an immediate and unwelcome marriage.

Mal.—(*Apart*). Out on it—What is this? it ill becomes
A maiden's honour.

Kam.—(*Entering.*).—How now.
My gentle child?

(*Malati throws herself into her arms.*)

Kam.—Look up! behold the youth who shared your sufferings,
Whose eyes first caught the flames; whose heart was next
To thee alone devoted; and whose frame,
Like thine emaciate, equal passion shows.
Behold him here! Dismiss this weak timidity—
Be love obeyed and destiny fulfilled.

Lav.—What marvel, dame, our friend should be alarmed!
This is, to say the truth, a fearful personage—
The conqueror of the fierce and impious wretch
Who braved his fatal army when on the night
No moon illumes, and with no good intent,
He trod the confines of the funeral ground.

Mak.—(*To himself.*) Well said, Lavangika, the double bond of love and gratitude is well suggested.

Mal.—Alas, my parents!

Kam.—Madhava my son.

Madh.—Command me.

Kam.—This is this dearest gem of *Bhurivasu*,
The mighty minister, whose feet are blazoned
With the bright diadems of prostrate princes,
Fate, pleased congenial merit to unite,
And love and I their instrument, confer
This treasure to your care. (*Weeps.*)

Mak.—Our hopes are gratified
By your kind aid.

Madh.—But why these tears?

Kam.—My son, long-cherished friendship has endeared
The interests of your house to me; and now
That love is consummated, for mine old
And tried affection, and for other causes,
I may demand you listen to my counsels.
Then, heed my words, and pledge your faith to me,
You cherish this dear child most tenderly,
When I no more behold her.

(*About to fall at the feet of Madhava.*)

Madh.—(*Preventing her.*) Forbear! forbear! your kindness overpowers me.

Mak.—Why should you need assurance, dame, of this—
The object of your praise—the living festival
Of human eyes—replete with warm affection
And brilliant worth—why, one were irresistible—
Their union is your surety.

Kam.—My son (*to Madhava*).

Madh.—Behold me!

Kam.—Malati, my child.

Lav.—She waits upon your will.

Kam.—Remember, children—

A virtuous wife and a respected lord
Are each to either all—kindred and friends,
Wealth, love, and life, and all the heart should covet.

Mak.—'Tis justly said,

Lav.—What further has the dame
To order?

Kam.—Makaranda, take these robes
And dress you for the bridal.

Mak.—As you will.
Behind this curtain I can make my toilet.
[*Retires.*

Madh.—But will not this expose my friend to peril?

Kam.—Out on thee—what hast thou to do in this?

Madh.—I trust me to your judgment.

Enter MAKARANDA *in female attire*

Mak.—My friend, behold your Malati

Madh.—(*Embracing him.*)—In truth,
The priestess highly favours Nandana,
To yield his admiration, for an instant,
A bride like this.

Kam.—Now my dear children (*to Malati and Madhava*),—leave
This temple by the sacred grove, and pass

Quick to the garden of my sanctuary.
In the pavilion Avalokita
Awaits your coming, with all means prepared
To celebrate the nuptial ceremony.
The rite accomplished, to the grove retire,
Where round the areka-trees the betel vine
Curls its pale leaves, as pallid as the cheek
Of the fair dames of *Kerala* who mourn
Their absent lords. The beauties of the scene,
Begirt with waving oranges, and musical
With the sweet tone of numerous choristers,
Who sip delightedly the jujube's juice,
Shall breathe a warmer rapture on your loves.
There loiter till your friend and his fair maid,
The princess Madayantika, shall join you.

Madh.—This were indeed to crown my happiness.

Kal.—If luck befriend us, this will surely be.

Madh.—There cannot be a fear.

Lav.—Heard you, my friend?

Kam.—Lavangika
And Makaranda, we must now depart.

Mal.—What! must you go, Lavangika?

Lav.—*(Smiling.)*—I must.
This is our way.

[*Exeunt Kamandaki, Lavangika, and Makaranda.*

Madh.—Like some fair lotus is this trembling hand,
Along whose slender stalk the downy filaments

Erect extend, and from whose leaflet fingers
The pearly drops from love engendered fall.
I clasp it now in mine—as with his tusk
The elephant entwines the tender flower,
And gently wrests it from native lake.
[*Exit with Malati.*

END OF THE SIXTH ACT.

ACT VII.

THE PALACE OF NANDANA.

Enter BUDDHARAKSHITA.

So far so well. Makaranda well became his disguise as Malati, and by the instructions and good fortune of the dame has played his part unsuspected, and has been wedded to Nandana in the palace of the minister. Kamandaki then took leave, and has gone home, anticipating that the attendants will all be wearied with the bustle of the festival of bringing the bride to her husband's house,[1] and that the evening will be favourable to the execution of our design. In the meantime, Nandana, impatient to possess his bride, first endeavoured to soothe her alarms, and humbled himself at her feet. Finding this in vain, he had recourse to violence; but he was so severely handled by the supposed maiden that he was compelled to desist. Enraged at the treatment, the tears starting from his eyes with pain and vexation, and his speech inarticulate with fury, Nandana vowed he would have no more to say to one who was no better than the wanton of a boy. With this determination he left the apartments, and with this opportunity we may bring Madayantika and Makaranda together.

[*Exist.*

SCENE II.—MAKARANDA *and* LAVANGIKA *on a couch in woman's attire discovered.*

Mak.—You are confident that Buddharakshita
Will make no blunder, and so disappoint
The project of the priestess ?

Lav.—Never fear :
And hark! the tinkling foot bells-that proclaim
Their near approach : quick, spread this mantle over you,
And seem sleep. (*He lies down as she covers him.*

Enter MADAYANTIKA *and* BUDDHARASKEITA.

Maday.—Is indeed my brother
So grievously displeased with Malati ?

Buddh.—No doubt.

Maday.—But this is unbecoming—let us go
And take to task this rude ill-mannered girl.

Buddh.—This is her chamber door.

Maday.—Lavangika,
Sleeps your fair friend ?

Lav.—Yes ; do not break her slumbers.
She has been sadly vexed of late, and now,

Her cares awhile forgot, she tastes repose.
Here, gently seat you on the couch.

Maday.—(*Sits down.*) Indeed
She may be vexed; that she is rude, I'm sure.

Lav.—How, should she not be fretted—with a husband
So gently kind, affectionate, and mild,
So skilled to win a maiden's confidence,
As is your brother?

Maday.—Hey, Buddharakshita,—
We blame her strange perverseness,

Buddh.—Perverse may not on all occasions be
Perverseness.

Maday.—How so?

Buddh.—'Tis true she treated with but scant respect
The husband prostrate at her feet; still this
Was maiden bashfulness, and might be pardoned.
You cannot deem so of your brother's anger,
Who in resentment of a coy resistance,
Such as became a virgin bride to offer
To boisterous violence, forgot all sense
Of his own dignity, and had recourse
To sheer abuse—such conduct is disgraceful
To you, not us. The poets well observe,
Women like flowers are of tender fabric,
And should be softly handled—they detest
The furious passion that would force their love,
Impatient, ere their confidence be won.

Lav.—Alas! who ever heard of such behavior?
In many a house, men of exalted rank
Are wedded unto maids of gentle birth.
But who, like fire the breeze blows into flame,
Is rendered furious by the chaste reluctance
Of his young, fair, and unoffending bride.
A husband's harshness renders home distasteful
To the desponding wife, tortures her heart
With poisoned shafts, and makes her wish for death.
Occurrences like these compel a family
To murmur sorely when a girl is born.

Maday.—(*To Buddh.*) Our freind Lavangika seems sadly grieved.
What fault so heinous is my brother charged with?

Buddh.—Did we not hear his words?

Maday.—What were they?

Buddh.—"I will nought
Of one no better than a stripling's wanton."

Maday.—Folly! insanity! my friend Lavangika,
It is with shame I look you in the face.
But I should have some voice in this affair;
So hear what I advise.

Lav.—I am attentive.

Maday.—Dismiss the memory of my brother's rudeness.
Remember only that he is the husband

Of our friend Malati: and to confess
The truth, you must admit there was some cause
For this intemperate language, though unmeet
For female ears.

Lav.—I know no cause.

Maday.—It has been noised abroad,
That Malati had plighted her affection
To the youth Madhava. This is no mystery.
But now, dear friend, exert your utmost skill,
That such ill-starred aversion to her husband
May utterly be rooted from her heart:
If not, a grievous shame will 'light upon her,
For wives, resentful and ungentle, plague
The hearts of men—this fear that I have hinted
You will not speak of.

Lav.—Hence, you heedless girl,
To be beguiled by loose report so easily:
I hold no further talk with you.

Maday.—Nay, nay,
Be not displeased: you need not hesitate
To own the truth—what, I suppose we knew not—
That Malati had nearly pined to death
On Madhava's account. We did not mark
The delicate beauty of her wasting form,
Like the young tender *ketaki*; we saw not
The animating influence of the wreath

Of *vakula* flowers, wove by the hand of
Madhava;
Nor did we note the evident sympathy
Each frame expressed, when either showed
as wan
As the moon's pallid disk when morning dawns.
You may forget, that I beheld their glances,
When in the garden of the flower-armed god
The youth and maiden met: their eyes
encountering,
Swam with delight, and brilliant flashes shot
From each soft orb, uttering intelligibly
The language prompted by the soft emotion
That played through every agitated limb.
Then, when the news arrived the king had
given her
In marriage to my brother, was not a change,
As if the hand of adverse fate had scorched
Her charms, and rudely from its living bands
Had wrung her heart, that moment manifest?
Nay I remember too——

Lav.—What more?

Maday.—When, by the shrewd suggestion of the dame,
The youth was counselled to give Malati
Some token of his happiness, that his friend,
The brave preserver of my life, was brought
Again to conscious being, he presented her
His heart, and life; and, if I heard aright,

Lavangika replied, "My friend esteems
These liberal gifts most worthy her acceptance"

Lav.—And who was he—the saviour of your life?
I have forgotten him.

Maday.—Think, think again.
When I was chased by the ferocious beast,
And had no hope—the guardian youth apeared,
And heedless of a person which enshrines
The worth of all the world, quick interposed
His powerful arm to snatch me from destruction.
For me he braved the monster's mighty blows,
Falling like thunder strokes; his manly breast
Was scored with wounds, and ruddier than a wreath
Of crimson roses. But the tiger plied
His fangs and claws in vain—the hero triumped—
The furious sagave fell beneath his sword,

Lav.—Ah, I remember now—'twas Makaranda.

Maday.—Whom, say you?

Lav.—Makaranda. (*Taking hold of her.*)
How now!
What, are we all alike? How chances it,
That one so free from passion should betray,
Without apparent cause, this agitation,
And blossom like the *kadamba* flower?

Maday.—Why laugh at me? I own I often think
Of that brave youth who, reckless of his safety,
Rushed to my aid and snatched me from the jaws

Of all-devouring fate I frequent view him,
As the sharp pain of his innumerous wounds
Forced the big drops his exhaused limbs,
And leaning on his sword awhile he stood,
Then closed his lotus eyes and fainting fell—
Content to leave this glorious living world
For Madayantika, and in her presence.
Should I think less of one who saved my life?

Buddh.—All this is in your person plainly told.

Maday.—Away, away! I have betrayed myself,
Depending on your faith.

Lav.—Nay, dear girl;
We know that which we know. Come, be composed,
Confess the truth; there should be no disguise
Amongst such friends as we are. Let us taste
The pleasure mutual confidence bestows.

Buddh.—Lavangika is right.

Maday.—Well, I must need
Obey my friend.

Lav.—Come, tell us how of late
You pass your time?

Maday.—Heare me:
Before I saw the youth I frequent heard
His praise from Buddharakshita, and pleased
By her description, let my fancy dwell
Upon his absent image till my heart
Was filled with anxious longing to behold him.

At length 'twas willed by fate that we should meet,
Though for brief interval. Oh, then I found
How deep a wound had Madana inflicted.
Life was distasteful to me—on my form
The scorching flames of passion fiercely preyed,
And filled my kind attendants with affliction.
The only remedy I saw was death;
And anxious sought such welcome liberation.
Still Buddharakshita opposed my purpose,
Assuaged my growing sorrows, and persuaded me
Still to endure this transitory world.
My dreams since comes to animate my hopes;
Place in my eyes the object of my wishes;
Bring to my ears the music of his voice,
Fold me within his grasp, and picture more
Than I dare tell you—till I wake and view,
Ah me! the world a lone and dreary waste.

Lav.—'Tis honestly avowed; and well I know,
It costs our friend here no small pains to hide
Some of these feeings from your tittering train.

Maday.—You chatter giddily—I have done with you.

Buddh.—Regard her not, be sure that Malati
Has for her ear some similar confession.

Maday.—Nay, nay, you must not laugh at Malati.

Buddh.—Well, I have done; and now my tender friend,

I have a question for you, if you promise me
Inviolate secrecy,

Maday.—What breach of trust
Have I commitred, that there needs such promise?
My heart is wholly yours and Lavangika's.

Buddh.—If Makaranda cross your sight again
By any accident, what would you do?

Maday.—My eyes wonld rest unwearied on his form,
And on my heart would heavenly rapture fall.

Buddh.—And if, by love directed, he should offer
Such gentle violence as *Rukmini*
Endured from *Purushottama*, and wrung
Your bridal vows from you?

Maday.—(*Sighing.*) Why tease me
With such vain hopes?

Buddh.—Nay, answer me.

Lav.—Those sighs,
Deep-drawn, betray the secrets of her heart,
And give you plain reply.

Maday.—What do you think of me?
He bought this body when he risked his own
And snatched me from the tiger—I am his.

Lav.—'Tis generously and gratefully resolved.

Buddh.—You will remember what you have now said.

Maday.—Hark! (*Drums without.*)
The drum proclaims the second watch begun;
I must disturb my friend, and try to soothe

Her indignation at my brother's conduct,
And then to rest. Why, Malati, asleep?
(*Goes to the couch, Makaranda shows his face and catches hold of her hand.*)
Hey, who is this?

Mak.—Fear nothing, gentle maid;
Let not that palpitating breast distress
Your slender waist. In me, behold your slave!
By your avowed affection elevated
To highest ecstasy.

Lav.—(*Holding up Madayantika's face.*)
Behold your lover!
The object of your hopes. Within the palace
The servants soundly sleep—the night is dark,
Now show your gratitude, let us take off
Our tinkling anklets and depart.

Maday.—Where should we go?

Buddh.—Where Malati has gone.

Maday.—What! has she fled?

Buddh.—She has; now let me see,
What I must think of you.
(*Madyantika weeps*).
(*To Mak.*) Noble youth,
My dear friend gives to you—herself.

Mak.—This is
A glorious conquest, and to-day I reap
The harvest of my youth—upon whose festival,
In proof of friendship, the fish-bannered god

Presents me in his bounty this dear maid.
Come, by this private entrance let us fly;
Our nightly journey will not want its pleasures.
The breeze that cool and fragrant sweeps along,
The lofty terrace or the palace top,
Reveals the joyous scenes it has surveyed,
As with the camphory balm, and flowery perfume,
And winey odours; redolent it blows.

[*Exeunt.*

END OF THE SEVENTH ACT.

ACT VIII.

THE MANSION OF KAMANDAKI.

Enter AVALOKITA.

Whilst my mistress has gone to the palace of *Nandana*, I will seek Madhava and Malati. Ah, there they sit, upon the marble platform crowning the steps of the lake, refreshing themselves after the heat of the day. I will join them.

[*Exit.*

THE GROVE.

MALATI *and* MADHAVA *discovered.—To them,* AVALOKITA.

Madh.—Night, ever friend to love, now spreads its shades.
Faint in the east the gentle moon-light gleams,
Pale as the palm's sear leaf, and through the air
The slowly rising breezes spread around
The grateful fragrance of the *ketaki*,
How shall I win this maid to confidence?
My dearest Malati, whilst I retain
The cooling influence of the evening bath,
You are oppressed with heat; the trembling drops,

Steal from your hair and quiver on your bosom,
And o'er your graceful form the down erect
Profusely rises. Whilst you suffer thus,
Come to my breast, let me but once embrace thee.
Why thus averse? Let those that confiding arms,
Upon whose taper length the sudden dews
Start with alarm as if the living gem,
Kissed by the moon distilled its gelid moisture,
Twine round my neck; and if this may not be,
Why may I not be blessed with your discourse?
What, if this frame, long scorched by southern gales
And by the lunar beams, may not aspire
To your embrace, yet let mine ear, distressed
By the wild *koil's* song, be now regaled
By your melodious voice, more musical
Than are the choirs of heaven.

Ava.—(*Advancing.*) What folly, this,—
What inconsistency!—late, in my presence,
When Madhava but a brief interval
Had disappeared, you were most miserable,
And thus exclaimed: "Where can my lord delay?

Would he were come, that I might gaze
upon him
With eyelids never veiled, and all reserve
Discarded wholly, I might fly to him
And clasp him in my arms!" Those were your
words;
And now, what contrast!
(Malati looks at her spitefully.)

Madh.—*(Apart.)* The dame's disciples,
Are all endowed with clear intelligence
And eloquence of speech. *(Aloud.)* How,
Malati,
Speaks Avalokita the truth?
(Malati shakes her head.)
Or are you sworn to silence, by the lives
Of those whom best you love?

Mal.—*(In a hesitating manner.)* How should I
know, my lord?

Madh.—Delightful, though imperfect sounds! But see!
(Pauses.)
What should this mean? The starting tear-
drop steals,
From those fawn eyes, and glisten on
that cheek,
Upon whose pallid hue the moon-beams play,
As if the lunar orb desired to quaff
The nectar of its beauty.

Ava.—Why is this?
Why start these tears?

Mal.—(*To her.*) How long must I regret
The absence of Lavangika ; is it
Not possible to gather tidings of her ?

Madh.—(*To Avalokita.*) What says my love ?

Ava.—You have recalled the memory of Lavangika,
And she is anxious for some news of her,

Madh.—It was but now, I ordered Kalahamsa
To go, and secretly collect intelligence
At Nandana's abode. Surely the plan
That was to win my friend a lovely bride
Cannot have failed ?

Ava.—Be sure of it,
But tell me, Madhava.
You gave your life and heart to Malati,
When brought again to consciousness—
suppressed
By fear for Makaranda's bleeding wounds.
Now, if that friend beloved should win the maid,
And thus your happiness should be increased,
What gift remains to speak your gratitude
To him who may impart the pleasing tidings ?

Madh.—She tells me what to do. (*Looking at his bosom.*)
This garland, wove
Of the sweet flowers of that beauteous tree
That graced the grove of Madana, beneath
Whose conscious shade I first saw Malati,
Shall be my free-will gift. It has been prest

Already to her bosom—from my hands
Conveyed by her dear friend Lavangika ;
And in her error, thinking that she gave
The garland to Lavangika again
To bear to me it came to me once more
From her, by whom all that I prize is given me.

Ava.—Malati, this garland ought to be
Something in your esteem—be on your guard
It do not pass into a stanger's hands.

Mal.—You counsel well.

Madh.—(*Looking out.*) 'Tis Kalahamsa.

Mal.—(*Approaching.*) Fate favours you, and Madayantika
Is won.

Madh.—(*Embracing her.*) The news is ecstasy.

(*Takes the garland from his neck and throws it on Malati's.*)

Ava.—The charge consigned to Buddharakshita,
Is well accomplished.

Mal.—And I see
Lavangika again,

Enter hastily KALAHAMSA, MADAYANTIKA, BUDDHARAKSHITA *and* LAVANGIKA.

Lav.—Help, prince ! the city-guard have stopped midway,
Your galland friend ; he checks pursuit alone'
That we with Kalahamsa might escape.

Kal.—And as we fled, we heard on every side
The gathering tumult; so that I fear fresh force
Has joined the guard.

Ava.—Alas! how sad a chance!
One hour produces happiness and terror.

Madh.—Come, Madayantika, my dwelling,
Is honoured by your presence. For my friend—
His prowess is well known—be not alarmed;
Dread not, though singly he contented with multitudes.
To such as he, odds are of little moment:
He needs no succour but his own right arm,
Resistless as the lion, when delightedly
He rings his clashing claws, and cleaves asunder
The elephant's broad temples, from whose hollows
The trickling dew flows over the shattered cheek.
Ambitious to pursue the glorious path
A hero treads, I haste to aid my friend.
[*Exit with Kalahamsa.*

Ava.—Assuredly these heroes will return
Unhurt.

Mal.—Do you and Buddharakshita
Apprise Kamandaki of this mischance.
Lavangika, overtake my lord; entreat him

That he and his brave friend will think of us,
And shun all needless danger—go, be speedy.
[*Exeunt the three.*

After a pause

Mal.—Lavangika delays—why comes she not?
This is a fearful interval; dear girl
(*To Madayantika*),
I will go forth along the road, and meet
Lavangika returning.

Maday.—My right eye throbs. [*Retires.*

As MALATI *is going, enter* KAPALAKUNDALA.

Kap.—Hold.

Mal.—(*Screams.*) Ah! husband! (*In an under-tone —stops terrified.*)

Kap.—Yes, call upon him.
Where is your love, the murderer of the pious,
The youthful paramour of wanton girls?
Let him, your husband, save you if he can.
Bird of the wild, that tremblest to behold
The hovering hawk, what canst thou hope,
long marked
My prey? I bear thee with me to *Sri Parvata*,
There to consign thee to a painful death,
Torn piecemeal—victim of my just revenge.
(*Carries off Malati.*)

Maday.—(*Coming forward.*)
I will even follow Malati.
Ha! Malati.

Lav.—(*Enters.*) 'Tis I, Lavangika.

Maday.—How! have you seen the princess?

Lav.—I have not.

Scarce had we left the garden's boundaries,
When hearing the increasing noise, the youth
Sprang speedily away, and in an instant
Was lost amidst the throng: in vain I followed,
And thought it better to retrace my steps.
As I returned, I heard from every house
Regret for Makaranda and his friend—
The citizens were grieving for their fate.
The king, they said, had been informed the youths
Had borne away the daughter of the minister,
And furiously incensed, had sent his guards
To seize the fugitives—himself awaiting
Upon the palace-terrace their return.

Maday.—Ah me, unhappy! I have heard my death.

Lav.—But where is Malati?

Maday.—She went to watch
The road you should return. I then pursued
Her steps, but have not seen her since. Most likely,
She has gone into the garden.

Lav.—Let us seek her. Hold! who comes here?
'Tis Kalahamsa: quick, your news,

Enter KALAHAMSA.

Kal.—We have got well out of the scuffle ! Oh, dear me ! I think I now see the glittering gleam of the polished sabres flashing in the moonlight—a pretty but awful appearance : and then what a tumult from the hostile force ! Assailed by the irresistible, merciless, and active Makaranda, they fled in dismay, and confusion, with a clamour which filled the whole space of heaven, like that emitted by the tossing waves of *Kalindi* when they were turned from their course by the mighty plough of *Balarama*, in fulfilment of the menace that wine had dictated. I shall not forget either the prowess of my master Madhava. He soon cleared the road of the soldiers : they ran with no little speed, those who could, while covering the road with heaps of various weapons, thrown away in their flight from the concentrated thunder-stroke of his formidable arm. The king has truly a regard for merit. His eye dwelt with complacency on the lovely countenances of Madhava and Makaranda, as they stood before him on the terrace, whither, after the affray was composed by the monarch's attendants, they had been respectfully conducted. Having heard their rank and connections from me, the youths received every honour ; and his majesty turning to Bhurivasu and Nandana, who stood nigh, their faces as black as ink with rage and disappointment, said to them very condescendingly : "How now ! are you not content with kinsmen such as these, ornaments of the world, eminent in worth and deseent, and handsome as the new moon ?" So saying, he withdrew to the interior, and Madhava and Makaranda were dismissed. They are now coming, and I have been sent on before to carry the tidings to the pious dame,

Lav.—(*To Madayantika.*) Delightful news for you, nor less acceptable
To our dear Malati: let us haste to find her,
[*Exeunt severally.*

Enter MADHAVA *and* MAKARANDA.

Madh.—I cannot choose but marvel at thy prowess,
So more than mortal—breaking thy way resistless
Through all opposing ranks; scattering the timid,
And levelling the fircest with thy arm.
On either hand the frightened troops retired,
As forced my friend a path amidst the wave
Of battle, tossing with innumerous heads.

Mak.—I do foresee the valiant will lose credit
With their fair nymphs, who in these festal nights,
Irradiated with the lunar beam,
Pledge deep the wine-cup, and impatiently
Court amorous dalliance from their lords returned.
They will declare that men are pithless grown,

When they shall find how ill the limbs are tuned.
To love, crushed, bruised, and mangled by thy vigour.

Madh.—We must not be unmindful of the clemency
The king displayed, whose favour overlooked
So readily our offences. Come, I long
To hear the story Kalahamsaka
Has told, I know full well, to both the damsels.
You must prepare to tell the tale again,
Whilst Madayantika declines her head
Veiling her eyes with modesty, afraid
To meet the sidelong smiling glance of Malati,
Here is the garden gate.

[*They enter.*

Madh.—How! all deserted!

Mak.—Alarmed, no doubt, at hearing our return
Was intercepted, they must have dispersed,
And hid themselves amid the garden shades.
Search we about.

They search, and enter LAVANGIKA *and* MADAYANTIKA.

Lav.—Ho, Madayantika!
Here's Malati. Ah no! yet fate is favourable;
The princely youths return.

Mak and Madh.—But where is Malati?

Lav.—Where Malati? Alas! we thought the tread
Of feet bespoke her here.

Madh.—My heart misgives me—
My mind, on that dear maid alone intent,
Desponds, and all my inmost soul gives way.
My left eye throbs, and then these words—ah me!
What hope remains?—she's lost to me ever!

Maday.—When you had left us, Malati despatched
The dame's attendants to their pious mistress—
Lavangika she bade convey her prayers
To her loved lord, to shun all needless peril.
Next, anxious for your tidings, she herself
Went forth to watch the road; and since that time
I saw her not. We were even now engaged
In quest of her, amidst the shady groves,
When we encountered you.

Madh.—My dearest Malati,
How many thoughts of evil omen crowd
Upon my spirit! If 'tis iu sport thou hidest,
Forego the barbarous pastime; if in anger,
Behold me humbled. If thou wouldst try my love,
The test is undergone: oh, yield reply;
My heart can bear no more—now thou art cruel!

Women.—O dearest friend, where art thou?

Mak.—(*To Madhava.*) Do not yield
Thus to despair—uncertain of her loss.

Madh.—Oh, think what agony she must have suffered,
In terror for my safety.

Mak.—That may be
But we have not yet thought to seek
The venerable priestess.

Women.—Let us fly to her.

Madh.—Yes, let us haste.

Mak.—(*Apart.*) If we should find the damsel with the dame,
Tis well; if not, I tremble for her life.
Alas! too often is the happiness
That kindred, friends, or lovers taste, as brief
As lightning's transient glare.

END OF THE EIGHTH ACT.

ACT IX.

THE VINDHYAN MOUNTAINS.

Enter SAUDAMINI.

From the tall mount *Sri-Saila*, I, Saudamini,
Have sought the royal city *Padmavati*,
And now the steps of Madhava pursue.
Unable to endure the scenes where late
His Malati was lost, the youth is wandering,
Attended by his ever faithful friend,
Amidst these rugged paths and rocky valleys.
(*Alights.*)
How wide the prospect spreads—mountain and rock,
Towns, villages, and woods, and glittering streams!
There where the *Para* and the *Sindhu* wind,
The towers and temples, pinnacles and gates,
And spires of *Padmavati*, like a city
Precipitated from the skies, appear,
Inverted in the pure translucent wave.
There flows *Lavana's* frolic stream, whose groves,
By early rains refreshed, afford the youth
Of *Padmavati* pleasant haunts, and where

Upon the herbage brightening in the shower
The heavy-uddered kine contented browse—
Hark! how the banks of the broad *Sindhu* fall,
Crashing, in the undermining current.
Like the loud voice of thunder-laden clouds,
The sound extends, and like *Heramba's* roar,
As deepened by the hollow echoing caverns,
It floats reverberating round the hills.
Those mountains coated with thick clustering woods
Of fragrant *sandal* and the ripe *malura*,
Recall to memory the lofty mountains
That southward stretch, where *Godavari*
Impetuous flashes through the dark deep shade
Of skirting forests, echoing to her fury—
Where meet the *Sindhu* and the *Madhumati*,
The holy fane of *Swarnavindu* rises,
Lord of *Bhavani*, whose illustrious image
Is not of mortal fabric. (*Bowing.*) Hail! all hail!
Creator of the universal world. Bestower
Of all good gifts. Source of the sacred *Vedas*;
God of the crescent-crested diadem. Destroyer
Of love's presumptuous power. Eldest lord
And teacher of mankind, all glory be to thee!
(*Going.*)
This mountain is, in truth, a grateful scene.
The peaks are blackened with dew dropping clouds,

And pleased the peafowl shriek along the groves.
The ponderous rocks upbear the tangled bowers,
Where countless nests give brightness to the gloom.
The inarticulate whine of the young bears
Hisses and mutters through the caverned hills;
And cool, and sharp, and sweet, the incense spreads,
Shed from the boughs the elephant's tusk has sundered.

(*Looking.*)

'Tis noon: the lapwing for the cassia's shade,
From the *Gambhari* wings its way. The pelican,
Whose beak has sipped the acid fruit beside
The stream, hastes now to plunge amidst its waters.
The *gallinule* creeps panting to the hollow
The *Tinisa* presents, and lower down,
Amidst the woods, the wild fowl make reply
To the soft murmuring of the mournful dove,
As in her nest she pours her frequent song.
Enough! I now will to the youths, and offer them
Such consolation as I may.

Enter MADHAVA *and* MAKARANDA.

Mak.—How dreary is the state, when nor the mind
Dare cherish hope, nor may indulge despair

Like helpless brutes, fate whirls us round
at will,
And ever plunges us in new misfortune.

Madh.—Ah Malati, where art thou? How so soon
Couldst thou desert me, ere my truth was
known?
Remorseless maid, relent—behold my sorows!
How canst thou prove thus cruel to that
Madhava,
Once so beloved! Behold me! I am he,
On whom thy hand, bound with the golden
thread,
Conferted in other days embodied bliss.
Alas! my friend, where in the world again
Shall equal tenderness be found? I long
Endured with withering limbs, like drooping
flow'rets
The feverish pangs of love, till in the end,
Unable further to sustain the conflict,
I was content to cast away my life
Like worthless grass. What then remained
for me
But to secure with gentle violence
That precious hand? Before the marriage rite,
Ere I had dared to hope, you may recall
My still increasing passion, sealed with tears,
Emaciate limbs, and heart-distracting anguish.
Such as I was, I am; and still my mind
Is tossed with agony. How strange it is,

This heart, that sorrow lacerates, does not break;
This frame, that sinks with anguish, cannot lose
Its conscious being; on my vitals preys
A burning fire, yet turns them not to ashes;
And fate, that piecemeal tears me, spares my life!

Mak.—As fierce as destiny, the flaming sun
Accords but ill with your exhausted strength.
Let us here rest awhile upon the marge
Of this wide lake, across whose shallow waters
Cool with the spray, and fragrant with the odours
Gleaned from the yet young lotus, gently blows
The fresh and friendly breeze. It will revive you.

(*They sit—Makaranda continues, to himself.*)
I will endeavour to divert his thoughts.
(*Aloud.*) My friend, a moment interrupt your tears.
Behold awhile the beauties of this lake,
Where on its slender stem the lotus trembles,
Brushed by the passing swan, as on he sails,
Singing his passion. (*Madhava jumps up.*)

Mak.—He heeds me not, and now would hence. My friend,
One instant pause—taste the delightful perfume

That o'er the wave the bending *bayas* scatters,
Or jasmine clustering round the flowery shore.
Observe, how smile the mountains, thickly set
With budding *kutajas*, up to the very peaks,
Where stretches dark the canopy of clouds,
Inspiring rapture in the dancing peafowl.
Thick on the hill's broad bosom the *kadamba*
Shows bright with countless blossoms: on the summit
Rest the black clouds in lengthening line: the streams
Descend through rows of budding *ketakas*,
And all the waving woods now laugh, emblazoned
With the *silindhra* and the *lodhra* flowers.

Madh.—I mark, my friend, the distant woods present
A beauteous sight—but what of that? Ah me!
What else should thought suggest? The days approach
When the long line of clouds shall shed on earth
Their amaranthine drops, trembling in the breeze
That from the east comes powerful, and embued
With the rich odours of the *sal* and *arjuna*,
Those days that boast the grateful interchange
Of heat and moisture, and the fragrant breath
The earth bestows, sprinkled with genial showers.

Ah! Malati, how can I bear to contemplate
The stooping clouds, as purple as the blossoms
Of young *tamala* trees; the rain-drops trembling
Before the cooling gale; the joyful cry
That echoes round, as pleased the peafowl hail
The bow of heaven propitious to their loves?
(*Faints.*)

Mak.—How hapless is the state of my dear friend!
My heart of adamantine mould could feel
Some taste of pleasure—now, alas, all hope
For Madhava is lost. How void of sense
He lies! Ah! Malati, how canst thou be
Thus unrelenting? Once for him you scorned
Your friends and ventured boldly. He has done
Now wrong to thee; then why this stern desertion?
He does not breathe. Fate robs me of my happiness.
My heart is rent—my fibres fall apart,
The world is blank. I burn with inward fires—
My soul sinks plunged into the glooms of hell,
And dim obscurity veils every sense.
What shall I do? The gentle source of pleasure
To friendship's heart—the orb whose radiance shed
Ambrosia on the eyes of Malati—the happiness

Of Makaranda—the bright ornament
Of all the world, now perishes. Alas!
My friend, my Madhava, thou wast to me
The *sandal* of my form, the autumnal moon
Of these fond eyes, and rapture to my heart.
Now am I slain— untimely fate uproots
A life that knew no other wish then thee—
Remorseless, deign to smile upon thy friend.
Speak to me; say, dost thou not know thy
friend,
Thy fond and faithful friend, thy Makaranda?

(*Madhava appears to recover.*)

Delightful shadows shedding on the world
New life—the cool refreshing drops that fall
From yon, cærulean cloud revive my friend.

Madh.—(*Recovering.*) Where in this thicket may I
hope to find
An envoy to my love? Ha! yonder winds
Around the mountain's brow the gathering
cloud,
Black as the tall *tamala*. As it stoops
From its high course, it pours its tribute down
Into the river bed, that gliding laves
The ebon *jambu* groves laden with fruit.

(*Rises and bows.*)

Thy form the lightning lovingly entwines;
Thy coming, thirsty *chatakas* proclaim;
The east wind fans thee with its gentle breath;
And *Indra's* bow irradiates thy course.

Hark! with deep voice he answers, and the sound
Mixed with the peacock's raptured cry reverberates
Along the echoing caves. He bids me speak.—
Majestic cloud—if haply as thou roamest
Free on thy airy path, thou shouldst behold
My love! allay the conflicts of her mind
Tell her her Madhava's distress, but heed,
You do not snap the slender thread or hope
That now alone sustains her fragile life.
He onward bends his course: I too will hence. (*Going.*)

Mak.—Alas! the reason of my noble friend
Is clouded by insanity. Pious dame,
Observe his state, and lend thy guardian aid.

Madh.—How now! the beauty of my love I view
In these young buds. Her eye the deer display—
The elephant has stolen her gait—her grace
The waving creeper shows—she has been slain,
And all her charms are scattered through the wild.
My love! my Malati! (*He faints.*)

Mak.—Obdurate heart, why break'st thou not, afflicted
By Madhava's affliction—as my friend,

The shrine of all desert, lord of my life,
The fellow of my childhood's sports, in youth
My fond associate, thus laments his love.

Madh.—*(Sighing and rising.)*—Such close similitude the hand of *Brahma*
Creates but sparingly—it must be so.
Ho! ye who tenant these high-towering rocks
And leafy woods, I call to you; awhile
Grant me attention. Tell me, have you seen,
Amidst these wilds a nymph of loveliest beauty,
Or know ye where she strays? I will describe
Her charms. Love rages tyrant in her bosom,
But lavishes his bounties on her form.—
Alas! the peafowl, as he dances wild
With rapture, drowns my sorrows with his cry—
With rolling eyeballs the *chakora* flies
After his mate—the ape his female's cheeks
Besmears with flowery dust. Whom should I sue to?
Vain the request unseasonably proferred.
There, leaning on the *rohin's* hollow stem, the elephant
Wearied supports his trunk upon his mate;
With the sharp points of his vast tusks he rubs
The corners of her eyes; he fans her form
With his broad ears, and thrusts into her mouth

The broken fragments of the incense bough.
How blest the master of the forest herd!
But yon dejected animal bewails
His absent female. To the muttering clouds
He breathes no murmured echo—from the lake
He gleans no grateful fodder, and he roams
With humbled brow, where silent sits the bee,
Deprived the nectar of the frontal juice.—
Enough of this despondence! I will hence.
This is, indeed, the proud [illegible]lting monarch
Of the huge herd: his mighty roar invites
Grateful his willing mate; down his broad cheek
The viscid fluid sheds such cooling odour
As from the newly ripe *kadamba* breathes.
He rends away the lotus leaf, and stem,
And roots, and filaments, as in the lake
He madly plunges, frightening from their nests
The osprey and the heron, and to the tune
Of his ferocious love, his ponderous ears
Waved dancing, lash the water into foam.
I will approach him.—Sovereign of the wild,
Thy youthful prowess merits praise no less
Than thine ingenuous fondness for thy mate.
With water fragrant with the rich perfume,
Drawn from the flowery lake, thou washest down
The savoury morsels of the lotus stalk,
With which thou erst hadst fed her—then in sport

Thou scatterest with thy trunk the silvery spray
Upon her brow ?—Ah shame ! why wav'st thou not
The straight-stemmed lotus over her, as a shade
Against the sun ?—Ah me ! upon the brute
I waste the hours due unto my friend.
Yet Makaranda I lament the most
In this, I grieve alone—nor would I taste
Of any pleasure that thou couldst not share.
Perish the day that is not spent with thee
And with my Malati ! False are the joys
That spring from any source but her and thee.

Mak.—Alas ! amidst his wanderings he recalls
The fervour of his friendship, and some chord
Awakes his love, though reckless of my presence.
(*Advances.*)—Behold me here ! your faithful, sorrowing friend.

Madh.—My friend, can it be true ? Oh, let me be
Convinced by thine embrace. Alas, I die.
I have no hope, my Malati is lost ! *(Faints.)*

Mak.—*(Looking.)* Alas ! the consciousness that my embrace
Had waked, again has flown—what hope is left me !
Alone, the sad conviction now survives
My friend is lost to me. Ah, Madhava,

I now may banish all those needless fears
For your tranquillity, my anxious heart
Has in its love unceasing entertained.
Ah, happier were the moments of distress
That still evinced perception. All is over ;
And now this body is a barren load.
Life is congealed, the faculties are dim,
And all the world a blank. Time is the source
Of ceaseless anguish, and the living world
Cold, dead, and cheerless, now that thou art gone.
Now what have I to do, beholding thus
The fate of Madhava ? It shall be so—
From this tall mountain summit will I plunge
Into the stream, the herald of my friend,
And glad precede him to the shades below.
(*Approaching and looking at Madhava.*)
Is this the form I have so oft embraced
Insatiate, and whose grace the eye of Malati,
Bewildered with a love till then unknown,
Delighted drank ? How wonderful, combined
Such countless merits with such early years.
Upon the world's tiara didst thou shine
The glittering gem ; and now thou fallst, a prey
To death—like the full moon to *Rahu's* jaws
Consigned—or like the volumed cloud, thin scattered
Before the driving breeze ; or like the tree,

That ere it puts its goodliest blossoms forth,
Consumes to ashes in the forest's blaze.
Let me once more embrace him, and address
My last farewell to my expiring friend.
Shrine of pure knowledge and of noblest worth,
Lord of the life of Malati; reflection
Of all surpassing loveliness; divinity
Of female hearts; autumnal moon, that swayed.
The tide of friendship's main, and charmed the days
Of Makaranda and the pious priestess—
My friend, my Madhava, accept this last,
This fond embrace, from him whose life began
Before thou wast, and who now terminates.
His blighted days. A little while he lives—
And do not thou forbid his fixed design.
Through life I have partaken of thy fortune,
And drank in childhood of thy mother's milk;
It must not be, that thou shalt quaff alone
The sad libations of thy sorrowing kin.

(*Leaves him and retires.*)

Deep underneath the precipice the stream
Flows rapid. Mighty lord of Gauri, hail!
Grant me with Madhava such future birth,
That, as in this life, I again may be,
In that to come, his follower and friend.

(*Going to precipitate himself, is withheld by Saudamini.*)

Forbear, my son! forego your desperate purpose.

Mak.—And who art thou, that seekest to stay my will

Saud.—Art thou not Makaranda?

Mak.—Let me go,
I am that luckless wretch!

Saud.—In me behold
The mistress of supernal power, and see
The vestiges of Malati.

(*Shows the Cakula garland.*)

Mak.—How! lives she?

Saud.—Do not fear. But what insanity
Is this, and how unwelcome to your friend:
Where is he?

Mak.—With despair o'ercome, even now
I left him—let us seek him—haste!

Madh.—(*Recovering.*) Who wakes.
My soul to sorrow once again—the wind,
Scattering the new and heavy laden clouds,
Regardless of my woes, has broke my slumbers

Mak.—Blest sight, my friend, revives!

Saud.—(*Looking at Madhava, then apart.*) The forms of both
These youths has Malati with truth described

Madh.—Hail, eastern gale! dissolve the dropping clouds,
And gratify the longing *chataka*—

Arouse the peafowl's rapture, and expand
The blossoms of the *ketaki*—awhile,
The absent lover, lost to sense, forgot
His misery; thou again hast called his soul
To conscious agony: what wouldst thou more

Mak.—The all-pervading wind diffuses life
To creatures animate.

Madh.—Celestial breeze,
Bear, with the fragrant odours thou hast wrung
From the *kadamba* blossoms, to my love,
The life of *Madhava*—or rather breathe
From her, impregnante with the cooling perfume
Of her delicious form—thou art alone
My hope.

(*Bows with joined hands applied to his forehead.*)

Saud.—This is the season to present
The well-known garland.

(*Throws it over his hands.*)

Madh.—Ha! the wreath I wove
Of *bakula* flowers, amidst the sacred shades
Of *Kama's* temple, and long fondly worn
Upon the bosom of my best beloved.
It is the same—this is the part
Lavangika was pleased to hear my Malati
Pretend was strung awry; a mere pretext,
To veil the irrepressible delight,
Her radiant countenance too plain revealed.

(*Jumps up.*)

Now Malati, behold! ah no, you heed not
My hapless state—my parting breath escapes,
My heart desponds—my body is on fire,
And darkness spreads around me—oh, be
quick;
You need not mock my sorrow—cast upon me
One bliss-diffusing glance—oh, be not pitiless.

(*Looking round, then at the garland.*)

How did she give me this—welcome, dear
wreath,
The favourite of my love, and long her friend,
Oh, whencesoever borne, welcome, most
welcome!
When on that gentle form, the scorching flame
Of love resistless preyed, and all her maidens
Despaired—thy grateful succour saved the days
Of Malati,—she clasped thee to her bosom,
And dreamt she pressed her lover to her heart.
Well I recall thy various passages.
Between my neck and that of my beloved,
Engendering tenderness, exciting hope,
And animating passion's glowing fires.

(*Puts his garland to his heart and faints.*)

Mak.—Revive, my friend. (*Fanning him.*)

Madh.—Ha, Makaranda!
Dost thou not see how Malati's affection
Is sealed with her fair hand—how chanced
it? say
Dost thou not know?

Mak.—This holy dame has brought
These traces of the maid.

Madh.—(*Bowing.*) With favouring ear.
Receive my prayers,—oh, tell me, Malati,
Say, does she live?

Saud.—Be of good cheer, my son;
She lives.

Madh.—How, where?—oh, speak!

Saud.—Some while ago it chanced,
Aghoraghanta at *Marala's* shrine
Fell by the arm of Madhava, in rescue
Oh his fair maid.

Madh.—Enough! I know the whole.

Mak.—How so?

Madh.—Kapalakundala, his partner—

Mak.—Is it e'en so?

Saud.—My son conjectures rightly.

Mak.—Alas! how beauteous did the union show
Of the bright moonlight and the lotus bed,
Till, like a dark unseasonable cloud,
Fate frowning came to intercept their joys.

Madh.—Into what dreadful hands has Malati.
Now fallen!—to what exposed!—O lovely maid,
How couldst thou bear the grasp unpitying
Of the fierce fined—like the pale struggling moon,
By hideous meteor seized? Kapalakundala,

Respect her tender form—repress thy spirit
Malign, and learn benevelence—the flow'ret
By nature delicate, should not be crushed
With blows, but gently twined around the brow.

Saud.—Enough! be calm. Remorseless as she is,
She dares not harm the maid—I will prevent her.

Madh. and Mak.—(*Bowing.*) Accept our thanks. Oh say, to what we owe
Thy friendly care?

Saud.—It is enough, at present,
To learn, that in your cause I will exert
The powerful knowledge, mystic rites and prayers,
Devout observance, and a sainted teacher,
Have armed me with. Come, Madhava, attend me.

(*Takes hold off Madhava, and they disappear.*)

Mak.—Astonishing reverse! the fearful gloom
Yields to the lightning flash of hope, and instant
The cheated eye resumed its wanted faculty.
(*Looks round.*)
How now, my friend not here! what can this be!
The dame is powerful in her magic rites,
But this alarms me. From one fear escaped.

Another comes to agitate my heart;
My mind is tossed amidst delight and dread,
And doubts one moment caused, subside the next.
I'll seek the priestess, who amidst the woods
Is roaming with her friends, and to her ear
Impart these wondrous chances.

[*Exit*.

END OF THE NINTH ACT.

ACT X.

ANOTHER PART OF THE FOREST.

Enter KAMANDAKI, MADAYANTIKA, *and* LAVANGIKA.

Kam.—My pride, my child, my Malati, where art thou?
Oh, yield me a reply. Your countless graces,
Your modesty, your elegance, your gentleness
Rise to my memory, consume my frame,
And rend my heart asunder. O my daughter,
I well recall your infant countenance,
Your pleasing prattle, and the transient tears
And smiles; that showed the young teeth budding forth.

Maday. and Lav.--O dearest friend, more radiant than the moon,
Ah, whither hast thou flown? can fate assail,
Remorseless thus, thy form as delicate
As the *sirisha* blossoms, and pursue thee
Unfriended and alone? O Madhava,
Thy promised joys are blighted in this world.

Kam.—Alas! my children, in your fond embrace
And new delight, fate, like a rising gale,
That fells the tree and tender vine together,
Has struck ye to the ground.

Lav.—Obdurate heart,
Despairing, still to torture me!

(Beats her breast, and falls on the ground.)

Maday.—Nay do not yet
Yield to despair.

Lav.—Alas, my life is bound
With bonds of adamant, and will not leave me.

Kam.—My dear child.
From birth, Lavangika was dear to thee,
And dost thou not compassionate her now?
Disdaining life, deprived of thee, her days
Are fading into gloom, as fluttering sinks
The lamp no oil supplies—How can'st thou quit
Kamandaki, within whose garb enfolded
Thy infant limbs to health and beauty grew!
From the maternal breast wast thou confided,
A delicate plaything, to my guardian care,
At first to ply thy sports, but more advanced
To learn the duties of thy state: now grown
To years mature, I have beheld thee wedded
To a loved busband, picked from all the world.
More than a mother's claims upon thy love
Have I—ingrate, thou leavest me to despair.
Ah me, I vainly hoped I should behold
A beauteous boy hang fondly at thy breast,
Or sport upon thy lap, his brow and forehead

White with protecting flour, His lovely face
Brightened with causeless smiles.

Lav.—Most holy dame,
I can no more endure this load of life :
This precipice relieves me of the burthen.
Grant me your blessing, that in after-life
I may once more behold my friend.

Kam.—My daughter,
Life is alike unwelcome to my bosom,
Deprived of my dear children, and despair
Invades my heart ; but different merits claim
A different birth, and if we should not gain
Reunion with our friends in days to come,
Abandonment of present life would yield
No fruit but vain repentance.

Lav.—Be it so.

Kam.—Daughter, Madayantika,

Maday.—Your commands—
If they direct me lead the way to death,
Behold, I am prepared.

Lav.—Dear friend, refrain
From self-destruction—keep me in your memory.

Maday.—Away, I am not subject to your will.

Kam.—*(Apart.)*—Alas! there is no hope.

Maday.—*(Apart.)* Dear husband, fare thee well.

Lav.—This is the loftiest point, and far below
The Madhumati twines its glittering zone.

Kam.—Enough—our purpose brooks not of delay.
(*They are about to cast themselves down.*)
(*Without.*) Astonishing reverse !—the fearful gloom
Yields to the lightning flash of hope.
Kam.—Who comes ?—
My son,

Enter MAKARANDA.

Without your friend!–say, how is the this ?
Mak.—A dame of more than mortal powers has used
Her art in our behalf.
(*Without.*) A fearful crowd is gathered—Bhurivasu,
Despising life and spurning worldly hopes,
Since he has learned his daughter's death, repairs,
To cast himself into the raging flames
At Swarnavindu's shrine.—Alas, we all
Shall mourn his fate.
Lav. and Maday. How short an interval
Rejoiced those lovers in each other's sight !
Kam. and Mak.—'Tis most miraculous ! what strange events
This day alternate! Drops of fragrant sandal
And sharp-edged swords in the same shower commingle;
And sparks of flame, and streams of heavenly nectar,
Descend together from unclouded skies.
The life-restoring drug with poison blends,

And light and gloom; and destiny entwines
The thunderbolt and lunar rays together.

Mal.—(*Without.*) Dear father, hold!! Oh, let me view again
The lotus of thy countenance—oh, turn
Thy gaze upon thy child. How, for my sake,
Canst thou desert thyself, the brilliant boast,
Of an auspicious race, whose fame pervades
Both earth and heaven? Ah, wherefore purpose thus
Again to plunge me into bitterest woe?

Kam.—My daughter, how is this? Art thou redeemed
From death, once more to be exposed to peril;
As lurk the demons of eclipse, to seize
The feeble moon scarce stuggling out of darkness?

Lav.—Behold our friend!

Enter MADHAVA *carrying* MALATI *senseless.*

Madh.—Alas! from danger rescued, has again
Fear fallen upon thee—who shall bar the gate
To shut out adverse destiny?

Mak.—My friend,
Where is the dame?

Madh.—With her we hither speeded
Swift from *Sri-Parvata*; but when we heard
The news the forester imparted to us,
I missed her suddenly,

Kam. and Mak.—O dame of power,
Befriend us still; why hast thou disappeared!

Maday. and Lav.—My Malati, I speak to thee, thy friend—
Priestess, preserve us; still she is insensible;
She does not breathe, her heart is still. Alas!
The sire and daughter are to each other,
In turn, the instrument of death.

Kam.—My dear child!

Madh.—My love!

Mak.—My friend!

Kam.—(*Looking up.*) What welcome drops are these
That fall from heaven to aid us?

Madh.—She revives—
Long sighs relieve her labouring breast; her heart
Resumes its pulse; her gentle eye unfolds;
And from unconscious stillness that dear face
Once more expands; as at the dawn of day
The lotus bears its bosom to the sun
(*Behind.*) Dear to the king's entreaties, and the prayers
Of Nandana though humbled at his feet,
Upon the flaming merge, the minister
By me has been [illegible]ed, and recalled
To life and joy.

Madh. and Mak.—(*Looking up.*) Mark, holy dame—from heaven,
The kind magician pours upon our hearts

The nectar of her tidings: they surpass
The virtue of the balmly shower.

Kam.—Blest news!

All.—Our happiness is now secure.

Kam.—My child!

Mal.—The priestess!

(*Falls at her feet. Kamandaki raises and embraces her.*)

Kam.—Restored to life, my child, to life restore
Your friends, and with your fond embraces, cool
As lunar rays, reanimate existence
In those who live for you.

Madh.—(*To Makaranda.*) My faithful friend,
This breathing world may now be well-endured.

Mak.—In sooth, it may.

Maday and Lav.—Dear Malati, confirm
The happiness we see, by your embrace.

Mal.—My dearest friends! (*Embraces them.*)

Kam.—Tell me, my sons, how chanced these strange events?

Madh.—Our past misfortunes were the wrathful work
Kapalkundala's revenge inspired;
And that we 'scap'd her toils, our thanks are due
To this propitious and all-powerful friend.

Kam.—Agharghanta's death was then the source
Of these mischances!

Maday. and Lav.—Strange vicissitude!
After repeated trials, adverse fate
In kindness terminates its chequered course.

Enter SAUDAMINI.

Sau.—(*To Kamandaki*:)
Hail, holy dame!—your scholar pays you homage,

Kam.—Saudamini, most welcome.

Madh. and Mak. Then we owe
Our succour to the priestess: this, her first
Disciple—all is clear.

Kam.—This is well done;
And many a life preserved has sanctified these.
'Tis long since we have met: dsmiss this reverence,
And let me grateful press thee to my bosom.
(*Embraces her.*)
Thou hast deserved the praises of the world,
Whose lofty powers, the harvest of the seed
By early study sown, are shown by deeds
That shame the mightiest masters.

Maday. and Lav.—Is this Saudamini?

Mal.—It is: by her,
The friend and pupil of my pious guardian,
The fierce Kapalakundala was foiled.
She bore me to her dwelling; and there living me
Secure, conveyed the wreath of *bakula* flowers
To snatch you from despair.

Maday. and Lav.—She has, indeed,
Been scarcely less propitious to us, than our old
And reverend preceptress.

Madh. and Mak.—The bright gem
That grants whatever is desired, demands
That suppliant's prayer; the dame's assistance came
All unsolicited.

San.—(*Apart.*) These thanks oppress me.—
Respected mistress, from the king I bear
A letter to the youth—it was inscribed
With Nandana's concurrence, and the assent
Of Bhurivasu. (*Gives her a letter.*)

Kam.—(*Takes it and reads.*)
"Unto all be health—
"The king commands—we are well pleased to greet
"A son in you, of noble race descended;
"Amongst the worthiest eminent, and late
"From great calamity redeemed: and more,
"In love and grace to you, we do permit
"Your well-loved friend to wed the youthful maid,
"Whom first affection yielded to his hopes.
You hear, my son?

Madh.—I do, and all I wished,
Thus hearing, have obtained.

Mal.—The lingering dart
Of fear is now extracted from our hearts.

Lav.—The loves of Malati and Madhava
Will now no more be thwarted.

Mak.—See, where come
Our other friends, and faithful Kalahamsa.

Enter AVALOKITA BUDDHARA KSHITA, *and* KALAHAMSA.

All.—(*Bowing.*) Glory to Kamandaki, the sage
Perfector of all aims! Glory to Madhava,
The moon that sheds delight on Makaranda!
Now fate propitious smiles.

Lav.—Who does not share
This general joy?

Kam.—And that our story,
Full of strange varied incidents, is closed
In happiness, deserves congratulation.

Sau.—And Devarata and his ancient friend,
Will see with joy their children now are joined
In that affiance they so long projected.

Mal.—(*Apart.*) Hey—how is this?

Madh. and Mak.—(*To Kamandaki.*)—How sorts the dame's discourse
With past events?

Lav.—(*Apart to Kam.*)—What's to be said?

Kam.—(*To her.*) We need no longer fear
The wrath of Nandana, now we obtain

His sister's aid, (*Aloud.*) 'Tis even as you have heard.
Whilst yet I taught your fathers, they agreed,
That when their children came to years mature,
Their hands should be united; and they left
Saudamini and me to take those cares
That might secure your union, hoping thus
To shun the anger of exalted rank.

Mal.—(*Apart.*) What marvellous secrecy!

Madh. and Mak.—It moves our wonder.
Yet must the schemes of the illustrious, planned
For virtuous ends, and prudently conducted,
Ever enjoy success.

Kam.—My son, What more remains?
The happiness that was your earliest hope,
By my devotions, and the skilful pains
Of my disciples, is at last ensured you.
The king and Nandana approve the suit
Of your dear friend, and hence no fear pevents
His union with his love. If yet there be
A wish ungratified, declare it, speak.]

Madh.—(*Bowing.*) My happiness henceforth is perfect: all
The wish I cherish more, is this; and may
Your favour, holy dame, grant it fruition:—
Still may the virtuous be exempt from error,

And fast to virtue cling—may monarchs, merciful
And firm in equity, protect the earth—
May, in due season, from the labouring clouds
The fertile showers descend—and may the people,
Blest in their friends, their kindred, and their children,
Unknowing want, live cheerful and content.
[*Exeunt all.*

THE END.

RATNAVALI;

OR

THE NECKLACE.

A DRAMA,

TRANSLATED FROM THE ORIGINAL SANSKRIT.

BY

H. H. WILSON.

PUBLISHED BY
THE SOCIETY FOR THE RESUSCITATION OF INDIAN LITERATURE.

Calcutta.

PRINTED BY H. C. DAS, ELYSIUM PRESS,
40, *Nayan Chand Dutt's Street.*

1901.

PREFACE.

The RATNAVALI is a play of different character from any of those which we have hitherto examined. Although the personages are derived from Hindu history, they are wholly of mortal mould, and unconnected with any mystical or mythological legend; and the incidents are not only the pure inventions of the poet, but they are of an entirely domestic nature. In this latter respect the RATNAVALI differs from the *Mrichchhakatika*, *Malati and Madhava*, and *Mudra-Rakshasa*, whilst its exemption from legendary allusion distinguishes it from the *Vikramorvasi* and *Uttara-Rama-Charita*.

Although, however, the RATNAVALI differs from its predecessors in these respects, and in others of still greater importance, it is well entitled to attention, as establishing an era in the history of both Hindu manners and literature, of which we are able to fix the date with precision.

The story of this drama appears to have been not wholly the invention of the author, but to have enjoyed very extensive popularity, at a period to which we cannot refer with confidence. The loves of VATSA, prince of *Kausambhi*, and VASAVA-DATTA, princess of *Ujjayini*, are alluded to in the *Megha-Duta*,' and are narrated in the *Vrihat-Katha* of *Soma Deva*. The last is a writer of the same period as the drama, but he does not pretend to have invented the story ; and the manner in which the tale is adverted to in the *Megha-Duta*, the date of which work is unknown, but which is no doubt anterior to the *Vrihat-Katha*, seems to indicate a celebrity of some antiquity. The second marriage of VATSA, which forms the business of the RATNAVALI, appears to be the invention of the writer, as it is very differently, told in the *Vrihat-Katha* ; the heroine being there named *Padmavati*, and being a princess of *Magadha*, not of Ceylon. the circumstances under which the marriage is effected are altogether distinct.

From whatever source, however, the plot of the drama may have been derived, it is very evident that the author is under considerable obligation to his predecessors, and especially to KALIDAS, from the *Vikrama* and *Urvasi*, of which writer several situations, and some of the dialogue even, are borrowed. At the same time, the manners described are very different, and the light aud loose principles of VATSA are wholly unlike the deep dignified passion of *Pururavas*. If we compare the RATNAVALI with the *Mrichchhakatika* or with the dramas of *Bhavabhuti*, the difference is still more striking, and it is impossible to avoid the conviction, that they are the productions of different ages, and different conditions of society ; the RATNAVALI indicating a wider deviation from manners purely. Hindu, more artificial refinement and more luxurious indulgence, and a proportionate deterioration of moral feeling.

The RATNAVALI, considered also under a purely literary point of view, marks a change in the principles of dramatic composition, as well as in those of social organization. Besides the want of passion and the substitution of intrigue, it will be very evident that these is in it no poetic spirit, no gleam of inspiration, scarce even enough to suggest a conceit in the ideas. The only poetry of the play, in fact, is mechanical. The structure of the original language is eminently elegant, particularly in the *Prakrit*. This dialect appears to equal advantage in no other drama, although much more laboured in the *Malati and Madhub* the Sanskrit style is also very smooth and beautiful without being painfully elaborated. The play is, indeed, especially interesting on this account, that whilst both in thought and expression there is little fire or genius, a generally correct and delicate taste regulates the composition, and avoids those absurdities which writers of more pretension than judgment, the writers of more recent periods, invariably commit. The RATNAVALI, in short, may be taken as one of the connecting links betweeu the old and new school; as a not unpleasing production of that middle region through which Hindu poetry passed from elevation to extravagance.

The place to which the RATNAVALI is entitled in the dramatic literature of the *Hindus* is the more interesting, as the date is verifiable beyond all reasonable doubt. It is stated in the prelude to be the composition of the sovereign, *Sri-Harsha-Deva*. A king of this name, and a great patron of learned men, reigned over Kashmir: he was the reputed author of several works, being, however, in fact only the patron, the compositions bearing his name being written, the author of the *Kavya-Prakasa* asserts by *Dhavaka* and other poets. That it was fashionable in his reign to take the adventures of Vatsa for the subject of fictitious narrative, we may infer from their being the groundwork of the *Vrihat-Kattha*, the author of which was a native of Kashmir ;and a contemporary of the prince. *Somadeva*, the author, states, that he compiled his collection of tales for the amusement of the grandmother of *Harsha-Deva*, king of Kashmir, the son of *Kalasa*, the son of *Ananta*, the son of *Samgrama*. His geneology is nearly identifiable with that of ABULFAZAL, which runs in GLADWIN'S translation of the *Ayeen Akbary*, (vol. ii. P. 154), *Sungram, Hurray, Anunt, Kulussder, Ungruss, Hurruss*. The two additional princes, *Hurray* and *Ungruss* reigned conjointly but forty-four days, and they are for all chronological purposes non-entities. But we have fortunately a better authority than either of the preceding, in the history of Kashmir by *Kalhana-Pandit*. The first portion of this work, down to the reign of *Samgrama-Deva*, in A. D. 1027, is translated summarily in the fifteenth volume of the

Asiatic Researches. Since its publication, the subsequent portion of the original has been procured in Kashmir, and presented to the Asiatic Society by the late enterprising travellor, *Mr. Moorcroft*. From this we are enabled to trace the successors of *Samgrama* with precision.

Samgrama reigned twenty-five years, and was succeeded by his son *Hari*, who enjoyed his elevation but twenty-two days, having been removed, it was supposed, by the practices of his mother, who aspired to the regency during the minority of a younger son. She was set aside by the chief officers of the state, under whose ministry *Ananta*, the next prince, reigned interruptedly fifty-three years, when he was succeeded by his son *Kalasa*. *Kalasa* reigned eight years, and being displeased with his son, *Harsha*, left the crown to a kinsman, *Utkarsha*. That prince, however, enjoyed his authority but twenty-two days, having been defeated, and invested in his palace, by the partisans of the legitimate heir, and putting an end to his existence rather than fall into their hands. *Harsha* succeeded. He consequenty ascended the throne. A. D. 1113; and the play must have been written between that date and A. D. 1125, the termination of his reign. No mention is made of the composition by the author of the history: but he dwells at much length, and with some acrimony, on *Harsha's* patronage of poets, players, and dancers. and the prince's conversancy with different dialects and elegant literature.

Harsha's propensities, indeed, were not likely to be regarded with a favourable eye by a Brahmanical historian, for in order to defray the expenses into which he was led by them, he made free with the treasures of the temples, and applied their gold and silver vessels and even the images of the gods, to his necessities. These measures, and others of an equally imprudent character, distracted the latter period of his reign with civil broils, and he perished in an insurrection which transferred the crown to a different dynasty. The date thus assigned for the composition refers to a period, which Mohammedan history and Hindu literature sufficiently establish, as pregnant with important changes in the political situation and national character of the natives of Hindustan.

The RATNAVALI has been translated in prose for the same reasons that the preceding dramas have been rendered in measured language: the fitness of the vehicle for the thoughts, and adaptation of the style to the pitch of the original ideas. Prose would have done scant justice to the merits of *Kalidasa* or *Bhavabhuti*, for with them it would have had to translate lofty imaginings: it is perfectly applicable to the level conceptions of *Sri-Harsha.* It may also form a not unacceptable variety, and it may likewise serve to convey some idea, how far the translator may be suspected of widely deviating from his text in the preceding dramas.

DRAMATIS PERSONÆ.

MEN.

Vatsa.—The king of *Kausambi.*

Yaugandharayana.—His chief minister.

Vasantaka.—The King's confidential companion.

Vasubhuti.—The ambassador of the king of *Simhala.*

Babhravya.—An envoy from *Vatsa* to the king of *Simhala.*

Samvara-Siddhi.—A magician.

Vijaya-Varman.—An officer of *Vatsa's* army.

WOMEN.

Vasavadatta.—The Queen of *Vatsa.*

Ratnavali, or Sagarika ... } Ths princess of *Simhala.*

Kanchanamala.—The Queen's principal attendant.

Susamgata.—The friend of Sagarika.

Nipunika,
Madanika,
Chutalatika,
Vasundhara. } Female attendants.

PERSONS SPOKEN OF.

Vikramabahu.—The king of *Simhala* or *Ceylon*, father of *Ratnavali*, and maternal uncle of *Vasavadattas.*

Rumanwat.—The General-in-Chief of *Vatsa.*

Scene.—The palace of *Vatsa* in *Kausumbi.*

TIME, Three days.

PRELUDE.

BENEDICTION.

May that presentation of the flowery offering, made by the mountain goddess to her mighty lord, preserve you! Trembling she raised herself to reach his brows, but agitated by his triple glance, and bowed downwards by her heaving bosom, she missed her aim, and dropped the fragrant wreath.

May *Gauri* ever be propitious to you! She who after new nuptials, yet scarce confiding, first hastened to her husband as remotely he advanced, then turned a verse from him as he approached, till gently forced to the embraces of the smiling god by her persuading damsels.

May *Shiva* ever be your trust! He who laughingly narrated to his goddess, how the sacrifice was disturbed, the holy fires were quenched by his flaming glances; how the Brahmans in terror were dragged by their turbans to the ground by his mischievous goblin legions; how *Daksha's* spouse implored in tears his pardon, and the gods, frightened, fled. Glory to the moon Reverence to the gods! Prosperity attend illustrious Brahmans! May the earth be fertile, and may the king of moon like loveliness shine ever resplendent as the monarch of the night.

Enter MANAGER.

Enough! I have been desired by the princes here assembled from various realms, recumbent at the feet of our illustrious monarch, *Sri-Harsha-Deva*, and who are collected together as this vernal festival; to represent for their entertainment the unequalled drama entiled *Ratnavali*, the elegant composition of our sovereign. "We have heard of this drama," they remark, "but have not yet witnessed its performance; and in compliance therefore with our wishes, and with defference to the king, who is the delight of all hearts, we request you to perform the piece as you best may. Very well: as soon as the decorations of the stage are ready I shall fulfil your desires.

That this whole assembly will be highly gratified, I make no doubt. *Sri-Harsa* is an eminent poet; the audience are judges of merit; the story of *Vatsa* is current in the world; and we, the actors, are experienced in the histrionic art; and I hope, therefore, that with so precious a poem, and such means of doing it justice, the opportunity afforded me of appearing before so distinguished an assembly will yield me the fruit of all my desires. Now then to my mansion, to call forth my dame. What, ho! mistress, come hither!

Enter ACTRESS.

Your commands sir?

Mana.—The drama of *Ratnavali* is to be represented before this princely audience—go, dress for your character.

Actr.—Ah, sir, you forget my only daughter has been betrothed by you to a husband who is abroad, and that the matrimonial rites cannot be performed in consequence of my son-in-law's absence in a foreign country: with so much anxiety on this account, how shall I be able to act?

Mana.—Oh, never sorrow for the absent. Propitious fate restores them to us from distant isles, from ocean's central waves and earth's extremest bounds.

Behind.—Son of *Bharata*, most truly uttered.

Mana.—*(Listening.)*—Away, child, away, no longer hesitate; here comes my brother as the noble Yaugandharayana. Come, come, we have no time to lose.

[*Exeunt.*

END OF THE PRELUDE.

RATNAVALI.

ACT I.

SCENE.—THE PALACE OF VATSA.

Enter YAUGANDHARAYANA.

'Tis true! fate, if propitious, soon restores the absent, and from remotest isles, the wastes of ocean, and the bounds of earth, safe gives them to us again—else how chanced it, that the fair daughter of the king of Lanka, whom as directed by the seer, we had sent to obtain, and who was by her father, with rich gifts, consigned a bride to our illustrious prince, escaped annihilation? Borne on a plank, the relique of her shattered bark, a merchant of Kausambi found her floating in mid sea. Her costly necklace spoke her of no common rank, whence with all honour she was treated, and to our capital conveyed. Fate still smiled upon our sovereign. I have transferred the maiden to the honourable keeping of the queen; and now I hear our chamberlain, Babhravya, and Vasubhuti, the minister of Simhala, who had accompanied the princess, having by some means reached the shore, are on their way hither, having been encountered by Rumanwat on his march to chastise the king of Kosola. I have little need to fear the end of this; but faithful service ever has its cares. The elevation of my master's power is my aim, and destiny co-operates with my design—neither can the seer prophetic err. The king himself alone I doubt, for still he loves to follow where his own inclinations lead. (*A noise behind.*) Hark! the mellow drum, accompanied with song and shouts, indicate the clamarous rejoicings of the multitude. I suspect the king has come forth to behold from his palace the frolic merriment with which his subjects celebrate the festival of *Kamadeva*. Ah, yes, I see him on the terrace; wearied of tales of war, and seeking most his reputation in his people's hearts, he issues forth attended by his companion Vasantaka, like the flower armed deity himself, descended to take a part in the happiness of his worshippers. I will retire to my dwelling, and meditate in tranquility the measures best adapted to ensure us a fortunate termination of the task we have begun.

[*Exit.*

(VATSA-RAJA *discoverd seated, dressed as for the spring festival, and attended by* VASANTAKA.)

Vatsa.—My friend!

Vas.—Your Majesty!

Vatsa.—I scarcely can express the content I now enjoy. My kingdom is rid of every foe, the burthen of my government reposes on able shoulders, the seasons are favourable, and my subjects prosperous and happy. In the daughter of Pradyota I have a wife whom I adore, and in thee, Vasantaka, a friend in whom I can confide. Attended by thee, thus, at such a season, and so disposed, I might fancy myself the deity of desire, and this vernal celebration held in honor of myself.

Vas.—Excuse me. Since you admit me to be a part of it, I shall even claim the whole ; and, so highly exalted by your regard, I shall maintain that the festival is mine. Observe the general joy. As if intoxicated with deight, the people dance along the streets, sporting merrily with each other's persons, and mutually scattering the yellow-tinted fluid. On every side, the music of the drum and the buzz of frolic crowds fill all the air. The very atmosphere is of a yellow hue, with clouds of flowery fragrance.

Vatsa.—Yon lofty mansion opposite to us is occupied by a merry band. I knew not that Kausambi was so wealthy!—She outvies the residence of the God of wealth. Her numerous sons are clad in cloth of gold, sprinkled with the fragrant dust of the colour of dawn or tinted with the safron dye, decked with glittering ornaments, and tossing their heads proudly with splendid crests, fit for Kama himself. The soil plashy with the frequent shower and tread of numerous feet, is converted into vermilion paste, as the artificial bloom is washed down from the cheeks of the maidens and mingled with the ground.

Vas.—See, where a coloured shower falls on a thick and struggling crowd, shrinking in vain from the mischievous pipes of those mirthful maids.

Vatsa.—I should compare the city to the subterranean world, where the snake gods dwell. The mischievous pipes are crested snakes—the scattering dust of yellow fragrance sheds unearthly dimness, and the gleaming tiaras dart through it such radiance as beams from the serpent jewels.

Vas.—Look, sir, where Madanika and Chutalatika, approach us their gestures indicate the influence of the divinity of the season.

Enter MADANIKA *and* CHUTALATIKA, *two of the Queen's Attendants, dancing and singing.*

Mad.—Cool from the southern mountains blowing,
Freshly swells the grateful breeze,
Round with lavish bounty throwing
Fragrance from the waving trees;
To men below, and gods above,
The friendly messenger of love.

Chut.—Lightly from the green stem shaken,
Balmy flowrets scent the skies—
Warm from youthful bosoms waken
Infant passions ardent sights.
And many a maid around is roaming,
Anxious for her lover's coming.

Both.—Nor alone the tender blossom
Opens to the smiling day,
Lordly man's expanding bosom
Buds beneath the genial ray,
Offering to the flowery dart,
Of love, a soft and yielding heart.

Vatsa.—I perceive, indeed, the influence of the season expressed in their appearance. The fillet of the one is loosened, and her long tresses float dishevelled to the air: the necklace of the other seems too weighty for her languid frame, though she plies her tinkling anklets with more than wonted activity.

Vas.—I will gird up my garb and join them, shall I, in compliment to the festival?

Vatsa.—If you please.

Vas.—*(Descends.)* Come, Madanika, teach me your poem.

Mad.—A poem, you simpteton! it is no poem.

Vas.—What is it, then?

Mad.—A ballad.

Vas.—Oh, a ballad! if that is the case, I wish you good by.

Mad.—You must not leave us.

Vas.—Consider my character. (*They hold him and sprinkle him with yellow powder, till he breaks away.*) Here I am at last, my good friend: I have been in jeopardy.

Chut.—Come, we have amused ourselves long enough, let us bear the queen's message to his Majesty.

Mad.—Come on. *(Approaching Vatsa.)*—Glory to your Majesty! So please you, the queen commands—I crave pardon, requests.

Vatsa.—Nay, Madanika, you are quite correct; the queen commands, particularly at a season sacred to the god of love. What are her orders?

Mad.—She is bound to-day to offer homage to the image of the flower-armed deity, which stands at the foot of the red *asoka* tree in the garden of the palace, and requests your Majesty's presence at her devotions.

Vatsa.—You see, my friend, how one festival begets another.

Vas.—Let us go thither. I will officiate as your priest, and I hope my benediction will not be wholly unproductive.

Vatsa.—Go, Madanika, and let the queen know that we shall meet her in the garden.

Mad.—As your Majesty's commands. [*Exeunt.*

Vatsa.—Come, my friend, lead the way to the garden. *(They descent and proceed.)*

Vas.—This is the place, sir. Behold the rich canopy of the pollen of the mango blossoms, wafted above our heads by the southern breeze, and the chorus bursts from the *koils* and the bees to hail your approach.

Vatsa.—The garden is now most lovely. The trees partake of the rapturous season—their new leaves glow like coral, their branches wave with animation in the wind, and their foliage resounds with the Clythe murmurs of the bee. The *bakula* blossoms lie around its root like ruby wine; the *champaka* flowers blush with the ruddiness of youthful beauty: the bees give back in harmony the music of the anklets, ringing melodiously as the delicate feet are raised against the stem of the *asoka* tree.

Vas.—No, no; it is not the bees who mimic the ringing of the anklets; 'tis the queen with her train approaching.

Vatsa.—You are right; they are at hand.

[*They retire.*

Enter VASAVADATTA *the queen*, KANCHANAMALA, SAGARIKA, *and other damsels attending.*

Vasava.—Now, Kanchanmala, where is the garden

Kanch.—This is it, madam.

Vasava.—And where the red *asoka* tree, at the foot of which I am to pay my offerings to Madana?

Kanch.—It is in sight. This is the *Madhavi* creeper, your Majesty's own plant; it is now rich with blossoms. This is the plant his Majesty takes such care of, the jasmine that he expects to blossom out of season:—now we pass it, and this is the tree.

Vasava.—Very well; where are the offerings?

Sagar.—Here madam. (*Presenting them.*)

Vasava.—(*Looking at her, then aside.*) What carelessness! an object I have hitherto so cautiously concealed, thus heedlessly exposed: it shall be so.

(*Aloud.*) How now, Sagarika, what make you here? Where is my favourite starling, that I left to your charge, and whom it seems you have quitted for this ceremony? Away! deliver the oblation to K chanamala and return.

Sagar.—As your Majesty pleases. (*Gives the offerings and withdraws to a short distance.*) The bird is safe with my friend Susamgata. I should like to witness the ceremony. I wonder if *Ananga* is worshipped here as in my father's mansion! I will keep myself concealed amongst these shrubs and watch them, and for my own presentation to the deity I will go cull a few of these flowers.

Vasava.—Now, place the divine *Pradyumna* at the foot of the tree.

Kanch.—(*Arranges the afferings.*) It is done, madam.

Vatsa.—Come, Vasantska, they are ready, let us join them. The queen stands by the side of the god of the fish-emblazoned banner, as slight and graceful as his own bow, and as delicate as the flowers that tip his shafts. My love, Vasavadatta!

Vasava.—My lord! victory attend him: let him honour our rites by his presence!—That is his regal seat.

Kanch.—Now, let her Majesty commence the ceremony, and to the god, whose station is the red *asoka* tree, present the accustomed gifts of sandal, saffron, and flowers.

Vasava.—Give them to me.

Kanch.—*(Presents them severally to the queen, who offers them to the image.)*

Vatsa.—Whilst thus employed, my love, you resemble a graceful creeper twining round a coral tree; your robes of the orange dye, your person fresh from the bath. As rests your hand upon the stem of the *asoka*, it seems to put forth a new and lovelier shoot. The unembodied god to-day will regret his disencumbered essence, and sigh to be material, that he might enjoy the touch of that soft hand.

Kanch.—The worship of the divinity concluded, be pleased, madam, to pay adoration to your lord.

Vasava.—Where are flowers and unguent ?

Kanch.—Here, madam.

(VASAVADATTA *worships the king.*)

Sagar.—(*Returns.*) I have idled my time whilst gathering these flowers, so that I fear the ceremony is over ; behind this tree I can observe them undiscovered. What do I see ? can this be true ? Does then the deity, whose effigy only we adore in the dwelling of my father, here condescend to accept in person the homage of his votaries ? I, too, though thus remote present my humble offering. (*Throws down the flowers.*) Glory to the flower-armed god : may thy auspicious sight both now and hereafter prove not to have been vouchsafed to me in vain ! (*Bows down, then rising looks again.*) The sight though oft repeated, never wearies. I must tear myself from this, lest some one should discover me.

(*Withdraws a little.*)

Kanch.—Approach, Vasantaka, and receive your portion.

Vasava.—Accept, most worthy sir, these propitiatory presents. (*Gives Vasantaka sandal, flowers and jewels.*)

Vas.—May prosperous fortune ever be your fate!

(*The Bard behind.*)

The sun from his diurnal road declines,
And in the west with flaming radiance glows—
Like some illustrious prince, whose glory shines
Intensest, as his days approach their close.
The moon comes forth amidst the evening sky,
With aspect as our youthful monarch's bright,
To soothe the night flower's love-empassioned sigh,
And at thy feet to shed his sacred ight.

Sagar.—How? (*Returning.*) Is this Udayana, to whom my father destined me a bride! The sight of him has purified my person from the contaminating gaze of others.

Vasta.—The twilight has drawn in, and we have been insensible of the course of time, our minds engrossed by holy and delightful duties. Look, madam, where the pale eastern sky, like a love-corn damsel, seems to sicken with impatience for the coming of her lord.

Let us rise, and return to the palace.

(*They rise.*)

Sagar.—They come! I must fly hence. Ah me, unhappy! no longer to behold him, whom I could gaze upon for ever.

Vatsa.—Come, love, thou puttest the night to shame. The beauty of the moon is eclipsed by the loveliness of thy countenance, and the lotus sinks humbled into shade; the sweet songs of thy attendant damsels discredit the murmur of the bees, and mortified, they hasten to hide their disgrace within the flowery blossom.

[*Exeunt.*

END OF THE FIRST ACT.

ACT II.

THE GARDEN OF THE PALACE.

Enter SUSAMGATA *with a Sarika, or talking bird, in a cage.*

What can have become of Sagarika ? she left this bird in my charge, and went I know not whither. Here coms Nipunika !

Enter NIPUNIKA.

These tidings his Majesty has charged me with, I must use despatch in conveying to the Queen. (*Going.*)

Sus.—How now, Nipunika ? what engrosses your thoughts, that you pass as if you saw me not ?—whither, in such haste ?

Nip.—I with tell you. We have a great sage come to court, the venerable Srikhanda Dasa, from *Sri-Parvata.* He has taught the king the craft of making flowers blossom at any season, and his Majesty being about to exercise his new art upon his favorite jasmine, sends me to request the queen's presence. But where are you going ?

Sus.—To look for Sagarika.

Nip.—I passed her just now ; she had a brush and dallet as if about to paint a picture, and went into the plantain bower: you will find her there, I dare say. Adieu! I must to our mistress.

[*Exeunt severally.*

A PLANTAIN BOWER OR HALL.

Enter SAGARIKA, *with a picture.*

Be still my foolish heart, nor idly throb for one so high above thy hopes. Why thus anxious again to behold that form, one only view of which has inspired such painful agitation? Ungrateful, too, as weak, to fly the breast that has been familiar to thee through life, and seek another, and as yet but once beheld, asylum. Alas! why do I blame thee! the terror of *Ananga's* shaft his rendered thee a fugitive;—let me implore his pity, Lord of the flowery bow, victor of demons and of gods! dost thou not blush to waste thy might upon a weak defenceless maiden, or art thou truly without form or sense? Ah me! I fear my heath impends, and this the fatal cause. *(Looking at the picture.)* No one approaches; I will try and finish the likeness I am here attempting to pourtray. *(Looking at the picture.)* My heart beats high, my hand trembles, yet I must try, and, whilst occasion favours me, attempt to complete these lineaments, as the only means to retain them in my sight.

(Draws.)

Enter SUSAMGATA.

This is the plantain bower. Ha! she is here, and apparently so intent upon some painting, that she does not notice my approach. I will keep out of her sight and look at what she is doing. *(Approaches gently and looks over Sagarika.)* How!—the king's picture! well-done, Sagarika! but so it is: the royal swan leaves not the lotus-crowded lake to sport elsewhere.

Sag.—It is finished, but in vain, my tears veil the picture from my sight. *(Raises her head, and beholding Susamgata hides the picture.)* How, Susamgata! sit down.

Sus.—Sits down and puts her hand upon the picture.) Who is this you have delineated?

Sag.—The deity of this festival, *Ananga.*

Sus.—It is cleverly done, but there wants a figure to complete it. Let me have it, and I will give the god his bride. *(Takes the paper and draws.)*

Sag.—*(Angrily.)* Hey, Susamgata! What mean you? you have sketched my likeness.

Sus.—Do not be offended without cause. I have given your *Kamadeva* my *Rati*, that is all. But come, away with disguise, and confess the truth.

Sag.—*(Apart.)* My friend, has discovered my secret. *(Aloud.)* My dear friend, I am overcome with shame—promise me that no body else shall be made acquainted with my weakness.

Sus.—Why should you be ashamed? Attachment to exalted worth becomes your native excellence. But be assured I will not betray you; it is more likely this prattling bird will repeat our conversation.

Sag.—Alas! my friend, my agitation overpowers me.

Sus.—(*Placing her hands on Sagarika's heart.*) Be composed, be composed! I will bring some leaves and fibres of the water-lily from this lake. (*Brings some leaves and fibres of the lotus, and binds the former with the latter upon Sagarika's bosom.*)

Sag.—Enough, enough, my friend, take away these leaves and fibres,—it is vain to offer me relief. I have fixed my heart where I dare not raise my hopes. I am overcome with shame—I am enslaved by passion—my love is without return—death my only refuge. (*Faints.*)

(*A noise behind.*)

The monkey has escaped from the stable, and rattling the ends of his broken chain of gold, he clatters along as if a number of famale feet, bound with tinkling anklets, were in sportive motion. Chased by the grooms and frightening the women, he has bounded through the inner gate. The unmanly eunuchs, lost to shame, fly from his path, and the dwarf takes shelter in the jacket of the chamberlain. The *Kiratas* who guard the surrounding walls are true to their designation, and bowing themselves lowly through fear, are ashamed to look each other in the face.

Sus.—Up, up, my dear friend! the wild brute is coming hither.

Sag.—What shall we do?

Sus.—Hide in the shade of this *tamala* grove: haste, he comes!

[*Exeunt.*

ANOTHER PART OF THE GARDEN.

Enter SAGARIKA *and* SUSAMGATA.

Sag.—What has become of the drawing? did you leave it behind? some one will discover it.

Sus.—Never heed the picture now. The ape has broken the cage to get at the curds and rice, and let the *sarika* fly: let us endeavour to recover her, or she will repeat what has passed between us.

(Behind).—Astonishing, astonishing!

Sag.—Hay, Susamgata, is that the ape coming?

Sus.—No, coward; it is the worthy Vasantaka, our royal master's friend. Let us hence, the *sarika* is far away.

Sag.—I attend you. [*Exeunt.*

Enter VASANTAKA.

Very strange, indeed! most marvellous! the power of Sri-khanda-Dasa is most surprising, by whose simple will the jasmine has been covered with countless buds, as if smiling disdainfully upon the queen's favourite *madhavi*. I will go and tell my friend what has happened. Ah! yonder he comes, Loing quite confident of his hopes, and as pleased as if he looked upon the jasmine blossoming in his presence. His eye sparkles with pleasure: I will join him.

[*Exit.*

Another Part of the Garden.

Enter Vatsa.

I shall make the queen turn pale with anger. She will look upon the creeper like a rival beauty, as the delicate shrub displays the brilliance of its nascent buds, and swells, as gently inflated with the zephyre's sighs.

Vas.—(*Approaches.*) Victory to your Majesty!—fortune is propitious.

Vatsa,—I doubt it not, my friend; for inconceivable is the virtue of drugs, and charms, and gems. Lead the way, and let these eyes this day obtain by the sight the fruit of their formation.

Vas.—This way,

Vatsa.—Precede.

Vas.—(*Advances and stops to listen: turns back in alarm.*) Fly, fly, sir;

Vatsa.—Why?

Vas.—There is a goblin in yonder *bakula* tree!

Vatsa.—Away, simpleton, go on, and fear not! how should any such being have power at this season to harm?

Vas.—He speaks quite distinctly—if you disbelieve me, advance and listen.

Vatsa.—(*Advances.*) I hear a distinct voice, and a sweet one, too, like that of a woman: from its small and sharp tone it must be a starling. (*Looking up.*) Ah! there she sits.

Vas.—A starling?

Vatsa.—(*Laughing.*) A starling, look there!

Vas.—And so, my good friend, your fears made you fancy a starling to be a goblin.

Vatsa.—Out on you, blackhead! would you accuse me of what you have done yourself?

Vas.—Well, now do not you interfere. (*Holds up his staff.*) You impertinent bird, have you no more respect for a Brahman? Stop a moment, and with this crooked staff I will bring you down from the tree like a ripe wood apple.

Vatsa.—Forbear, forbear! how prettily she talks!

Vas.—Yes; now I listen again: she says, give this Brahman something to eat.

Vatsa.—Something to eat is ever the burthen of the glutton's song. Come, say truly, what does she utter?

Vas.—(*Listening and repeating.*) "Who is this you have delineated? Do not be offended without cause; I have given your *Kamadeva* my *Rati.*" Hey, sir! what should this mean?

Vatsa.—Oh, I suppose some female has been drawing her lover's portrait, and passing it off on her companion as the picture of the god of love: her friend has found her out, and ingeniously exposed her evasion, by delineating her in the character of *Kama's* bride.

Vas.—Very likely,

Vatsa.—Be still; she speaks again. (*They listen.*)

Vas.—(*Repeating.*) "Why should you be ashamed! attachment to exalted worth becomes your native excellence."

Vatsa.—Likely, likely!

Vas.—Nay, do not you presume upon your scholarship; I will expound all she says, when she has finished. The lady that is pictured is very handsome.

Vatsa.—We shall have leisure to satisfy our curiosity; let us now listen.

Vas.—Very well; do you hear what she says? "Take away these lotus leaves and fibres—it is in vain you strive to offer me relief."

Vatsa.—I hear and understand.

Vas. How the jade chatters to-day! but I will explain all I hear.

Vatsa.—Very likely; but now listen.

Vas.—Hey!—I declare she speaks in measure, like a Brahman skilled in the four Vedas.

Vatsa.—What said she? I did not hear.

Vas.—"I have fixed my heart where I dare not raise my hopes;—I am overcome with shame and despair, and death is my only refuge."

Vatsa.—With the exception of yourself, my worthy friend, what learned Brahman would call this speaking in measure.

Vas.—Why, what is it?

Vatsa.—Prose.

Vas.—Prose! Oh, very well! and what does it mean?

Vatsa.—Some young female may be supposed to have spoken the sentence, indifferent to life, because uncertain of her affection being returned.

Vas.—(*Laughing loudly.*) You may as well drop these evasive interpretations; why not say at once, "The damsel doubts my returning her passion?" Who but yourself could have been delineated as the god of the flowery bow! (*Claps his hands and laughs.*)

Vatsa.—Peace, simpleton! your obstreperous mirth has frightened the bird away; see! there she flies.

Vas.—She has perched on the plantain bower: let us follow her.

Vatsa.—Oppressed by the shafts of Kama, the delicate maid entrusts her companions with the sorrows of her breast: the tattling parrot or imitative starling repeats her words, and they find an hospitable welcome in the ears of fortunate

[*Exeunt.*

THE PLANTAIN BOWER.

Enter VATSA *and* VASANTAKA.

Vas.—Here is the bower; let us enter: but what has become of the starling? No matter; let us rest on this bench, where the breeze breathes cool and soft amidst the waving leaves of these *bananas.*

Vatsa.—As you please. (*They sit.*)

Vas.—What is yonder? It looks like the cage of the starling—broken to pieces most probably by the monkey.

Vatsa.—See what it is.

Vas.—I will. (*Looking about.*) What's here?—a picture. (*Takes it up.*) Ha, ha! my friend, you are in luck.

Vatsa.—What is that?

Vas.—Just what I said: here is your likeness. Who but yourself could have been delineated as the god of the flowery bow?

Vatsa.—Give it me.

Vas.—Stop a little. What! is such a jewel of a girl as is here pictured to be seen for nothing?

Vatsa.—Take this. (*Gives him a golden bracelet, and Vasantaka delivers the picture.*) Ha! behold, my friend, what lovely swan is this that wings her flight to *Manasa*, in whose sports the lotus trembles, who declares such auspicious fortune shall befall us, and whose face might be taken for the full moon by *Brahma*, when he first emerged from his lotus throne? (*Looking at the picture.*)

Enter SUSAMGATA *and* SAGARIKA.

Sus.—It is hopeless to follow the bird; let us get the drawing again, therefore, and go in.

Sag. By all means.

Vas.—(*To the king.*) Well, my friend, who is this damsel, think you, that seems to bend her head so humbly?

Sus.—Hark! I hear Vasanta talking—I suspect to the king. Let us conceal ourselves amongst the plants and hear what they are talking of. (*They hide behind the plantain trees.*)

Vatsa.—*Brahma*, when he first emerged from his lotus throne, had taken such a face for the unrivalled orb of the moon.

Sus.—(*To Sagarika.*) You are in luck, girl; your lover is dwelling upon your praises.

Sag.—How can you make so light of me as to treat me as matter for your mirth?

Vas.—Why should she hang down her head in this manner?

Vatsa.—Has not the starling told us all?

Sus.—There! I told you so; that bird has repeated our conversation.

Sag.—(*To herself.*) What will he reply? I hang between life and death.

Vas.—Well; and does she please your eyes?

Vatsa.—Please my eyes, say you! My sight insatiate rests upon her graceful limbs and slender waist: reluctantly it rises to her budding bosom, and thence ascending, fixes on those soft expressive orbs, where tremulously hangs the crystal tear.

Sus.—Did you hear?

Sag.—Did you hear? he praises the artist's skill!

Vas.—Well, sir, and what dulness must there be in you, not to perceive that in this, the object of the damsel's affection, your resemblance is exhibited?

Vatsa.—I cannot deny that she has flatteringly delineated my likeness, nor doubt her sentiments,—for observe the traces of the tear that has fallen upon her work, like the moist dew that starts from every pore of my frame.

Sag.—(*To herself.*) Heart, be of good cheer! your passion is directed to a corresponding object.

Sus.—My friend, you are fortunate; we must treat you now with the deference due to her whom our master loves.

Vas.—(*Looking round.*) Here are other traces of her passion: the lotus leaves she has applied to her heart whilst revealing her affection to her friend.

Vatsa.—You have guessed well. Where it has been in contact with her form the leaf has faded, but is still green where the contour of her well-proportioned shape has interposed an interval between the verdure and her person. The central freshness of the lotus leaf that has reposed upon her bosom reveals not the fervour of her love, but these two pallid circles on either side betray the violence of her affection.

Vas.—(*Picking up the fibre.*) Here is another vestige—it has bound the lotus leaf upon her bosom.

Vatsa.—(*Applying it to his heart.*) It still dispenses its cooling freshness. Say, fibre, art thou withered, because thou art no longer cherished between those palpitating orbs, whose friendly contiguity scarce leaves room for the lodgment of a silken thread, much less for thee.

Sus.—(*Apart.*) His Grace must be violently affected to talk thus incoherently. It will not become me to leave him to these fancies. (*To Sagarika.*) Well, my friend, what you came for is before you.

Sag.—Why, what did I come for, pray?

Sus.—The picture, what else? there it is—take it.

Sag.—(*Angrily.*) As I don't understand what you say, I shall leave you. (*Going.*)

Sus.—How now, impatient! stop a moment, and I will recover the drawing before we leave this place.

Sag.—Do so.

(*Susamgata comes forward, so as to be seen by Vasantaka.*)

Vas.—Hide the picture, here in this plantain leaf—here comes one of the queen's damsels. (*Vatsa covers it with his mantle.*)

Sus.—(*Advancing.*) Glory to the king!

Vatsa.—Welcome, Susamgata; sit down. How knew you that I was here?

Sus.—That is not all my knowledge; I am acquainted with secret of the picture, and some other matters, of which I shall apprise her Majesty. (*Going.*)

Vas. (*Apart to Vatsa.*) It is all blown—she is a great tattler—better bribe her to be silent.

Vatsa.—Stay, Susamagata; accept these ornaments. (*Takes off his bracelet, etc.*). This is but a matter of sport, not to be mentioned to the queen.

Sus.—Your Grace is bountiful ; you need not fear me, I was but in jest, and do not want these jewels. The truth is, my dear friend, Sagarika, is very angry with me for drawing her picture, and I shall be much obliged to your Majesty to intercede for me and appease her resentment.

Vatsa.—(*Springing up.*) Where is she? Lead me to her.

Vas.—Give me the picture—I will take care of it ; it may again be wanted.

Sus.—This way. (*They advance.*)

Sag.—He is here—I tremble at his sight, I can neither stand nor move—what shall I do !

Sas.—(*Seeing her.*) A most surprising damsel, truly ; such another is not to be found in this world. I am confident that when she was created, *Brahma* was astonished at his own performance.

Vatsa.—Such are my impressions. The four mouths of *Brahma* must at once have exclaimed in concert, bravo, bravo ! when the deity beheld these eyes more beauteous than the leaves of his own lotus ; and his heads must have shaken with wonder, as he contemplated loveliness, the ornament of all the world.

Sag.—(*To Susamgata.*) This is the picture you have brought. (*Going.*)

Vatsa.—You turn your eyes upon your friend in anger, lovely maid ; yet such is their native tenderness they cannot assume a harsh expression. Look thus, but do not leave us, for your departure hence will alone give me pain.

Sus.—She is very angry, sir, I assure you; take her hand and pacify her.

Vatsa.—You advise me well. (*Takes Sagarika by the hand*).

Vas.—I congratulate you, sir; you enjoy unprecedented fortune.

Vatsa.—You say rightly—she is the very deity Lakshmi herself: her hand is the new shoot of the *parijata* tree, else whence distil these dew drops of ambrosia.

Sus.—It is not possible, my dear friend, you can remain inexorable whilst honored thus with his Grace's hand.

Sag.—(*Frowning.*) Will you not forbear, Susamgata?

Vatsa.—You must not be angry with your friend.

Vas.—Why, like a hungry Brahman, should you thus be out of humour, lady?

Sus.—Very well, my friend, I will say nomore.

Vatsa.—This is not right, resentful girl, to be so unforgiving to your intimate companions.

Vas.—Hey; here again is Madam Vasavadatta.

The Raja lets go Sagarika's hand in alarm.

Sag.—(*To Sus.*) What shall I do?

Sus.—We can escape unperceived behind this *tamala* tree (*They go off hastily.*)

Vatsa.—(*Looking round.*) Why, my friend, where is the queen, where is Vasavadatta?

Vas.—I do not know. I said, here again is Madam Vasavadatta; I meant in testiness of temper.

Vatsa.—Out on thee! thou hast rudely snapped the string of splendid gems, that fate and acknowledged love had hung around my neck.

[*They retire.*

Enter VASAVADATTA, *the queen, and* KANCHANAMALA, *an Attendant.*

Vasava.—Well, girl, how far from hence is my lord's favourite jasmine tree?

Kanch.—It is but a little way farther: we shall see it after passing this plantain bower.

Vasava.—Let us hasten.

Kanch.—It is bat a little way further: we shall see it after passing this plantain bower.

Vasava.—Let us hasten.

Kanch.—I think I see his Majesty. Yes there he is; will it please you join him?

Vasava.—(*Approaching* Vatsa.) Glory to my lord!

Vatsa.—(*To* Vasantaka.) Hide the picture-quick.

(*Vasantaka takes it and holds it under his arm.*)

Vasava.—Has the jasmine budded yet, my lord?

Vatsa.—I have been waiting your arrival and have not yet seen it; we will now visit it together.

Vasava.—Oh no—I see by your countenance that it has flowered; that is sufficient, I will go no further.

Vas.—Then your Grace acknowledges we have conquered! Huzza! (*Waves his hand and dances; the picture falls; the Raja observes it, looks at him angrily, and points to the picture.*)

Vas.—(*Apart to* Vatsa.) Be calm; I will manage it.

Kanch.—(*Picking up the picture and shewing it to the queen.*) See, madam, whose portrait is this?

Vasava.—(*Looking at it and apart.*) This is my lord; and is not this Sagarika? (*Aloud to* Vatsa.) Pray what is this, my lord.

Vatas.—(*To* Vasanta.) What shall I say?

Vas.—(*To* Vatas.) Fear not, leave it to me. (*Aloud to* Vasavadatta.) I was observing, madam, that it would be very difficut to hit my friend's likeness, on which his Majesty was pleased to give me this specimen of his skill.

Vatsa.—It is as Vasantaka tells you.

Vasava.—And this female standing near you—I suppose this is a specimen of Vasantaka's skill?

Vatsa.—What should you suspect? That is a mere fancy portrait, the original was never seen before.

Vas.—I will swear to this, by my Brahmanical cord, that the original was never before seen by either of us.

Kanch.—(*To the queen, apart.*) Why should he speak evasively, madam? There is no need to be angry.

Vasava.—(*To her.*) My honest girl, you do not understand his prevarications. I know Vasantaka. (*Aloud.*) My lord, excuse me. Looking at this picture has given me a slight headache. I leave you to your amusements. (*Going*).

Vatsa.—What can I say to you, dearest? I really am at a loss! If I ask you to forgive me, that is unnecessary, if you are not offended; and how can I promise to do so no more, when I have committed no fault—although you will not believe my assertions.

Vasava.—(*Detatching herself gently and with politeness.*) You mistake, my lord; I assure you my head aches; on that account I take my leave.

[*Exit with Kanchanamala.*

Vas.—Your Majesty has had a lucky escape. The queen's anger has dispersed like summer clouds.

Vatsa.—Away, blockhead, we have no occasion to rejoice: could you not discover the queen's anger through her unsuccessful attempts to disguise it? Her face was clouded with a passing frown. As she hung down her head, she looked on me with an affected smile. She gave utterance to no angry words, 'tis true, and the swelling eye glowed not with rage—but a starting tear was with difficulty repressed; and although she treated me with politeness, struggling indignation lurked in every gesture. We must follow, and endeavour to pacify her.

[*Exeunt.*

END OF THE SECOND ACT.

ACT III.

A CHAMBER IN THE PALACE.

Enter MADANIKA, *one of the queen's Attendants.*

Ho! Kausambika! tell me if Kanchanamala is with the queen? (*Listening.*) What say you? she came in some time since and went out again! where can she be? Oh, she comes.

Enter KANCHANAMALA.

Kanch.—Bravo, Vasantaka, bravo! you are a deeper politician than the prime minister himself.

Mad.—How now, fellow Kanchanamala, what has Vasantaka done to merit your praises?

Kanch.—What occasion is there for your asking? you are not able to keep the secret!

Mad.—I swear by the feet of the queen, I will not mention it to any body.

Kanch.—On that condition you shall hear. As I was passing from the palace to-day, I overheard Vasantaka and Susamgata in conversation behind the door of the picture gallery.

Mad.—What is the subject?

Kanch.—Vasantaka said, Sagarika alone is the cause of my friend's indisposition; do you, Susamgata, devise a remedy.

Mad.—And what replied she?

Kanch.—She said, the queen having discovered what was going forward by finding the picture, but not suspecting me, has placed Sagarika under my charge—giving me, to insure my vigilance, some of her own clothes and ornaments. With these I will equip Sagarika as the queen, and myself as Kanchanamala, and thus disguised will meet his Majesty at the *Madhava* bower about sunset: do you come to this place and conduct us thither.

Mad.—Very well plotted, Susamgata; but you are mistaken, if you think to deceive a mistress so kind to her attendants.

Kanch.—And where are you going?

Mad.—I was coming to look for you. You were so long in bringing us an answer about his Majesty's illness, that the queen was very anxious, and sent me to see what had become of you.

Kanch.—Her Majesty is too simple, to be so easily deceived. But the king, whose only illness is love, is sitting in the pavilion over the ivory gate. Come along, let us carry this news to the queen.

[*Exeunt.*

THE PAVILION.

VATSA *discovered.*

Vatsa.—Endure, my heart, the fever love has kindled, and which the maid I sigh for can alone allay. Why approach me with my folly; for seeking to subdue thy farvours with the cooling sandal, instead of that lovely hand which was awhile in my grasp! The mind from its natural unsteadiness should be a difficult mark to hit; how happens it that the archer-god has lodged all his shafts in mine. Deity of the flowery bow, innumerable are those who may be struck with thy five arrows, and such as I am are notoriously thy aim. But in this is the usual state of things reversed, that I, singly, am pierced with thy countless darts, and am about to perish. Yet I suffer less on my own account than for poor Sagarika. She shrinks from every gaze, suspecting that her secret is discovered. If she observe two of her companions in conversation, she fancies herself the subject; and if they laugh, she thinks she is the object of their mirth. Alas, my love! thy uneasiness excites my compassion, and I share the dread thou sufferest from the glances of the queen, as they bend on thee with ill dissembled indignation.—How long Vasantaka delays! I have sent him to obtain some tidings of the maiden.

Enter VASANTAKA.

Vatsa.—(*To himself.*) Ha, ha! my friend, you will be better pleased to-day than when you ascended the throne of Kausambi, when you hear the agreeable news I bring you. Oh, there he is, he seems expecting me. Joy, joy, my friend; fortune is propitious, and promises to accomplish your desire.

Vatsa.—How is Sagarika?

Vas.—In a little time you may judge for yourself.

Vatsa.—What, may I hope to see her soon?

Vas.—Why not? Am not I your counsellor—I who laugh at the wisdom of Vrihaspati?

Vatsa.—Admitted—there is nothing you cannot manage; but come, tell me, I long to hear the particulars.

Vas.—(*Whispers in his ear.*) There you have the whole.

Vatsa.—This merits reward. (*Gives him a bracelet.*)

Vas.—(*Takes it and puts it on.*) Very becoming; a golden bracelet suits my arm. I will go and show it to my wife. (*Going.*)

Vatsa.—Stop, my friend, stop, another time will serve your purpose. How much of the day remains?

Vas.—(*Looking.*) See my friend, the lord of a thousand rays approaches the bowers of the western mountain.

Vatsa.—True, the lord of the one-wheeled car having performed the circuit of the world, now purpose to suspend his labours till the morrow's dawn, and halting on the mountain's brow, he calls in the scattered rays, whose golden lines converging round his chariot, look like the radiant spokes that shoot to their centre from the wide circumference of the spheres. As with assembled beams he rests upon the summit of the western hill, the lord of the day thus breathes his farewell to the lotus: "Adieu, my beloved, my hour is come and I must depart: sleep dwell upon thy lids, till I again distrub thy slumbers." Let us therefore away to the *Madhabi* bower, and be punctual to the time appointed by my fair.

Vas.—I attend you. The interval that separates the trees of the grove is lost, and they seem to form one close compacted mass. A dusky hue, like that of the hide of the buffalo or wild boar besmeared with mire, extends over the garden, and thick glooms spreading above the east, obscure the horizon.

Vatsa.—True: first gathering in the east, the deepening gloom successively obscures the other regions of the sky: becoming intenser as it proceeds, it steals the hue of *Shiva's* neck, and mountains, trees, and towns, the heavens and the earth, are hidden from our sight. Let us to the garden.

[*Exeunt.*

The Garden.

Enter Vatsa *and* Vasantaka.

Vas.—This clump of trees should be the *makarandra* grove, but I am not quite certain: how shall we find the way?

Vatsa.—Go on, we are right, I know the path. The *champaka* trees are here, I smell their fragrance; and now the *sindhuvaras*; we now pass the cluster of *bakulas*, and here are the *patala* trees: their various odour indicates their situation, and would enable us to track the walk were they concealed by twice the present gloom.

Vas.—Ha! here we are, this is the *madhavi* bower.

I know it by the perfume of the buds so tempting to the bees, and the smoothness of the emerald pavement. Do you remain here whilst I go for Sagarika; I shall soon be back.

Vatsa.—Do not be long.

Vas.—Do not be impatient, my friend. I am back already. [*Exit.*

Vatsa.—I wait you on this emerald seat. Who will take part with the inconstant swain, that abandons his old love for a new? The timid damsel that comes to her first assignation, casts but a sidelong glance upon her beloved, and though she shrink not from his embrace, averts her countenance from his gaze. "Let me go," she murmurs repeatedly; "I will leave you!" but still submits to the gentle violence that prevents her departure. What heightened charms does a stolen interview bestow upon the amorous maid! How long Vasantaka delays! Surely Vasavadatta has not heard of our design. [*Retires.*

A CHAMBER.

Enter VASAVADATTA *and* KANCHANAMALA.

Vasava.—Can it be possible, wench, that Sagarika has promised to meet my lord disguised in my attire?

Kanch.—I have told your Majesty; but if we find Vasantaka at the door of the picture gallery, your doubts, I hope, will be removed.

Vasava.—Let us thither. [*Exeunt.*

CHAMBER LEADING TO THE PICTURE GALLERY.

Enter VASANTAKA, *disguised.*

Vas.—I thought I heard the tread of the feet Sagarika approaches.

Enter VASAVADATTA *and* KANCHANAMALA.

Kanch.—This the place, madam. Now to see if Vasantaka is here. (*Snaps her fingers.*)

Vas.—(*Approaching.*) Ha, Susamgata! well done: I declare I should have taken you for Kanchanamala. Where is Sagarika.

Kanch.—(*Pointing to Vasavadatta.*) There.

Vas.—Why, this is the very queen herself.

Vasava.—(*Alarmed and apart.*) How! am I recognised?

Kanch.—(*To the queen.*) All's safe, madam. (*Pointing to Vasantaka.*) Ah! rogue, you will have cause to remember your word.

Vas.—Haste, haste, Sagarika! the deer-marked deity rises in the east.

A GROVE.—VATSA *discovered.*

Why is my heart so agitated when I expect an interview with my fair? or is it that the flame of love burns fiercest as it approaches its gratfication, as the days are hottest when the rains are about to descend?

Entor VASANTAKA, VASAVADATTA, *and* KANCHNAMALA.

Vas.—(*To Vasava.*) Lady Sagarika, I hear my friend muttering to himself his anxiety for your appearance; I will announce your arrival. (*Vasavadatta nods assent.*) Fortune is propitious to your Majesty; Sagarika is here!

Vatsa.—(*Approaching her.*) My beloved Sagarika, thy countenance is radiant as the moon, thy eyes are two lotus buds, thy hand is the full blown flower, and thy arms its graceful filaments. Come thou, whose whole form is the shrine of ecstasy, come to my arms, and allay the feverish pangs inflicted by the shapeless god.

Vasava.—(*Weeping, apart to Kanch.*) Ah! girl, my lord now speaks his honest self—how soon will his tone be changed. Is not this incomprehensible?

Kanch.—It is so, indeed, madam; there is nothing so bad, that it may not be expected from these abominable men.

Vas.—Come, Sagarika, take courage, speak to his Majesty. We have had the harsh tones of the angry queen Vasavadatta grating in our ears today; let them be now regaled with the melody of your sweet voice.

Vasava.—(*To Kanchan apart.*) Hey, girl! am I accustomed to speak harshly? The worthy Vasantaka is very complimentary.

Kanch.—He will have cause to recollect this.

Vas.—See, my friend, the moon is up, and casts on everything his rays as pallid as the maiden's cheek that whitens with resentment.

Vatsa.—See, love, the lord of night now stands

upon the mountain's crest, and throws his scattered rays around to emulate the radiance of thy cheek. But idle is his coming; does not thy countenance shame the beauty of the lotus? do not thine eyes diffuse dearer delight? What aid can he bring to the influence of the fish-bannered god, which is not wrought by a single glance of thine? Why should the moon show himself whilst thy resplendent charms are visible? And if he rises, proud of his store of nectar, does he not know thy lips may boast too of ambrosia?

Vasava.—*Throwing off her veil.*)—Believe me still Sagarika, my good lord; lyour heart is so fascinated by her, you fancy you behold Sagarika in everything.

Vatsa.—(*Apart.*)—How! the queen Vasavadatta! What is this?

Vas.—My life is in jeopardy—that is—what is this.

Vatsa.—(*To the queen.*)—Forgive me, dearest.

Vasava.—Address not this to me, my lord—the epithet is another's property.

Vas.—(*Apart.*)—What is to be done? (*Aloud.*) Nay, madam! you are of too generous a spirit not to forgive this first offence of my dear friend.

Vasava.—Worthy Vasantaka, the offence is mine, who have presumed to interrupt this intended interview.

Vatsa.—It is of no use to deny it. But hear me:

I bow me to thy feet, and mark my forehead with their vermil dye, in hope to transfer thither the hue with which anger discolours thy moon-like countenance. (*Falls at her feet.*)

V*asava.*—Rise, my lord, rise! that wife must be unreasonable indeed, who, with such evidence of her lord's affection, can presume to be offended. Be happy, I take my leave. (*Going.*)

V*as.*—Nay, madam, be merciful; I am sure, if you quit his Majesty in this posture, you will hereafter repent it.

V*asava.*—Away, fool, I know no reason for mercy nor repentance. [*Exit with Kanchanamala.*

V*as.*—Your Majesty may get up, the queen is gone. What is the use of weeping in a wood?

V*atsa.*—What, gone, without relenting!

V*as.*—Not so either, for our limbs are whole.

V*atsa.*—Out, simpleton! do you make a jest of this? you, by whose blundering this untoward accident has happened! The genuine regard, our long and tender union has inspired, will now appear pretended, and the impression of my inconstancy may render her unable to endure existence. No pang is so intolerable as that of unrequited affection.

V*as.*—The queen is angry, that is a clear case; as to what she will do, that is by no means certain. In the meantime, is Sagarika alive or not?

V*atsa.*—I was thinking of her. [*They retire.*

Enter SAGARIKA *(behind), dressed as the queen.*

Sag.—I have luckily got clear of the music hall, and have come so far in this disguise without being observed. But, alas! what shall I do now?

V*as.*—Why thus lost in thought, something must be devised.

V*atsa.*—But what?

Sag.—(*Behind.*)—'Twere better far, that I should put an end at once to my sufferings and my life: the queen will then know nothing of my purpose, and Susamgata and I shall both escape disgrace. This tree will do.

V*atsa.*—I see nothing left for it but to appease the queen. Come, let us go in.

V*as.*—Stop, I heard steps! perhaps she has thought better, and returns.

V*atsa.*—She is a woman of a generous spirit—it may be so. Quick, ascertain!

Sag.—With the fibres of the *madhavi.* I will suspend myself to this bough. Alas! my dear friends, far, far away, alone and unfriended, I thus terminate my miserable existence. *(Fastening the noose around her neck.)*

V*as.*—Who is there?—Ha, the queen! Hey why, what! haste, haste, my friend, or Vasavadatta will destroy herself.

V*atsa.*—(*Advancing hastily.*)—Where, where is she?

V*as.*—Behold!

Vatsa.—(*Rushing to her and tearing off the tendril.*)—Intemperate woman! what horrid act is this? My own life trembles in my throat: existence is not yours to abandon! forego such desperate thought.

Sag.—(*Apart.*) My lord! His presence inspires the love of life; at least my last wish is accomplished, and having seen him, I shall die content. (*Aloud.*) Let me go, sir, you forget my dependent station; I may not find again an opportunity to end this hated being. Beware how you displease the queen.

Vatsa.—Can it be, my own Sagarika! No more of this despair? away with this fatal bands, and to arrest my fleeting life, twine round my neck the noose of these dear arms. (*Embraces her.*) My friend, it rains without a cloud.

Vas.—Very true, if the queen does not return like a sudden squall, and spoil our fine weather.

Enter VASAVADATTA *and* KANCHANAMALA.

Vasava.—I treated my lord too disrespectfully, girl, as he condescended to cast himself at my feet; I must therefore see him again, and behave to him with more temper.

Kanch.—Who could think in this way but your Grace? However, better the king fail in decorum than Your Majesty, so let us seek him.

Vatsa.—Say, fair maid, may not our affection hope to be returned?

Kanch.—I hear his Majesty's voice; he is probably seeking for you in hopes to pacify your anger.

Vasava.—Let us approach gently from behind; I will cast my arms round his neck, and tell him I forgive him.

Vas.—Take courage, Sagarika, make my friend a reply.

Vasava.—(*Apart.*) Sagarika here! Keep back, let us listen; I will presently be of the party.

Sag.—Why, sir, will you thus pretend regard you do not feel, and wantonly risk the displeasure of the queen, who, I know, is dearer to you than your life.

Vatsa.—You utter what is not quite true, my love. When her bosom swells with sighs, I express concern, when she is sullen, I soothe her; when her brows are bent, and her face is distorted with anger, I fall prostrate at her feet. These marks of respect are due to the queen's exalted station; but the regards that springs from vehement affection, that is yours alone.

Vasava.—(*Coming forward.*) I believe you, my lord, I believe you.

Vatsa.—How now, madam, is it you? Why, then, you need not be offended. Cannot you perceive that I have been attracted hither, and misled by the resemblance of your dress and person? Be composed, I beg you. (*Falls at her feet.*)

Vasava.—Rise, rise! let not my exalted station put you to such unnecessary inconvenience.

Vatsa.—(*Aside.*) She has overheard me—there is no chance then of appeasing her.

Vas.—It is very true, madam, I assure you, that deceived by the belief that you were attempting to destroy yourself, I brought my friend to this spot, to preserve, as I thought, your life. If you doubt me see this noose. (*Takes up the noose.*)

Vasava.—Kanchanamala, girl, take the twisted tendril and secure that Brahman, and make this hussy go on before us.

Kanch.—As you command. (*Puts the noose over Vasantaka's neck and beats him with the other end of it.*) Now, sir, see what is the consequence of your ingenuity. You have had the queen's harsh voice grating in our ears, have you? do you recollect this? Come, Sagarika, do you go on before,

Sag.—Why did I not perish when I sought to die!

Vas.—Think of me, my dear friend, who am thus carried off an unfortunate captive by the queen.

Exeunt all but Vatsa.

What an unlucky business this is! What is to be done? How shall I dissipate the rage that clouds the smiling countenance of the queen! how rescue Sagarika from the dread of her resentment, or liberate my friend Vasantaka? I am quite bewildered with these events, and can no longer command my ideas.—At any rate, it is useless to stay here: I will in, and endeavour to pacify Vasavadatta. *Exit.*

END OF THE THIRD ACT.

ACT IV.

A Chamber.

Enter Susamgata *with a diamond necklace in her hand.*

Alas, alas! my dear friend Sagarika, my timid, my tender, my generous friend! whither, lovely maiden, are you gone? Shall I not again behold you? Pitiless destiny, why shouldst thou have endowed her with such unrivalled charms, to consign her to so hapless a fate? Despairing of her life, she has begged me to give this necklace to some Brahman. Whom shall I present it to? Eh, here comes Vasantaka, I will give it to him.

Enter Vasantaka.

Vas.—So, I am well out of that scrape. Appeased by my excellent friend's intercession, her Majesty has not only restored me to freedom, but has regaled me with cakes from her own fair hands, and presented me with a dress and these earrings. Now then to seek the king.

Sus.—Worthy Vasantaka, one moment.

Vas.—Hey, Susamgata, what's the matter? why do you weep? no bad news, I hope, of Sagarika?

Sus.—It is of her I wished to speak. It is said that the queen ordered her off to Ujjayin, and she was taken away at midnight; but whither she is gone I know not.

Vas.—Alas, poor Sagarika, a damsel of such unequalled charms, and of such a gentle disposition! I much fear the violence of the queen.

Sus.—She herself despaired of life, poor girl, and left with me this diamond necklace, to be presented to the worthy Vasantaka. Pray you, accept it.

Vas.—(*Covering his ears.*) Excuse me, I could not stretch out my hand to take so sad a memorial. (*Weeps.*)

Sus.—For her sake, let me entreat you.

Vas.—I tell you what: I will take it to the king. It will relieve the sorrow into which the loss of Sagarika has plunged him. (*Susamgata gives it to him he looks at it attentively.*) Why, where could she have procured such a valuable necklace?

Sus.—That excited my curiosity, and I asked her.

Vas.—And what replied she?

Sus.—She looked me in the face, and sighed, and said, Ah, Susamgata, it is now of no avail to tell my sad story,—and then burst into tears.

Vas.—Although she has not confessed it, yet such an ornament is a proof that she belongs to some distinguished family.—Where is the king?

Sus.—He went from the queen's apartments to the crystal alcove. Do you go to him—I must to her Majesty.

[*Exeunt severally.*

THE CRYSTAL ALCOVE.

VATSA *discovered seated.*

Deceitful vows, tender speeches, plausible excuses, and prostrate supplications, had less effect upon the queen's anger than her own tears; like water upon fire, they quenched the blaze of her indignation. I am now only anxious for Sagarika. Her form, as delicate as the petal of the lotus, dissolving in the breath of inexperienced passion, has found a passage through the channels by which love penetrates, and is lodged deep in my heart. The friend to whom I could confide my secret sorrows is the prisoner of the queen; in whose presence can I now give vent to my tears?

Enter VASANTAKA.

V*as.*—Yonder is my friend, emaciate with care, but graceful still, radiant as the newly-risen moon. Health to your Grace! fortune favours you. I have got out of her Majesty's clutches, and these eyes have again the pleasure of beholding you.

V*atsa.*—My friend Vasantaka, embrace me. (*Embraces him.*) Your dress declares you restored to the goodGraces of the queen. Tell me, what news of Sagarika? (*Vasantaka hangs down his head.*) I pray you speak.

V*as.*—I cannot utter such unpleasant tidings.

V*atsa.*—What tidings, speak? Alas, it is too plain, she is no more! Sagarika! (*Faints.*)

Vas.—(*Alarmed.*) My friend, revive—revive!

Vatsa. (*Recovering.*) Leave me, existence—I willingly resign you—haste, or you will be forcibly expelled. Already is that graceful maid far off.

Vas.—You are alarmed unnecessarily. I was about to tell you, the queen has sent her to Ougein:—this I called unpleasant tidings.

Vatsa.—To Ougein! Ah cruel Vasavadatta. Who told you this?

Vas.—Susamgata;—and more, she gave me this necklace to bring to your Majesty. She knows why.

Vatsa.—To alleviate my despair; what else. Give it me. (*Vasantaka gives him the necklace which he applies to his heart.*) This has once hung upon her neck, and is now far removed from her: it is a friend that shares a similar fortune with myself, and will speak comfort to my sorrows: wear it, my friend, that as it meets my gaze I may acquire fortitude.

Vas.—As you command. (*Ties the necklace round his neck.*)

Vatsa.—Alas, I shall never again behold my love.

Vas.—Speak not so loud—some one approaches.

Enter VASUNDHARA, *a Female Attendant, with a sword.*

Vasun.—Glory to your Majesty!—So please you, the nephew of Ramanwat, Vijayavarman, desirous of communicating to you some acceptable tidings, is the door.

Vatsa.—Let him enter.

VASUNDHARA *goes out, and returns with* VIJAYAVARMAN.

Vij.—Glory to your Majesty! Your Majesty's fortune is propitious in the triumphs of Rumanwat.

Vatsa.—Are the *Kosalas* subdued?

Vij.—By your Majesty's auspices.

Vatsa.—Rumanwat has well performed his task, and speedily achieved an arduous labour. Let me hear the circumstances of our truimph.

Vij.—On receiving your Majesty's commands, the general of the state, Rumanwat, soon collected a mighty army of foot, and horse, and elephants, and marching against the king of *Kosala*, surrounded him in a strong position in the *Vindhya* mountains.

Vatsa.—Proceed.

Vij.—Impatient of the blockade, the *Kosala* monarch prepared his troops for an engagement.

Vas.—Your slowness sets my heart in a flutter.

Vij.—Issuing from the heights, the enemy's forces came down upon us in great numbers, and the points of the horizon were crowded with the array of mighty elephants, like another chain of mountains; they bore down our infantry beneath their ponderous masses those who escaped the shock were transpierced by inmerable arrows, and the enemy flattered himself the for once disappointed our commander's hopes labour shed from the blows of contending heroes another heads were cloven in twain—the broken armour and scattered weapons were carried away in torrents of blood, and the defiance of the king of *Kosala*, in the van of his army, was heard by our warriors; when—

Vatsa.—How! was our force discomfited?

Vij.—Our chief alone confronted him, and slew the monarch on his furious elephant with countless shafts.

Vas.—Victory! victory! we have truimphed!

Vatsa.—And honour to our gallant foe, the king of *Kosala*; for glorious is the warrior's death when his enemies applaud his prowess. What next?

Vij.—Rumanwat then appointed my elder brother, Sanjayavarman, to govern the country of *Kosala*, and making slow marches in consequence of the number of his wounded, returned to the capital. He is now arrived.

Vatsa.—Vasundhara, go apprise Yaugandharayana to distribute the treasures of my favour.

Vasundh.—You are obeyed.

[*Exit with* Vijayavarman.

Enter KANCHANAMALA.

Kan.—Glory to your grace! the queen sends you word, that Samvara-Siddhi, a magician, is arrived from Ougein: will your Majesty be pleased to see him?

Vatsa.—By all means; I take much pleasure in this cunning—bring him hither. (*Kanchanamala goes,—and returns with the magician, Samvara-Siddhi, carrying a bunch of peacock's feathers in his hands.*)

Kan.—Here is the king.

Sam.—(*Waving the feathers and laughing.*)—Reverence to Indra, who lends our art his name, and on whom *Samvara* and *Vivara* attend! What are your Majesty's commands? would you see the moon brought down upon earth, a mountain in mid air, a fire in the ocean, or night at noon? I will produce them—command.

Vas.—My good friend, be careful,—take heed what sort of a person this conjuror may be.

Sam.—What need of many words? By the force of my master's spells I will place before your eyes the person whom in your heart you are most anxious to behold.

Vatsa.—Go, girl, to the queen, and tell her that as the magician is her servant, I do not wish to witness his performances alone, but will see them in her company.

Kanch.—She is here.

Enter VASAVADATTA.

Vasava—(*Apart to Kanchanamala.*) Girl, this man is from Ougein: think you he is a friend to me?

Kanch.—Fear not, madam, he is well disposed to your Grace's family.

Vasava.—(*Advances.*) Victory to my lord!

Vatsa.—Come, madam; the sage promises much: let us behold his cunning. (*Leads her to a seat, and sits beside her.*) Now, sir, display your power.

Sam.—You shall be obeyed. (*Waves his plume.*) *Hari*, *Hara*, *Brahma*, chiefs of the gods, and thou their mighty monarch, *Indra*; with the host of heavenly spirits, *Siddhas* and *Vidyadharas* appear rejoicing and dancing in heavens. (*The king and queen look up and rise from their seats.*)

Vatsa.—Most wonderful!

Vas.—Extraordinary indeed!

Vatsa.—Most strange!

Vas.—See, love, that is *Brahma* throned upon the lotus.—That, *Samkara* with the crescent moon, his glittering crest—that, *Hari* the destroyer of the demon race, in whose four hands the bow, the sword, the mace, and the shell are borne.—There, mounted on his stately elephant, appears the king of *Swarga*; around them countless spirits dance merrily in mid air, sporting with the lovely nymphs of heaven, whose anklets ring responsive to the measure.

Vasava.—It is very marvellous.

Vas.—(*Apart.*) The son of a slave—this conjuror! —what do we want with gods and nymphs—if he would treat us with a pleasant sight: let him show us Sagarika.

Enter VASUNDHARA.

Vasundh.—So please your Majesty the minister Yaugandharayana begs to inform you, that the king

Vikramabahu has sent you, along with your messenger who returns, the councillor Vasubhuti: be pleased to receive him, as the season is auspicious. Yaugandharayana will also wait upon you as soon as he is at leisure.

Vasava.—Suspend this spectacle, my lord. Vasubhuti is a man of elevated rank; he is also of the family of my maternal uncle, and should not be suffered to wait; let us first see him.

Vatsa.—Learned sir, be pleased to repose awhile.

Sam.—(*Waves the brush.*) I obey. (*Going.*) But we have yet some sights for your Majesty to be hold.

Vatsa.—We will see them.

Vasava.—Make him a present, Kanchanamala.

Kanch.—I shall, madam. [*Exit with the Magician.*

Vatsa.—(*To Vasantaka.*) Go and conduct Vasubhuti hither.

(*Retires with the queen; Vasantaka goes out, and returns with* VASUBHUTI *and* BABHARAVYA.)

Vas.—This way.

Vasu.—The avenues of this palace do in truth present a splendid scene. The eye is bewildered amongst the stately steeds and mighty elephants of war; the ear is regaled with harmonious sounds, and the heart is gratified by mixing with the throng of attending princes. The state of the king of *Simhala* is here effaced, and the magnificence of the entrance into every court betrays me into rustic admiration.

Babh.—The idea of seeing my master again after so long an absence, diverts my thoughts from every other object. Age and agitation together make my limbs tremble, my eyes are dimmed with involuntary tears, and I stutter and stumble in my speech.

Vas.—(*In advance of them.*) Come on, sirs.

Vasu.—(*Observing the necklace.*) Babhravya, we should know that necklace: it was presented by the king to his daughter on her departure.

Babh.—It is very like—shall I ask Vasantaka where he got it?

Vasu.—No, no; it is not very surprising that princely families should possess jewels of a similar appearance.

Vas.—The king,—advance.

Vasu.—Victory to your Majesty!

Vatsa.—I pay you reverence.

Vasu.—Prosperity ever attend your Highness!

Vatsa.—A seat for the minister.

Vas.—This is a seat. (*Spreads his upper garment on the floor.*)

Babh.—Babhravya pays his respects to your Majesty.

Vatsa.—(*Puts his hand on his shoulder.*) Babhravya, sit here.

Vas.—Minister, the queen Vasavadatta.

Vasava.—I salute your Excellency.

Vasu.—May your Highness have a son like his father!

Babh.—Madam, Babhravya bows to you.

Vatsa.—Now, Vasubhuti, how is it with the sovereign of Simhala?

Vasu.—(*Sighs.*) I know not what reply to offer.

Vasava.—(*Apart.*) Alas! what can he have to communicate?

Vatsa.—What is the meaning of this concern?

Babh.—(*Apart to Vasubhuti.*) It is useless to hesitate—say at once what must be said.

Vasu.—It is with difficulty, Sir, that I can relate what has chanced, but thus it is. In consequence of the prophecy of the seer, that whoever should wed Ratnavali, my master's daughter, should become the emperor of the world, your Majesty's minister, as you are aware, solicited her for your bride :- unwilling, however, to be instrumental to the uneasiness of Vasavadatta, the king of Simhala declined compliance with his suit.

Vatsa—.(*Apart to Vasavadatta.*) What strange untruths are these, my love, your uncle's envoy relates.

Vasava.—I cannot pretend to judge, my lord, who is to be believed here.

Vas.—(*To Vasubhuti.*) Well, and where is the princess now?

Vasu.—My master, understanding at last that the queen was deceased, consented to give his daughter to Vatsa. We were deputed to conduct her hither, when alas, our vessel was wrecked, and—(*weeps.*)

Vasava.—Alas, unhappy that I am! Loved sister Ratnavali, where art thou, hear me and reply.

Vatsa.—Be composed: the fate that causes, may remove, our sorrows. [Have not these escaped? (*Pointing to Vasubhuti and Babhravya.*)

Vasava.—Oh, that it may prove so, but fate is no friend to me.

(*Behind.*) The inner apartments are on fire. The flames spread over the palace top a roof of gold; they wind around with clouds of smoke; thy shed intolerable heat, and fill the female train with affright. Alas! the former false report, that at Lavanaka the queen was burnt, will now is become a pitiable truth.

Vatsa.—(*Starting up wildly.*) Vasavadatta burnt to death! my queen, my love!

Vasava.—What extravagance is this—behold me at your side. But ah! help, help, my lord.

Vatsa.—(*Embracing her.*) Be calm, my love.

Vasava.—I think not of myself, but poor Sagarika. She is in bonds: my cruelty has kept her captive—and she will be lost without some aid—haste, haste, and save her!

Vatsa.—Sagarika in peril! I fly to her rescue!

Vasu.—What desperate purpose is this, Sir? the fatal folly of the moth.

Babhr.—Hear Vasubhuti, Sir.

Vas.—(*Catching hold of his robe.*) Forbear! this is madness.

Vatsa.—Let me go, fool! Sagarika will perish—think you I shall survive her?

Babhr.—What! shall the race of Bharata be imperilled for such trifling cause? But be that as it may, I will do my duty.

Vatsa.—Stop, thou devouring flame! withhold thy veiling smoke, as high in air thy circling brilliancy revolves, behold! I come to share the destiny of Sagarika. The fire nears the prison of the maid—I shall the more quickly discover her. [*Rushes off.*

Vasava.—My inconsiderate speech has inflicted this anguish on my lord. I cannot bear his loss, and will follow,

Vas.—Wait, Madam, I will lead the way.

[*Exit with the queen.*

Vasu.—Vatsa has precipitated himself into the flames. After having witnessed the fate of the princess, what remains but that I also offer up my life.

[*Exit.*

Babhr.—And must the race of Bharata thus causelessly perish?—But why do I delay—I will at least give proof of my fidelity. [*Exit.*

THE PALACE ON FIRE.

SAGARIKA, *in chains, discovered.*

The blaze encompasses me on every side: thanks, lord of flame, thou puttest a period to my sorrows.

Enter VATSA.

Vatsa.—The light shows me Sagarika—'tis she, alone, without assistance.

Sag.—The prince! The sight of him inspires me with the hope of life. (*Aloud.*) Preserve me, Sire!

Vatsa.—Fear not: support one moment these investing vapours—ha! the scarf on your bosom is on fire. (*Snatches it off.*) Your fetters impede your path, —let me support you. Dearest,—cling to me. (*Takes her in his arms.*) Already is the heat allayed,—be of good cheer: the fire cannot harm thee, love, whose very touch abates its intensity. (*Pauses—looks round —closes his eyes, and re-opens them.*) Why, what is this? where are the flames? they have disppeared, and there stands the palace unharmed! Ha! the daughter of Avanti's monarch.

Enter VASAVADATTA, VATSA'S *arms who runs into.*

Vasava.—My dearest lord!

Enter VASUBHUTI, VASANTAKA *and* BABHARVYA.

Vatsa.—My friends!

Vasu.—Fate is propitious to your Majesty.

Vatsa.—This must have been a dream, or is it magic?

Vas.—The latter, no doubt: did not that conjuring son of a slave say he had still something for your Majesty to see.

Vatsa.—(*To the queen.*) Here, madam, is Sagarika, rescued in obedience to your commands.

Vasava.—(*Smiling.*)—I am sensible of your obedience, my lord.

Vasu.—(*To Babhravya*).—That damsel is wonderfully like the princess.

Babhr.—So it struck me.

Vasu.—Excuse me, Sire, permit me, ask,—whence is this maiden?

Vatsa.—You must ask the queen.

Vasu.—(*To Vasavadatta.*) Will your grace inform me?

Vasava.—Yaugandharayana presented her to me, and told me she had been rescued for the sea 'twas hence we designated her, the Ocean Maid.

Vatsa.—(*Apart.*) Presented by Yougandharayana and without mentioning it to me—what could have been his motive.

Vasu.—(*Apart to Babhravya.*) The likeness—the necklace—the recovery of the damsel from the sea—leave no doubt that this is the daughter of the king of Simhala, Ratnavali. (*Advances to her.*) Lady Ratnavali, do I find you in this condition?

Sag.—(*Looking at him.*) Ha! the minister Vasubhuti!

Vasu.—I die! (*Faints.*)

Sag.—Unfortunate that I am, I perish: my beloved parents, hear me; reply to your child. (*Faints.*)

Vasava.—What! Babhravya, is this my sister, Ratnavali?

Babhu.—It is.

Vasava.—Revive, dear sister, revive.

Vatsa.—Is this the daughter of Vikramabahu of the house of Udatta, the sovereign of Simhala.

Vas.—*(Apart.)* I knew this necklace was the property of no ordinary person.

Vasu.—(*Recovering.*) Revive, dear lady,—be composed; see your elder sister grieves! Console her sorrows with your embrace.

Ratna. (*Or Sagarika.*)—I have offended the queen, how shall I look her in the face again!

Vasava.—Come hither, unrelenting girl—behold in me a sister! come to my arms. (*As Ratnavali goes to embrace the queen she stumbles. Vasavadatta apart to Vatsa.*)—My good lord, I blush for my cruelty. Quick undo these horrible bonds.

Vatsa.—Be composed, I will remove them. (*Takes the chains off Ratnavali's feet.*)

Vas.—Youndharayana is most to blame in this; he must have known the truth, and yet said not a syllable to any one.

Enter YAUGANDHARAYANA.

The temporary absence of her husband, and the contraction of marriage bonds with another wife, cannot fail to be displeasing to the queen: she may thank me for these favours, and I am ashamed to face her. Yet I am confident she will forgive me, when she considers my motives, and will be well pleased that the king obtains by these means the sovereignty of the world. However, happen what may, duty to a master must be performed without regard to such considerations.—They are here: I will approach.—Glory to the king! Pardon me, Sire, if I have accomplished any object affecting your interest, without previously consulting you.

Vatsa.—What have you done, inform us?

Yaugan.—Please your Majesty to be seated, and I will tell you. It was formerly announced to us by a holy seer, that the husband of the princess of Simhala should become the emperor of the world: we therefore earnestly applied to her father to give her hand to our sovereign; but unwilling to be the cause of uneasiness to to the queen, the monarch of Simhala declined compliance with our request: we therefore raised a report that Vasavadatta had perished by a fire at Lavanaka, and Babhravya was despatched with the news to the court of Simhala.

Vatsa.—I have heard what ensued. But why place the princess with the queen in so unsuitable a station?

Vas.—I can guess his object, he expected you would see her in the inner apartments, and take pleasure in her sight.

Vatsa.—Has Vasantaka stated your purpose correctly?

Yaugan.—Your Majesty has said.

Vatsa.—I suppose, too, you have some concern in the appearance of the conjuror?

Yaugan.—What other means remained of restoring the damsel to your presence, or how else was Vasubhuti to have seen and recognised the princess?

Vatsa.—(*To Vasavadatta, laughing.*) Well, Madam, it remains with you to say how we shall dispose of the sister you have acknowledged.

Vasava.—My lord, you might as well speak out, snd say, make Ratnavali over to me?

Vas.—Your Majesty very accurately conceives the minister's design.

Vasava.—Come, here, Ratnavali, appear as becomes my sister. (*Puts on her her own jewels, then takes her by the hand and presents her to Vatsa.*) Accept Ratnavali, my lord.

Vatsa.—(*Taking her hand.*) Who would not prize the favours of the queen?

Vasava.—And remember, my lord, she is far away from her natural relations; so treat her, therefore, that she may never have occasion to regret them.

Vatsa.—I shall obey.

Vas.—Victory to your Majesty! The world is now in the posssion of my friend.

Vasu.—Princess, pay respectful reverence to Vasavadatta. (*Ratnavali bows.*) Madam, you justly possess the title of queen.

Vasava.—(*Embracing Ratnavali.*) Glory to your Majesty.

Vatsa.—My cares are all rewarded.

Yaugan:—What else can we perform to gratify your Highness?

Vatsa.—What more is necessary? Vikramabahu is my kinsman. Sagarika, the essence of the world, the source of universal victory, is mine, and Vasavadatta rejoices to obtain a sister. The *Kosalas* are subdued: what other object does the world present for which I could entertain a wish? This be alone my prayer: may Indra with seasonable showers render the earth bountiful of grain; may the presiding Brahmans secure the favour of the gods by acceptable sacrifices; may the association of the pious confer delight until the end of time, and may the appalling blasphemies of the profane be silenced for ever.

THE END.

THE

MRICHCHHAKATI,

OR

THE TOY-CART.

A DRAMA.

TRANSLATED FROM

THE ORIGINAL SANSKRIT.

BY

H. H. WILSON, M. A. F. R. S.

PUBLISHED BY

THE SOCIETY FOR THE RESUSCITATION OF INDIAN LITERATURE.

40, Nayan Chand Dutt's Street, Calcutta.

CALCUTTA.

PRINTED BY H. C. DAS, ELYSIUM PRESS,

40, Nayan Chand Dutt's Street.

1901.

INTRODUCTION.

THE drama of which the translation is now published is a work of great interest, both in the literary and national history of the Hindus.

Although not named by the authority from which we have principally drawn our general view of the Hindu dramatic system, the "Dasa-Rupaka," it is unquestionably alluded to in the test of that work, and we may therefore feel assured that this play was written earlier than the tenth century; there is every reason to infer much earlier.

The introduction of the "Mrichchhakati" attributes the composition to a king named Sudraka, and gives him a high character both in arms and letters: he lived, it is said, a hundred years and then burnt himself, leaving his kingdom to his son.

Over what kingdom Sudraka ruled is not mentioned. The writer of the "Kamandaki" says it was Avanti or Ougein; tradition, especially in the Dekhin, includes him amongst the universal monarchs of India, and places him between Chandragupta and Vikramaditya, without specifying his capital. The late Col. Wilford. (*As. Res.* Vol. ix.) considers him the same with the founder of the Andhra-dynasty of Magadha kings, succeeding to the throne, by deposing his master, the last of the Kanwa race, to whom he was minister; but these averments are very questionoble. The circumstances are in fact attributed, it is said (p. 116), to a prince named Balihita, or Sipraka, or Sindhuka, or (p. 103) Mahakarni—and the identification of Sudraka, with either or of all of these, rests upon chronological data by no means satisfactorily established. From these (p. 100), it appears, that the first Andhara king of Magadha reigned 456 years earlier than the last, or Pulimat, who, it is said, died A. D. 648 (p. 111), consequently the former reigned about A. D. 192. But it is stated, that in a work called the Kumarika-Khanda, a portion of the "Skanda-Purana," it is asserted that in the year of the Kali 3300—save 10—a great king would reign (it does not appear where) named Sudraka. This date in our era is 190; the date of the first Andhra king, as mentioned above, is 192; *therefore* Sudraka must be that king a deduction which may possibly be correct, but which depends too much upon the accuracy of a work very little known, and upon a calculation that yet requires to be revised, to be considered as decidedly invalidating the popular notion, that Sudraka preceeded Vikramaditya, and consequently the era of Christanity by a century at least.

The attribution of a play to a regal author is not a singular occurrence. The "Ratnavali," as will be hereafter noticed, is ascribed to a bard of like dignity: whether truly or not, whether the monarch was not rather the patron than the poet, is immaterial to the chronology of the drama ;.as, if the work of Sudráka's reign, it may be considered as the oldest extant specimen of the Hindu drama, and á composition of respectable antiquity. The play contains abundant internal evidence of an ancient date.

The style, though not meagre, is in general simple and unartificial, and of a day evidently preceding the elabrate richness of Hindu writing, not to speak of the fantastic tricks and abuses which began to disgrace Sanskrit composition apparently in the ninth and tenth centuries. This may be considered a safe indication in a work of such pretence as one attributed to a regal bard; and although it could not be admitted alone as conclusive, yet, as associated with the name and date of Sudraka, it is a strong confirmation of the latter, at least, being correct.

Another circumstance in favour of the antiquity of the drama is derived from a peculiarity in the language of one of the chief characters. Samsthanaka, the *Raja's* brother-in-law, affects literature, with which he has so little conversancy, that his citations of poetic personages and events are as erroneous as frequent. Now it is a remarkable circumstance that all his citations are from the "Ramayana" and "Mahabharata," and that he never alludes to the chief actors in the Pauranik legends, as Dhruba, Daksha, Prahlada, Bali, etc. There can be no good reason why he should not cite from a Purana as well as from either of the poems which bear a similarly holy character, and it is not likely that the author of the drama, who was thoroughly familiar with the poems, should not have been acquainted with the Puranas if they had existed, or been equally in circulation: we have great reason therefore to suspect that the "Mrichchhakati" was written prior to the composition of the Puranas, or at least before the stories they contain had acquired by their aggregation familiar and and popular currency.

Peculiarities in manners contribute to a similar conclusion and the very panegyric upon Sudraka, specifying his voluntary cremation when arrived at extreme old age, praises him for an act prescribed in the Kali, or present period of the world. By all current legal authorities, except the text of the most ancient, suicide is prohibited everywhere except at Prayaga, and is there allowed only under certain circumstances. The prohibition may be disregarded, it is true, but such a breach of the law could not with any decency have been made the theme of public eulogium by a Brahman in the Sanskrit language, and therefore the event most probably preceded the law.

The subject of the peace, the love of a respectable Brahmana for a courtesan, is also in favour of a period of some remoteness, although it may be allowed to mark a state of social demoralisation, a decline from the purity of Hindu institutions; at the same time, it seems probable that the practice of antiquity, as regarded the intercourse of the sexes, was much more lax than it pretends to be in modern days. The laws of Manu recognise the cohabitation of a Sudra female with a Brahman, as an inferior kind of wife, or a hand maid. Now this association is prohibited in the Kali age, and its occurrence in the play, in which Vasantasena, who may be supposed to be a Sudra, becomes the wife Charudatta, indicates a period anterior to the law prohibiting the marriage of a Sudra by a Brahman. The choice of such an event for the subject of a dramatic performance, renders it likely that such a prohibition could not have been then even contemplated.

The most unquestionable proof, however, of high antiquity, is the accuracy with which Bauddha observances are adverted to, and the flourishing condition in which the members of that sect are represented to exist. There is not only absolute toleration, but a kind of public recognition; the ascetic who renders such essential service to the heroine being recommended or nominated by authority, chief of all the 'vihars' or Bauddha establishments of Ujjayin.

At what period could this diffusion and prosperity of the Bauddha faith have occurred, and when was it likely that a popular work should describe it correctly? Many centuries have elapsed since Hindu writers were acquainted with the Bauddhas in their genuine characters. Their tenents are preserved in philosophical treatises with something like accuracy, but any attempt to describe their persons and practices invaiably confounds them with the Jainas. The "Mrichchhakati" is as yet the only work where the Bauddhas appear undisguised. Now we know from the Christian writers of the second century, that in their days the worship of butta or Bauddha was very prevalent in India. We have every reason to believe, that shortly after that time the religion began to decline, more in consequence of the rise and growth of the Jains, probably, than any persecution of the Bauddhas; and as it is clear that the drama was written in the days of their prosperity, it follows that we cannot fairly assign it a later date than the first centuries of the Christian era.

From the considerations thus stated, we cannot but regard the "Mrichchhakati" as a work of considerable antiquity, and from internal evidence may very safely attribute it to the period when Sudraka the sovereign reigned, whether that be reduced to the end of the second century after Christ, or whether we admit the traditional chronology, and place him about a century before our era.

The revolution in the government of Ujjayin which forms an under plot in the piece, is narrated with so little exaggeration, that it is probably founded on fact. As the simple narrative of a simple event, it is the more entitled to our credence; and it is not at all unlikely that the Brahmans offended by their sovereign Palaka's public disregard of them, brought about a change of the government, employing a hermit and a cow-boy, or young peasant, as their instruments. This plain story is not improbably the origin of the obscure allusions which exercised the industry of Colonel Wilford, and in which, and in the purport of the word Arya, the name of the cowherd in the play, and in general acceptation a little of respect, he thought he could trace a reference to the history of Christianity in India. (*As. Res.* Vol. X., "Essay on the Sacred Isles of the West.") There is also an Arya of some renown in the history of Cashmir, whom the same learned and laborious, but injudicious writer, identified with Salibahana. The real character of that personage may now be more accurately appreciated.—("Essay on the History of Cashmir," *As. Res.* Vol. XV. p. 84.

The place which the "Mrichchhakati" holds in the dramatic literature of all nations will, however, be thought matter of more interest by most readers than its antiquity or historical importance. That it is a curious and interesting picture of national manners every one will readily admit; and it is not the less valuable in this respect, that it is free from all exterior influence or adulteration. It is a portrait purely Indian. It represents a state of society sufficiently advanced in civilisation to be luxurious and corrupt, and is certainly very far from offering a flattering similitude, although not without some attractive featues. There will probably be more variety of opinion on its merits as a literary composition, and its title to rank with the more polished dramas of the West may be called in question by competent judges. As observed by the spirited translator of Aristophanes, it is no longer the fashion for translators to direct the taste of their readers, and they must be left to condemn or approve for themselves. I shall therefore refrain from any further observations on this head; and if, in imitation of high authority, I venture to subjoin my own sentiments by way of epilogue, I shall do so as briefly as possible, and without any hope to bias the judgment of the public.

DRAMATIS PERSONÆ.

OF THE PRELUDE.

MANAGER. ACTRESS.

OF THE PLAY.

MEN.

Charudatta.—A Brahman of a wealthy and respectable family, reduced to poverty by his munificence, beloved by Vasantasena.

Rohasena.—The son of Charudatta, a boy.

Maitreya.—A Brahman, the friend and companion of Charudatta, the Vidusaka, or Gracioso of the piece, a character of mixed shrewdness and simplicity, with an affectionate disposition,

Vardhamana.—The servant of Charudatta.

Samsthanaka.—The brother-in-law of the Raja, an ignorant, frivolous, and cruel coxcomb.

The Vita.—The attendant, tutor, or parasite of the preceeding.

Sthavaraka.—The servant of the Prince.

Aryaka.—A cowherd and insurgent, finally successful.

Sarvilaka.—A dissipated Brahman, the friend of the preceeding in love with Madanika.

The Samvahaka.—A man whose business it has been to rub and knead the joints, but who becomes a Bauddha mendicant or Sramanaka.

Mathura.—The keeper of a gaming-house.

Darduraka.—A Gambler.

Another Gambler.

Karnapuraka.—Vasantasena's servant.

The judge.

The Sreshtin.—Or Provost.

The Kayastha.—Scribe or Recorder.

Chandanaka ... } Captains of the Town Guard.
Viraka ... }

The Vita.—Or parasite attendant of Vasantasena.

Kumbhilaka.—A servant of Vasantasena.

Two Chandalas.—Or Public Executioners.

Officers of the Court.

WOMEN.

The wife of Charudatta.

Vasantasena.—A Courtesan, in love with Charudatta, and beloved by him: the object also of Samsthanaka's addresses.

The Mother of Vasantasena;

Madanika.—The attendant of Vasantasena, beloved by Sarvilaka.

Radanika.—The servant of Charudatta's house.

PERSONS SPOKEN OF.

Palaka.—King of Ujjain.

Rebhila.—A Musician.

The Siddha or Seer who has prophesied Aryaka's triumph.

Passengers, Attendants, Guards, etc.

SCENE.—Ujjain, the city and the suburbs.—

TIME.—four days.

THE MRICHCHHAKATI,

OR

THE TOY CART.

ACT I.

PRELUDE.

BENEDICTION.

I. MAY that profound meditation of Sambhu protect you! (*the audience*) which is intent on Brahman, the absorbing end of every effort of abstract vision; as he contemplates with the eye of wisdom, spirit, in himself, detached from all material instruments; his senses being restrained by holy knowledge, as he sits ruminating with suspended breath, whilst his serpents coil with the folds of his vesture round his bended knees.

II. May the neck of Nilkantha, which resembles a dark cloud in hue, and which is decorated by the entwining arms of Gauri, as brilliant as the lightning, be ever your protection.

Enter MANAGER.

Enough: delay not longer to gratify the curiosity of this assembly. Saluting, therefore, this gentle audience, I apprise them that we are prepared to enact the drama entitled the Toy-Cart.

There was a celebrated poet whose gait was that of an elephant, whose eyes resembled those of the *Chakora*, whose countenance was like the full moon, and who was of stately person and profound veracity; chiefest of the Kshatriya race and distinguished by the appellation of Sudra: he was well versed in the Rig-, and Sama-, Vedas, in mathematical sciences, in the elegant arts, and the management of elephants. By the favour of Siva he enjoyed eyes uninvaded by darkness, and beheld his son seated on the throne: after performing the exalted *Aswamedha*, having attained the age of a hundred years and ten days, he entered the fatal fire. Valiant was he in war, and ready to encounter with his single arm the elephant of his adversary; yet he was void of wrath, eminent amongst those skilled in the Vedas, and affluent in piety: a prince was Sudraka. In this drama, written by him, it is thus related.

In Avanti lived a young Brahman of distinguished rank, but of exceding poverty; his name was Charudatta. Of the many excellences of Charu-

enamoured, and the story of their loves is the subject of king Sudraka's drama, which exhibits the infamy of wickedness, the villainy of law, the efficacy of virtue, and the triumph of faithful love.

(*Walks round the stage.*)

Hey! the boards are deserted: where can all the actors have vanished? Ah, I understand. Empty is the house of the childless—empty is the heart of one that has no friends; the universe is a blank to the blockhead, and all is desolate to the poor. I have been chanting and reciting until my eyes ache, the pupils twinkling with hunger, like the seeds of the lotus shrivelled in the hot weather by the rays of a scorching sun. I will call one of my wenches, and see if there be anything in the house for breakfast. What ho there—Here am I! But I had better talk to them in a language they can understand.—What ho—I say! What with long fasting and loud shouting my limbs are shrivelled like dry lotus stalks. It is high time to take myself home, and see what is prepared for my coming. This is my mansion—I will go in.

Enters.

Hey day!—Some new frolic is going on in this mansion of mine. The ground, like a young damsel fresh from her toilet, wears a *tilaka* smeared with the discoloured water of the rice that has been boiled in the iron kettle, and is perfumed with most savoury smells. Verily, my hunger increaseth. What, in the name of wonder, have my people found a treasure—or from the promptings of my appetite do I fancy everything smacks of boiled rice? If there be no breakfast for me at home, this hunger will be the death of me. Yet everything puts on a new face: one hussy is grinding perfumes, another is stringing flowers: the meaning of all this must be inquired into. Come hither one of you.

Enter ACTRESS.

Act.—Here am I, sir.

Man.—Welcome, welcome.

Act.—What are your commands?

Man.—Hark ye, girl, I have been bawling myself both hoarse and hungry: is there anything in the house for me to eat?

Act.—There is everything, sir.

Man.—Indeed; and what is there?

Act.—For example—there is rice, dressed or undressed, sugar, curds; in short, there is sustenance for a century so may the gods comply with all your desires.

Man.—Hark ye, my girl, is all this in my house, or do you jest?

Act.—(*Apart.*) Oh, as he doubts, I will have a laugh at him. (*Aloud.*) Indeed and indeed, sir, there is all that I have mentioned—in the market.

Man.—Ah, you hussy! May you be so disappointed. The deuce take you—you have hoisted me up like a ball on a turret top, that I might tumble down again.

Act.—Patience, sir, patience, I did but jest.

Man.—Then what is the meaning of all this unusual preparation; this grinding of perfumes and stringing of chaplets? The ground is strewed with offerings of flowers of every dye.

Act.—We hold a solemn fast to-day.

Man.—A fast, for what?

Act.—That we may have a desirable master.

Man.—In this world, or the next?

Act.—Ah in the next, to be sure.

Man.—Here, gentles (*to the audience,*) here is pretty usage: these damsels would engage a new manager in another world at my expence in this!

Act.—Be appeased, sir. I have observed the fast, in order that I might have you again for my master in a future birth.

Man.—That alters the case. But, pray, who directed you to hold this fast?

Act.—Your particular friend, Churnavriddha.

Man.—Oh, you son of a slave, I shall see you, Churnavriddha, some day or other, fast bound by king Palaka, like the perfumed tresses of a new-married girl.

Act.—Pardon us, dear sir; this fast was observed to secure the future felicity of our worthy Manager. *(Falls at his feet.)*

Man.—Rise; enough. We must now consider by whom this fast is to be completed.

Act.—We must invite some Brahman of our own degree.

Man.—Well, go, finish your preparations; I will seek the Brahman. [*Exit.*

Act.—I obey.

MANAGER.

Alas! in such a flourishing city as Ujjayin, where am I to find a Brahman who is not of a superior rank to mine? (*Looking out.*) Yonder comes Maitreya, the friend of Charudatta. I will ask him; he is poor enough. What, ho! Maitreya; condescend to be the first to eat in my house to-day.

MAITREYA (*behind the sences*).

Call some other Brahman; I am particularly engaged.

Man.—Food is provided; no enemy is in the way, and you shall have a present into the bargain.

Mait.—(*Behind.*) I have already given you an answer. It is useless to disturb me.

Man.—I shall not prevail upon him, and must therefore set off in quest of some other Brahman.

[*Exit.*

(The scene is supposed to represent a street on one side, and on the other the first court of Charudatta's house: the outside of the house is also seen in the part next the street.)

MAITREYA *enters the court with a peace of cloth in his hand.*

Truly, Maitreya, your condition is sad enough, and well qualified to subject you to be picked up in the street and fed by strangers. In the days of Charudatta's prosperity, I was accustomed to stuff myself till I could eat no more, on scented dishes, until I breathed perfume; and sat lolling at yonder gateway, dyeing my fingers like a painter's, by dabbling amongst the coloured comfits, or chewing the cud at leisure like a high-fed city bull. Now, in the season of his poverty, I wander about from house to house, like a tame pigeon, to pick up such crumbs as I can get. I am now sent by his dear friend Churnavriddha with this garment that has lain amongst jasmine flowers till it is quite scented by them: it is for Charudatta's wearing, when he has finished his devotions.—Oh, here he comes, he is presenting the oblation to the household gods.

Enter.—CHARUDATTA *and* RADANICA.

Char.—*(With a sigh.)*

Alas! how changed; the offering to the gods,
That swans and stately storks, in better time
About my threshold flocking, bore away,

Now a scant tribute to the insect tribe,
Falls midst rank grass, by worms to be devoured.

(*Sits down.*)

Mait.—I will approach the respectable Charudatta. Health to you; may you prosper.

Char.—Maitreya, friend of all seasons, welcome sit you down.

Mait.—As you command. (*Sits down.*) This garment, perfumed by the jasmines it his lair amongst, is sent to you by your friend Chrunavriddha, to be worn by you at the close of your devotions.

Char.—(*Takes it and appears thoughtful.*)

Mait.—On what do you meditate?

Char.—My friend—

The happiness that follows close on sorrow,
Shows like a lamp that breaks upon the night
But he that falls from affluence to poverty,
May wear the human semblance, but exists
A lifeless form alone.

Mait.—What think you preferable then, death or poverty?

Char.—Had I the choice,

Death, and not poverty, were my election:
To die is transient suffering; to be poor,
Interminable anguish.

Mait.—Nay, never heed. The loss of your wealth, lavished upon your kind friends, only enhances your merit; as the moon looks most lovely when reduced to the slender fragment that the draughts of the gods for half a month have left it.

Char.—I do not, trust me, grieve for my lost wealth :
But that the guest no longer seeks the dwelling,
Whence wealth has vanished, does, I own, afflict me.
Like the ungrateful bees, who wanton fly
The elephants broad front, when thick congeals
The dried-up dew, they visit me no more.

Mait.—The sons of slaves! your guest is ever ready to make a morning meal of a fortune: he is like the cow-boy, who, as if afraid of gad-fly, drives his herds from place to place in the thicket, and sets them to feed always in fresh pasture.

Char.—'Tis true.—I think not of my wasted fortune.
As fate decrees, so riches come and vanish.
But I lament to find the love of friends
Hangs all unstrung because a man is poor.
And then with poverty comes disrespect;
From disrespect does self-dependence fail,
Then scorn and sorrow, following, overwhelm
The intellect; and when the judgment fails
The being perishes; and thus from poverty
Each ill that pains humanity proceeds.

Mait.—Ah well, it is but waste of thought to send it after the wealth-hunters; we have had enough of this subject.

Char.—But poverty is aye the curse of thought.
It is our enemy's reproach ; the theme
Of scorn to our best friends and dearest kin.
I had adjured the world and sought the
hermitage,
But that my wife had shared in my distress.
Alas, the fires of sorrow in the heart
Glow impotent ; they pain but burn not.
My friend, I have already made oblation
Unto the household gods—Go you to where
The four roads meet, and there present it
To the Great Mothers.

Mait.—Not I, indeed.

Char.—Why not ?

Mait.—Of what use is it ? You have worshipped the gods : what have they done for you ? it is labour in vain to bestow upon them adoration.

Char.—Speak not profanely. It is our duty. And
the gods
Undoubtedly are pleased with what is offered
In lowliness of spirit and with reverence,
In thought, and deed, and pious self-denial :
Go therefore and present the offering.

Mait.—I will not go, indeed ; send somebody else. With me every part of the ritual is apt to get out of its place, and a in the reflection of a mirror, the right becomes left and the left right. At this time of the evening, too, the royal road is crowded with loose persons, with cut-throats, courtiers, and courtesans.

amongst such a set I shall fare like the unhappy mouse, that fell into the clutches of the snake which was lying in ambush for the frog. I cannot go, indeed. Why not go yourself? You have nothing to do but to sit here.

Char.—Well, well—attend then whilst I tell my beads. [*They retire.*

(*Behind the scenes.*) Stop, Vasantasena, stop!

Enter VASANTASENA *pursued by* SAMSTHANAKA, *the King's brother-in-law, the* VITA, *and his own servant.*

Vita.—Stop, Vasantasena, stop! Why, losing your gentleness in your fears, do you ply those feet so fast, that should be nimble only in the dance? You run along like the timid deer from the pursuing hunter, casting tremulous glances fearfully around.

Sams.—Stop, Vasantasena, stop! Why do you thus scamper away, stumbling at every stop? Be pacified, you are in no danger. With love alone is my poor heart inflamed; it is burnt to a cinder, like a piece of meat upon the blazing coals.

Ser.—Stop, lady, stop! Why, sister, do you fly? She runs along like a pea-hen in summer with a tail in full feather, whilst my master follows her, like the young hound that chases the bird through the thicket.

Vita.—Stop, Vasantasena, stop! You tremble like the young plantain tree, whilst the ends of your red vesture wanton on the wind. The seeds of the red lotus are put to shame by your glowing eyes, and the bed of orpiment, when first penetrated by the axe, is rivalled by the complexion of your cheeks.

Sams.—Stop, Vasantasena, stop! Why do you thus fly from a liking, a love, a passion which you inflame? My nights you deprive of rest, and you avoid me by day. It is unavailing: you will trip and tumble into my hands as Kunti fell into those of Ravana.

Vita.—Why, Vasantasena, do you grace my steps by leaving traces for them to obliterate? Like a snake from the monarch of the birds, you glide away from me, but vain is your flight. I could outstrip the wind in such a chase, and shall I not overtake so delicate a fugitive?

Sams.—Most worthy sir, I have invoked her by ten names. I have called her the taper lash of that filcher of broad pieces, Kama; the fish-eater, the figurante, the pug-nosed untamable shrew. I have termed her love's dining-dish—the gulf of the poor man's substance—the walking frippery—the harlot—the hussy—the baggage—the wanton. I have addressed her by all these pretty names, and yet she will have nothing to say to me.

Vita.—Why, Vasantasena, do you fly us? The trembling pendants of your ears toss agitated against your cheeks, and make such music as the lute to a master's touch. You fly like a female crane that starts away from the sound of thunder.

Sams.—Your ornaments jingle to your paces as you run from us, as Draupadi fled from Rama. But I shall have you; I will dart upon you like Hanumat upon Subhadra, the lovely sister of Viswavasu.

Ser.—Relent, relent, be gracious to the prince's friend; accept the flesh and the fish. When they can get fish and flesh, the dogs prey not upon carrion.

Vita.—What should have so strangely alarmed you? Believe me, you look like the guardian goddess of the city, as round your slender waist sparkles with starlike gems that tinkling zone, and your countenance is pale with terror.

Sams.—As the female jackal is hunted by the dogs, so run you, and so we follow: You run along with your prey, and bear off from me both heart and pericardium.

Vas.—(*Calling for her female attendants.*) What ho! Pallava, Parabhritika.

Sams.—(*In alarm to the Vita.*) Eh, sir, sir! men, men!

Vita.—Never fear.

Vas.—Madhavika, what ho!

Vita.—Blockhead; she is calling her servants.

Sams.—What, her women?

Vita.—To be sure.

Sams.—Who is afraid? I am a hero—a match for a hundred of them.

Vas.—Alas, alas! my people are not within hail I must trust to myself alone for my escape.

Vita.—Search about, search about.

Sams.—Vasantasena, what is the use of your bawling there, for bud and blossom, or all spring together! Who is to preserve you when I pursue? What could Bhimasena do for you, or the son of Jamadagni, or the son of Kunti, or Dasakandhara himself? I would take them, like Duhsasana, by their hair, and, as you shall see, with one touch of my well-sharpened sword off goes your head. Come, come, we have had enough of your running away. One who is desirous of dying cannot be said to live.

Vas.—Good sir, I am only a weak woman.

Vita.—True, therefore you may live.

Sams.—True, you shall not die.

Vas.—(*Apart.*) His very courtesy appals me. It shall be so. (*Aloud.*) Pray, sirs, why do you thus pursue me, or why address such language to me? Do you seek my iewels?

Vita.—Fie, fie, what have we to do with your ornaments? Who plucks the blossoms of the creeper.

Vas.—What is it, then, you require?

Sams.—That I, who am a person of celestial nature, a mortal Vasudeva, obtain your affections.

Vas.—Get you gone; you talk idly.

Sams.—(*Claps his hands and laughs.*) What think you of that, sir? Here how this gentle damsel regards me: she bids me go and rest myself, no doubt, after my fatigue in running after her; but I swear by your head and my feet, that I have gone astray neither in town nor village, but have kept close to your heels all the way, by the which I am wearied.

Vita.—(*Apart.*) The blockhead! he misapprehends the whole. (*Aloud.*) Why, Vasantasena, you act quite out of character: the dwelling of a harlot is the free resort of youth: a courtesen is like a creeper that grows by the road-side—her person is an article for sale, her love a thing that money will buy, and her welcome is equally bestowed upon the amiable and disgusting. The sage and the idiot, the Brahman and the outcast, all bathe in the same stream, and the crow and the peacock perch upon the branches of the same creeper.

The Brahman, the Kshattriya, the Vaisya, and all of every caste are ferried over in the same boat; and like the boat, the creeper, and the stream, the courtesan is equally accessible to all.

Vas.—What you say may be just, but, believe me, merit alone, not brutal violence, inspires love.

Sams.—Sir, sir, the truth is, that the baggage has had the perverseness to fall in love with a miserable wretch, one Charudatta, whom she met in the garden of Kamadeva's temple: he lives close by here on our left, so take care she does not slip through our fingers.

Vita.—(*Aside.*) Confound the fool, he lets out everything he ought to conceal. In love with Charudatta—humph! no wonder; it is truly said, pearls string with pearls: well, let it be so, never mind this simpleton. (*Aloud.*) What say you, is the house of Charudatta on our left? the deuce it is.

Sams.—Very true, I assure you.

Vas.—(*Aside.*) Indeed! the house of Charudatta so near! These wretches have unintentionally befriended me, and promoted a meeting with my beloved.

Sams.—Sir, sir, Vasantasena is no longer visible; she is lost in the dark, like an ink-cake in a pile of black beans.

Vita.—It is very dark, indeed! The gloom cheats my eye-sight of its faculty; my eyes open only to be closed by it; such obscurity envelops everything, as if the heavens rained lamp-black: sight is as unavailing as the service of a worthless man.

Sams.—I must search for Vasantasena.

Vita.—Indeed! (*Aloud.*) Is there not anything by which you may trace her?

Sams.—What should there be?

Vita.—The tinkling of her ornaments; the odour of her perfumes; and the fragrance of her garland.

Sams.—Very true; I can hear with my nostrils the scent of her garland spreading through the darkness, but I do not see the sound of her ornaments.

Vita.—(*Apart, in the directions of Vas.*) Very well, Vasantasena. True, you are hidden by the gloom of the evening, like the lightning between gathering clouds, but the fragrance of your chaplet, the music of your anklets, will betray you—do you hear?

Vas.—(*To herself.*) I hear and comprehend. (*Takes off her garland and the rings from her ankles.*) If I am not mistaken, the private entrance is in this direction: by carrying my hands along the wall—(*feels for the door*)—ah, it is shut.

Char.—(*Within the court.*) My prayer is finished; now, Maitreya, go, present the offering to the divine mothers.

Mait.—I tell you I will not go.

Char.—Alas it does embitter poverty—

That then our friends grow deaf to our desires,
And lend a keener anguish to our sorrows.
The poor man's truth is scorned: the tender light
Of each mild virtue languishes; suspicion
Stamps him the perpetrator of each crime
That others are the authors of: no man seeks
To form acquaintance with him, nor exchange
Familiar greeting or respectful courtesy.
If e'er he find a place in rich men's dwellings
At solemn festivals, the wealthier guests
Survey him with disdainful wonder; and
Whene'er by chance he meets upon the road

With state and wealth, he sneaks into a
corner,
Ashamed of his scant covering, till they pass,
Rejoicing to be overlooked. Believe me,
He who incurs the guilt of poverty
Adds a sixth sin to those we term most
heinous.
In truth, I mourn e'en poverty for thee,
Whose cherished dwelling is this wasting
frame,
And oft I sadly wonder what asylum,
When this shall be no more, shall then receive
thee.

Mait.—Ah! Well, if I must go, I must; but let your maid Radanika go along with me.

Char.—Radanika, follow Maitreya.

Rad.—As you command, sir.

Mait.—Here, Radanika, do you take the offerings and the lamp, while I open the back door. (*Opens the door.*)

Vas.—(*On the outside.*) Luckily for me, the door is opened: I shall now get in. Ah the lamp. (*Brushes it out with her scarf, and enters.*)

Char.—What was that?

Mait.—Opening the door let in a gust of wind, which has blown the lamp out: never mind—go on, Radanika. I will just step into the house and re-light the lamp, and will be with you again immediately.

Sams.—(*On the outside.*) What can have become of Vasantasena !

Vita.—Search, search.

Sams.—So I do, but cannot find her—I have her. (*Lays hold of the* Vita.)

Vita.—Blockhead, this is I.

Sams.—Stand out of the way then. (*Lays hold of the servant.*) Now then I have caught her.

Ser.—No, your honour has caught me.

Sams.—Here then, this way, this way, here, master, servant, servant, master, here, here, stand here. (*Lays hold of Radanika by the hair as she comes out.*) Ha, ha ! now I have her indeed. I detected her endeavouring to escape by the scent of the garland. I have her fast by the hair, as Chanakya caught Draupadi.

Vita.—Very well, young lady, very pretty ; running after honest men's sons, in the pride of youth, with your head full dressed with flowers ; you are caught in the fact.

Sams.—You are the young girl, I believe, that was caught by the hair of the head : now call, and cry, and scream, and curse, and abuse Siva, Sambhu Sankara, and Iswara.

Rad.—(*In alarm.*) Bless me, gentlemen, what do you mean ?

Vita.—How now ! the voice is that of another person.

Sams.—Oh, sir, your female can change her voice when she will, as the cat mews in a different key when she attempts to steal cream.

Vita.—Such a difference can scarcely be, and yet it is possible. Yes, it may be she has been taught to disguise her voice in the way of her profession, both for the purposes of deception and the articulation of the gamut.

Enter MAITREYA.

Mait.—How funnily the lamp burns; it goes flutter, flutter, in the evening breeze, like the heart of a goat just caught in a snare. (*Seeing Radanika and the rest*) They, Radanika!

Sams.—Holloa, master—a man.

Mait.—What is all this?—it is not right; not right at all—although Charudatta be poor, yet strangers are not to come into his house without leave.

Rad.—See here; Maitreya, here's disrespect to me.

Mait.—Not you merely, but all of us. To me as well as you.

Rad.—You, indeed—how can that be?

Mait.—Why, have they been rude to you?

Rad.—Rude indeed—to be sure, rude enough.

Mait.—No, really.

Rad.—Yes, really.

Mait.—(*In wrath and taking up a stick.*) Then I will do for them; this is quite unbearable every dog will bark in his own kennel, and why not a Brahman? With this dry bamboo staff, as crooked as our fortunes, will I batter that head of thine, thou abominable villain.

Vita.—Patience, patience! worthy Brahman.

Mait.—(*To him.*) Eh! this cannot be the offender. (*Turns to Samsthanaka.*) Oh! here he is. Oh, you king's brother-in-law! you abominable miscreant: have you no decency? Do not you know that, notwithstanding the worthy Charudatta be poor, he is an ornament to Ujjayin, and how dare you think of forcing your way into his house and maltreating his people? There is no disgrace in an untoward fate; disgrace is in misconduct; a worthless man of wealth is contemptible.

Vita.—Worthy Brahman, pardon us, we mistook the person: we intended no affront, but looking for a female.

Mait.—For her? (*Pointing to Radanika.*)

Vita.—Heaven forbid!—No, no for a girl her one mistress, who has run away. Searching for her, we lighted upon this damsel, and committed an unintentional indecorum. We beg your pardon, and submit ourselves to whatever you may please to ordain. (*Gives his sword and falls at Maitreya's feet.*)

Mait.—You are a man of sense; arise. I knew not your quality when I addressed you so roughly; now I am aware of it, I shall treat you with proper politeness.

Vita.—You are entitled to our respect. I will only rise on one condition.

Mait.—Declare it.

Vita.—That you will say nothing to Charudatta of what has chanced.

Mait.—I will not say anything to him on the subject.

Vita.—I will place your kindness, Brahman, on my head; armed with every excellence, you are invincible by arms.

Sams.—What do you mean, my friend, by putting your hands together and falling at the feet of such a contemptible fellow?

Vita.—I am afraid.

Sams.—Of what?

Vita.—Of the eminent virtues of Charudatta.

Sam.—Very eminent, indeed, when they cannot afford his visitors a dinner.

Vita.—Never mind that; he has become impoverished by his liberality; like the lake in the summer which is exhausted by relieving the thirst of the travellers; in his prosperity he was kind to all, and never treated any one with disrespect.

Sams.—Who is this slave, the son of a slave? Is he a warrior, a hero? Is he Pandu, Swetaketu, the son of Radha, Ravana, or Indradatta? Was he begotten on Kunti, by Rama, or is he Ashwathaman, Dharmaputra, or Jatayu.

Vita.—No, you wiseacre, I will tell you who he is: he is Charudatta, the tree of plenty to the poor, bowed down by its abundant fruit. He is the cherisher of the good, the mirror of the wise, a touchstone of piety, an ocean of decorum, the doer of good to all, of evil to none, a treasure of manly of virtues, intelligent, liberal, and upright; in a word, he only is worthy of admiration: in the plentitude of his merits he may be said to live indeed; other men merely breathe. So come, we had better depart.

Sams.—What, without Vasantasena?

Vita.—Vasantasena is lost.

Sams.—How lost?

Vita.—Like the sight of the blind, the health of the sick, the wisdom of the fool, and the prosperity of the sluggard; like the learning of the dull and dissipated, and the friendship of foes.

Sams.—Well, I will not go hence until I recover her.

Vita.—You may as well. Have you never heard the saying:

An elephant may be held by a chain,
A steed be curbed by his rider's art;
But even go hang, if you cannot gain
The only bond woman obeys—her heart.

You may as well, therefore, come away.

Sams.—Go, if you please; I shall stay where I am.

Vita.—Very well, I will leave you. [*Exit.*

Sams.—Let him go; who cares? (*To Maitreya.*) Now, you crow-foot pated pupil of mendicity, down with you.

Mait.—We are cast down already.

Sams.—By whom?

Mait.—By destiny.

Sams.—Get up then.

Mait.—So we will.

Sams.—When?

Mait.—When fortune smiles.

Sams.—Weep, weep.

Mait.—So, we do.

Sams.—What for?

Mait.—Our misfortunes.

Sams.—Laugh, blockhead, laugh

Mait.—So we shall.

Sams.—When?

Mait.—When Charudatta is again in prosperity.

Sams.—Hark ye, fellow; do you carry a message from me to the beggar Charudatta. Say to him thus from me: A common wanton, hight Vasantasena, covered with gold upon gold, like the chief of a troop of comedians about to act a new play, saw you in the garden of Kamadeva's temple, and took a fancy to you. Having put us to the trouble of using violence to secure her, she fled, and has taken refuge in your house. If you will give her up, and put her yourself into my hands without any litigation, her delivery shall be rewarded with my most particular regard; but if you will not put her forth, depend upon my eternal and exterminating enmity. Consider that a preserved pumpkin, a dried potherb, fried flesh, and boiled rice that has stood for a night in the cold weather, stink when kept too long. Let him then not lose this opportunity. You speak well and distinctly; you must, therefore, speak my message so that I may hear you, as I sit in the upper terrace of my house, here adjoining. If you do not say what I have told you, I shall grind your head between my teeth, as I would a nut beneath my door.

Mait.—I will deliver your message.

Sams.—Is the worthy Vita really gone?

(*To the servant.*)

Serv.—He is, sir.

Sams.—Then let us follow him quick.

Serv.—Please to take your sword.

Sams.—No, carry it after me.

Serv.—This is your honour's sword.

Sams.—Ah, very well, give it me. (*Takes it by the wrong end.*) I bear it on my shoulder, sleeping in its pink sheath; and thus go I home as a jackal retires to his lair, followed by the yell of all the dogs and bitches of the village. [*Exit.*

Mait.—My good Radanika, say nothing to Charudatta about your having been insulted in this currish place, by that king's brother-in-law: he frets already about his affairs, and this business, I am sure, would double his vexation.

Rad.—I am only Radanika, Maitreya; I can hold my tongue.

Mait.—Nay, nay, not so. [*They retire.*

Char.—(*Within the house, to Vasantasena.*) Radanika, my boy Rohasena must have enjoyed the breeze long enough; he will be chilled by the evening dews; take him in, and cover him with this cloth.

Vas.—(*Apart.*) He mistakes me for one of the servants. (*Takes the cloth and smells it.*) Scented jasmine flowers! Ha, then, he is not all a philosohper.

[*Retires.*

Char.—Radanika, carry Rohasena to the inner apartments.

Vas.—(*Apart.*) Alas! my fortune gives me no admission to them.

Char.—What! No reply, Radanika?—Alas! when a man has been unfortunate enough to have outlived his means, his best friends lose their regard, and old attachments change into dislike.

Enter MAITREYA *and* RADANIKA.

Mait.—Here, sir, is Radanika.

Char.—Here—then who is this? Not knowing her, I have degraded her by the touch of my vestment.

Vas.—(*Apart.*) Degraded; no, exalted.

Char.—She looks like the waning moon, half-hidden by autumnal clouds; fie, fie, another's wife this is not a meet object for my regards.

Mait.—(*Recognising* Vasantasena.) A wife indeed, a pretty wife! Why, sir, this is Vasantasena, a lady, who, having had the felicity of seeing you in the gardens of Kamadeva's temple, has taken it into her head to honour you with her affection.

Char.—(*Apart.*) Indeed; is this Vasantasena?

What now avails it to return her love
In my declining fortunes; let it sink
Suppressed in silence, as a coward checks
The wrath he dares not utter.

Mait.—I have a message, too, from the king's brother-in-law.

Char.—What?

Mait.—Thus he says: "A common wanton, hight Vasantasena, covered with gold upon gold, like the chief of a troop of comedians about to act a new play, saw you in the garden of Kamadeva's temple, and took a fancy to you. Having put us to the trouble of violence to secure her"—

Vas.—"Violence to secure her!" Oh I am honored by such words.

Mait.—"She fled, and has taken refuge in your house. If you will give her up, and put her yourself into my hands without litigation, her delivery shall be rewarded with my most particular regard; but if you will not put her forth, depend upon my eternal and exterminating enmity.

Char.—(*With disdain.*) He is a fool.

(*To himself.*) She would become a shrine—

The pride of wealth
Presents no charm to her, and she disdains
The palace she is roughly bid to enter;
Nor makes she harsh reply, but silent leaves
The man she scorns, to waste his idle words.
Lady—I knew you not, and thus unwittingly
Mistaking you for my attendant, offered you
Unmeet indignity, I bend my head,
In hope of your forgiveness.

Vas.—Nay, sir, I am the offender, by intruding into a place of which I am unworthy; it is my head that must be humbled in reverence and supplication.

Mait.—Very pretty on both sides; and whilst you two stand there, nodding your heads to each other like a field of long grass, permit me to bend mine, although in the style of a young camel's stiff knees, and request that you will be pleased to hold yourselves upright again.

Char.—Be it so; no further ceremony.

Vas.—(*Aside.*) How kind his manner, how pleasing his expression! But it is not proper for me to remain longer: let me think. It shall be so. (*Aloud.*) Sir, respected sir, if truly I have found favour in your sight, permit me to leave these ornaments in your house; it was to rob me of them, that the villains I fled from pursued me.

Char.—This house, lady, is unsuited to such a trust.

Vas.—Nay, worthy sir, you do not speak me true. Men, and not houses, are the things we trust to.

Char.—Maitreya, take the trinkets.

Vas.—You have obliged me.

Mait.—Much obliged to your ladyship.

(*Taking them*).

Char.—Blockhead, this is but a trust.

Mait.—(*To him apart.*) What if they should be stolen ?

Char.—They will be here but a short time.

Mait.—What she has given us is ours.

Char.—I shall send you about your business.

Vas.—Worthy sir, I could wish to have the safeguard of this your friend's company to return home.

Char.—Maitreya, attend the lady,

Mait.—Go yourself ; you are the properst person ; attending her graceful form as the stately swan upon his mate. I am but a poor Brahman, and should as soon be demolished by these libertines as a meat-offering in the market-place by the dogs.

Char.—Well, well, I will attend her, and for further security on the road let the torches be prepared.

Mait.—What ho ! Vardhamana,—(*enter Servant*)—light the flambeaus.

Vardh.—(*To him.*) You dunderhead, how are they to be lighted up without oil ?

Mait.—(*Apart to Charudatta.*) To say the truth,

sir, our torches are like harlots; they shine not in poor men's houses.

Char.—Never heed; we shall not need a torch.

Pale as the maiden's cheek who pines with love,
The moon is up, with all its starry train—
And lights the royal road with lamps divine,
Whilst through the gloom its milk-white rays descend,
Like streamlets winding o'er the miry plain.

(*They proceed.*) This, lady, is your dwelling.

Vasantasena makes an obeisance and exit.

Come, my friend, let us return—
The road is solitary, save where the watch
Performs his wonted round: the silent night—
Fit season only for dishonest acts—
Should find us not abroad.
As to this casket, let it be your charge
By night, by day, it shall be Vardhamana's.

Mait.—As you command. [*Exeunt.*

END OF THE FIRST

ACT II.

SCENE.—VASANTASENA'S HOUSE.

Enter A FEMALE ATTENDNT.

I am sent to Vasantasena with a message from her mother, I will therefore enter and deliver it to her. Ah, there she sits. She seems uneasy. I must approach her.

(*Vasantasena discovered seated, Madanika attending.*)

Vas.—Well, girl, you must then—

Mad.—Then—when—madam? You have given me no orders.

Vas.—What said I?

Mad.—You said, girl, you must then—

Vas.—True.

Atten.—(*Approaches.*) Madam, your mother desires that you will perform your ablutions and come to worship.

Vas.—Tell my lady mother, child, that I shall not attend to-day; let the Brahman complete the ceremony.

Atten.—As you command. [*Exit.*

Mad.—Dear madam, affection, not malice, compels me to ask what you meant to say?

Vas.—Why, Madanika, what think you of me?

Mad.—I should guess from your being so absent that you are in love.

Vas.—Well said, Madanika; you are a judge of hearts, it should seem.

Mad.—Excuse me, but Love is a resistless god, and holds his holiday in the breast of youth: so tell me, what prince or courtier does my lady serve?

Vas.—I pretend, Madanika, to be a mistress, not a slave.

Mad.—What young and learned Brahman, then, is it that you love?

Vas.—A Brahman is to be venerated, not loved.

Mad.—It must be a merchant then, rich with the collected wealth of the many courtiers he has visited.

Vas.—Nay, Madanika, it were very ill-advised to fix my affections on a trader to foreign lands. His repeated absence would subject me to a life of incessant grief.

Mad.—Neither a prince nor a courtier, a Brahman nor a merchant; who then can he possibly be?

Vas.—Madanika, you were with me in the garden of Kamadeva's temple.

Mad.—I was, madam.

Vas.—Then why do you ask me, as if you knew nothing?

Mad.—Ah! now I know—he in whose house you told me you had taken refuge.

Vas.—How is he called?

Mad.—He lives near the Exchange.

Vas.—I asked you his name.

Mad.—His well-selected name is Charudatta.

Vas.—Right, Madanika; right, girl, now you know all.

Mad.—Is it so! (*Aside.*) But, lady, it is said that he is very poor.

Vas.—I love him, nevertheless. No longer let the world believe that a courtesan is insensible to a poor man's merit.

Mad.—Yet, lady, do the bees swarm in the mango-tree after it has shed its blossoms.

Vas.—Therefore are they called wantons.

Mad.—Well, if he is the object of your affections, why not contrive an interview?

Vas.—I have provided for it: the scheme must succeed; and although it is not easy to get access to him, yet it may it may be managed.

Mad.—I suppose it was with this view that your ornaments were deposited in his hands?

Vas.—You have a shrewd guess, wench.

[*They retire.*

SCENE.—A STREET, WITH AN OPEN TEMPLE; *noise behind.*

Halloa, sirs, halloa! Yon gambler has lost ten *suvarnas*, and is running off without paying—stop him! stop him! Ah, I see you, there you go—stop! stop!

Enter the SAMVAHAKA *hastily.*

Curse on my gambling propensities: I am kicked by an ass, as it were by a she-ass just broke away from her first halter; I am picked up by a pike like Ghatotkacha by the dart of Karna; no sooner did I see the master of the table intent upon the writings, than I started. Now I have got away from them, where can I conceal myself? The gamester and the master are at my heels. Here is an empty temple; I will walk backwards into it, and take my stand as its deity. (*Enters the temple.*)

Enter MATHURA, *the keeper af the Gaming-house and the Gambler.*

Math.—Halloa, sirs! stop him, stop him.

Gam.—Though you hide in hell, or take shelter with Indra, you shall not escape. Rudra himself cannot protect you. The keeper of the gaming-house is your only chance.

Math. Whither, you deceiver of a courteous publican, have you flown. You, are shaking with fear, every limb of you; I know it by your irregular footmarks, as your feet have slipped and stumbled over the ground, blackening your family and fame.

Gam.—So far he has run, but here the track is lost.

Math.—Hey, the footmarks are all reversed. This temple had no image in it. Oh, the villain, he has walked backward into it.

Gam.—Let us after him.

Math.—Agreed. (*Enter the temple, and signify in dumb show to each other the discovery of the Samvahaka.*

Gam.—Is this image, think you, of wood ?

Math.—No, it appears to me to be of stone. (*They shake and pinch the Samvahaka.*) Never mind it, let us sit down and play out our game. (*They play.*)

Sam.—(*Who gradually expresses an interest in watching the game.*) The rattling of the dice are as tantalising to a man without a penny, as the sound of a drum to a king without a kingdom. I shall not play, I know. Gambling is as bad as being pitched from the top of mount Meru : and yet, like the Coil's song, the sound of the dice, is really bewitching.

Gam.—The throw is mine.

Math.—No, no, it is mine.

Sam.—(*Forgetting himself and jumping off the pedestal.*) No, no, it is mine.

Gam.—The man is taken.

Math.—(*Seizing the Samvahaka.*) Now, you scoundrel, we have you ; where are the ten *suvarnas* ?

Gam.—I will pay them in the course of the day.

Math.—Pay them now.

Gam.—Have patience, and you shall be paid.

Math.—I must be paid immediately.

Sam.—Oh, dear, oh, lord, my head. (*Falls down as in a swoon. They beat him.*)

Math.—You are fast now in the gaming ring.

Sam.—(*Rising and expressing pain.*) It is very hard that you will not give me a little time; where am I to get the money?

Math.—Give me a pledge then.

Sam.—Very well. (*Taking the Gamester aside.*) I tell you what, I will pay you half the money if you will forgive the rest.

Gam.—Agreed.

Sam.—(*To Mathura aside.*) I will give you security for half the debt, if you cry quits for the other half.

Math.—Agreed.

Sam.—(*To the Gamester aloud.*) You let me off half the debt?

Gam.—I do.

Sam.—And you give up half? (*To the Sabhika.*)

Math.—Yes, I do.

Sam.—Then, good morning to you, gentlemen. (*Going.*)

Math.—Halloa, not so fast, where are you going?

Sam.—See here, my masters—one has forgiven me one-half, and the other has let me off another half; is it not clear that I am quits for the whole?

Math.—Hark ye, my friend, my name is Mathura. I know a thing or two, and am not to be done in this way: so down directly with the whole sum.

Sam.—Where am I to get it?

Math.—Sell your father.

Sam.—Where is my father?

Math.—Sell your mother.

Sam.—Where is she?

Math.—Sell yourself.

Sam.—Well, well, be pacified, take me upon the highway.

Math.—Come along! (*They proceed.*) What ho, good worthy friends; pray, some one buy me of this gambler for ten *suvarnas.*

Passenger.—What noise is that?

Sam.—I will be your servant, your slave. Gone, and no reply—well, try again: who buys, who buys; will no one buy me of this gambler for ten *suvarnas*? He has passed and not said a syllable! Ah, luckless me, ever since the noble Charudatta came to poverty, I prosper only in misfortunes.

Math.—Come, come—give me the money.

Sam.—How should I give it? (*Falls and is dragged along by Mathura.*) Murder, murder! help—protect me.

Enter DARDURAKA.

Gambling is to the gamester an empire without a throne; he never anticipates defeat, but levies tribute from all, and liberally disburses what he obtains; he enjoys the revenues of a prince, and counts the opulent amongst his servants; money, wife, friends, all are to be won at the gaming-table, and all is gained, all possessed, and all lost at play. Let me see: Tray carried off everything; Deuce set my skin crawling; Ace settled the point, and Doublets dished me completely. Ha! here's my acquaintance, the keeper of the gaming-house, Mathura: I cannot avoid him, so I will wrap myself up so as not to be known. Eh! this vest is rather threadbare; it is embellished with sundry holes. It makes but a sorry covering, and looks best folded up. (*Folds up his uppercloth after examining it, and puts it under his arm.*) Never mind him; what can he do to me? I can stand with one foot on the ground, and the other in the air, as long as the sun is in the heavens.

Math.—Come, come; your money.

Sam.—Whence it is to be got?

Dar.—What is going on here?

Passen.—This gambler is getting a thrashing from the Sabhika, and nobody will take his part.

Dar.—Indeed! then I must interfere, I see. (*Approaches.*) Make way, here; heigh, sirs: Mathura, that rogue, and the Samvahaka; the wretch, whose head is hanging below his heels at sunset, whose back is variegated with stripes and bruises, and whose legs are daily nibbled by the dogs; what has he, with his lank emaciated carcase, to do with gambling? I must appease Mathura. Good day, Mathura.

Math.—Good day, good day.

Dar.—What are you at here?

Math.—This fellow owes me ten *suvarnas*.

Dar.—A trifle, a trifle.

Math.—(*Snatching Darduraka's ragged cloth from him.*) See here, my masters; here is a pretty fellow, in a ragged robe, to call ten *suvarnas* a trifle.

Dar.—Why, you blockhead, how often do I stake ten *suvarnas* on a throw. What is a man to do with his money? carry it in his waistband? But you; you are villain enough, for the sake of ten *suvarnas*, to demolish the five senses of a man.

Math.—Keep your *suvarnas* for your morning meal, if you like: this is my property.

Dar.—Very well; hear me! Give him other ten *suvarnas*, and let him play you for the whole.

Math.—How so?

Dar.—If he wins, he shall pay you the money.

Math.—And if he lose?

Dar.—Then, he shall not pay.

Math.—Go to; you talk nonsense. Will you give it? My name's Mathura; I am a cheat, and win other men's money unfairly: what then? I am not to be bullied by such a blackguard as you.

Dar.—Whom do you call a blackguard?

Math.—You are a blackguard.

Dar.—Your father was a blackguard. (*Makes signs to the Samvahaka to escape.*)

Math.—You son of a slave! are you not a gamber yourself?

Dar.—Me? do you call me a gambler?

Math.—Enough, enough. Come, do you pay the ten *suvarnas*. (*To the Samvahaka.*)

Sam.—I will pay them to-day.

[*Mathura drags him along.*

Dar.—You villain! no one shall maltreat the poor in my presence.

[*Mathura gives the Samvahaka a blow on the nose; it bleeds: the Samvahaka, on seeing his blood, faints and falls on the ground. Darduraka approaches, gets between him and Mathura, and a scuffle ensues: they pause.*

Math.—You villain! you son of a slave! yo shall suffer for this.

Dar.—You fool! you have assaulted me on the king's high-way; you shall see to-morrow, in court, whether you are to beat people in this manner.

Math.—Ah, ha! yes, yes, I shall see; depend upon it.

Dar.—How so! how will you see?

Math.—How! why, so, to be sure. (*Thursting his face forward.*)

[*Darduraka throws a handful of dust into his eyes; Mathura cries out with pain and falls; the Samvahaka recovers, and according to Darduraka's gesticulations makes his escape.*

Dar.—Mathura is a man of some weight here, that's certain; I had better therefore take myself off. My friend Sarvilaka told me that a cunning man has prophesied to a cow-herd named Aryaka, that he shall be king, and people like myself are flocking to him accordingly: my plan is to join him with the rest.

[*Exit.*

Scene—Vasantasena's House.

(*Outside and inside.*)

Enter the Samvahaka, wandering about.

(*Interior.*)—The door of this house is open; I will enter it. (*Enters and sees Vasantasena.*) Lady, I seek protection.

Vas.—It is offered you; fear nothing. Madanika, shut the door. What do you fly from?

Sam.—A creditor.

Vas.—Secure the door. (*To Madanika.*)

Sam.—(*To himself.*) She seems to be as much afraid of a creditor as myself; so much the better; he that takes a burthen suited to his strength will not slip by the way, nor perish in the thicket. My situation is duly known here, it seems.

Enter (outside of the House.) Mathura *and the* Gambler.

Math.—(*Rubbing his eyes.*) The money, I say; I will have the money.

Gam.—Sir, whilst we were struggling with Darduraka, the other rogue has run off.

Math.—The villain! but I have flattened his nose for him; we shall track him by the blood.

Gam.—He has entered here.

(Stops at Vasantasena's door.)

Math.—The ten *suvarnas* are gone.

Gam.—Let us complain to the prince.

Math.—In the meantime the scoundrel will come forth and escape. No; let us wait here; we shall have him yet.

Inside of the House.

Vas.—(*Makes signs to Madanika.*)

Mad.—*(To the Samvahaka.)* My mistress, sir, wishes to know whence you are; who you are; what you are; and what you are afraid of.

Sam.—I will tell you. I was born, lady, at Pataliputra; I am the son of a house-holder, and follow the profession of a Samvahaka.

Vas.—Were you trained to this effiminate occupation?

Sam.—I learnt the practice, lady, to get a livelihood.

Mad.—So far so good. Proceed.

Sam.—Whilst living in my father's house, I heard traveller's talk of distant countries, and felt curious to visit them myself. Accordingly, I came to Ujjayin, where I entered into the service of a distinguished person, whose like for an engaging figure and courteous speech never yet acknowledged kindness or forget offence—enough said; he only values his consequence as it enables him to do good and cherish all who seek his protection.

Mad.—Who is this that so graces Ujjayin, having stolen the good qualities my lady loves ?

Vas.—Right, Madanika, my heart suggests to me the same inquiry.

Mad.—Proceed.

Sam.—This gentleman having by his munificent bounty—

Vas.—Lavished all his wealth.

Sam.—How should your ladyship know ? I have not yet told this.

Vas.—I need no telling : worth and wealth are rarely found together. The pool is full to the brim, whose water is unfit for drinking.

Mad.—Oblige us with his name.

Sam.—To whom is the appellation of that earthly moon unknown, entitled to universal eulogium ? his habitation is near the Exchange ; his name is Charudatta.

Vas.—(*Springs from her seat.*) Girl, girl, a seat. This house is yours, sir ; pray be seated. A fan ! wench—quick ; our worthy guest is fatigued.

Sam.—(*To himself.*)—Such respect from the simple utterance of Charudatta's name ! Bravo ! excellent Charudatta ! you in this world live ; other men only breathe : (*Falls at Vasantasena's feet.*) Pray, lady, resume your seat.

Vas.—(*Sitting down.*) Where is your wealthy dun ?

Sam.—He is truly wealthy, who is rich in good acts, although he own not perishable riches. He who knows how to honour others, knows how his honour may be best deserved.

Vas.—Proceed.

Sam.—I was made by that gentleman one of his personal attendants; but in his reduced circumstances being necessarily discharged, I took to play, and by a run of ill-luck have lost ten *suvarnas*.

Math.—(*Without.*) I am rubbed! I am plundered!

Sam.—Hear, lady, hear; those two gamblers are lying wait for me; what is your ladyship's will?

Vas.—Madanika, the birds are fluttering about and rustling in the leaves of the adjoining tree; go to this poor fellow's pursuers, and say to them that he sends them this jewel in payment.

Mad.—As you command.

[*Exit.*

(*Outside of the House.*)

Math.—I am robbed!

(MADANIKA *enters by the side door unobserved.*)

Mad.—These two, by their casting such anxious looks up to the house, their agitation, their close conference, and the diligence with which they watch the door, must be the gambler and the keeper of the gaming-house. I salute you, sir.

Math.—Joy be with you, wench.

Mad.—Which of you two is the master of the gaming house?

Math.—He, my graceful damsel, whom you now address with pouting lip, soft speech, and wicked eye; but get you gone; I have nothing for you.

Mad.—If you talk thus, you are no gambler. What! have you no one in your debt?

Math.—Yes, there is a fellow owes me ten *suvarnas*: what of him?

Mad.—On his behalf, my mistress sends—nay, I mistake—he sends you this bracelet.

Math.—Ha, ha! tell him I take this as a pledge, and that he may come and have his revenge when he will. [*Exeunt severally.*

Inside of the House.

Enter MADANIKA.

They have gone away, madam, quite pleased.

Vas.—Now, my friend, depart, and relieve the anxiety of your family.

Sam.—If there be anything, lady, in which I can be of use to you, employ me.

Vas.—There is a higher claim upon your service; you should still be ready to minister to him by whom you were once employed, and on whose account your skill was acquired.

Sam.—The lady discards me; how shall I requite her kindness! (*Aloud.*) Lady, as I find my profession only begets disgrace, I will become a Bauddha mendicant; I tell you my design, and beg you will keep it in your recollection.

Vas.—Nay, friend, do nothing rashly.

Sam.—I am determined, lady. (*Going.*) In bidding adieu to gambling, the hands of men are no longer armed against me: I can now hold up my head boldly as I go along the public road. (*A noise behind the scenes.*) What is the matter now!

(*Behind the scenes.*) Vasantasena's hunting elephant has broken loose.

Sam.—I must go and see this furious beast;—yet why should I, as I purpose a pious life?

[*Exit.*

A Continued clamour without till KARNAPURAKA *enters hastily.*

Kar.—Where is my lady?

Mad.—You uumannerly fellow! what ails you? Cannot you see your mistress and address her fittingly?

Kar.—Lady, I salute you.

Vas—Karnapuraka, you seem highly pleased with something; what is it?

Kar.—You have lost a great deal to-day in not witnessing your humble servant's achievement.

Vas.—What achievement?

Kar.—Only hear. Your ladyship's fierce elephant Khuntamoraka killed his keeper and broke his chain; he then scoured off along the high road, making a terrible confusion. The people shouted and screamed,

"Carry off the children, get up the trees, climb the walls, the elephant is coming!" Away went girdles and anklets; and pearls and diamonds were scattering about in all directions. There he was, plunging about in Ujjayin, and tearing everything to pieces with his trunk, his feet, and his tusks, as if the city had been a large tank full of lotus flowers. A mendicant came in his way; the elephant broke his staff, water-pot, and platter, sprinkled him with water from his trunk, and held him up between his tusks; all cried out, "The holy man will be killed."

Vas.—Alas! alas!

Kar.—Don't be alarmed; only hear. Seeing him thus at large, and handling the holy man so roughly, I, Karnapuraka, my lady's humblest slave, determined to rescue the mendicant and punish my gentleman; so I quickly snatched up an iron bar, and approaching him sidelong, made a desperate blow at the animal.

Vas.—Go on.

Kar.—Big as he was, like the peaks of Vindhya, I brought him down and saved the saint.

Vas.—You have done well.

Kar.—So every body said, "Well done, Karnapuraka, well done!" for all Ujjayin, in a panic, like a boat ill-laden, was heaped on one spot, and one person, who had no great matter of dress to boast of himself, turning his eyes upwards, and fetching a deep sigh, threw his garment over me.

Vas.—Does it smell of jasmines ?

Kar.—The smell of the elephant's frontal moisture is still in my nostrils; so I cannot tell how the garment smells.

Vas.—Is there any name on it ? see, see !

Kar.—Here are letters ; your ladyship will best be able to read them.

Vas.—(*Reads.*) Charudatta ! (*Throws the cloth round her with delight.*)

Mad.—How well the garment becomes our mistress, does it not ?

Kar.—(*Sulkily.*) Yes, it becomes her well enough.

Vas.—Karnapuraka, be this your recompense. (*Gives him an ornament.*)

Kar.—(*Puts it to his head and bows.*) Now indeed the garment sets as it should do.

Vas.—Where did you leave Charudatta ?

Kar.—Going home, I believe, along this road.

Vas.—(*To Madanika.*) Quick, girl, quick ; up on this terrace, and we may yet catch a glimpse of him.

[*Exeunt.*

END OF THE SECOND ACT.

ACT III.

CHARUDATTA'S HOUSE.

(*Outside and inside.*)

Enter VARDHAMANA *(inside)*.—

A worthy kind master, even though he be poor, is the delight of his servants; whilst a morose haughty fellow, who has only his wealth to boast of, is a constant vexation. There is no changing nature; nothing can keep an ox out of a field of corn, nor stop a man who covets another's wife. There is no parting a gamester from the dice, and there is no remedy for an innate defect. My excellent master has gone to a concert. It is not quite midnight, I suppose. I need not expect his return yet awhile; I shall therefore take a nap in the hall. (*Sleeps.*)

Enter (outside) CHARUDATTA *and* MAITEYA.

Char.—Excellent, excellent indeed; Rebhila sang most exquisitely.

Although not ocean-born, the tuneful *vina*
Is most assuredly a gem of heaven—
Like a dear friend, it cheers the lonely heart,
And lends new lustre to the social meeting.
It lulls the pain that absent lovers feel,
And adds fresh impulse to the glow of passion.

Mait.—Come, sir, let us get home.

Char.—In truth, brave Rebhila, 'twas deftly sung.

Mait.—Now, to me, there are two things at which I cannot choose but laugh, a woman reading Sanskrit, and a man singing a song: the woman snuffles like a young cow when the rope is first passed through her nostrils; and the man wheezes like an old Pandit who has been repeating his bead-roll till the flowers of his chaplet are as dry as his throat: to my seeming it is vastly ridiculous.

Char.—What my good friend, were you not pleased to-night with Rebhila's fine execution?—

Smooth were the tones, articulate and flowing
With graceful modulation, sweet and pleasing,
And fraught with warm and passionate expression;
So that I often thought the dulcet sounds
Some female, stationed covertly, must utter.
Still echoes in my ears the soothing strain,
And as I pace along, methinks I hear
The liquid cadence and melodious utterance.
The *vín's* sweet notes, now gently undulating,
Now swelling high, now dying to a close—
Sporting awhile in desultory descant,
And still recurring to the tasteful theme!

Mait.—Come, my friend, the very dogs in the high road through the market place are fast asleep; let us go home. See, see, the moon descends from his mansion in the skies, making his way through the darkness.

Char.—True have you said. From his high palace bowed,
And hastening to his setting, scantly gleams
The waning moon, amdist the gathering gloom;
In slender crescent, like the tusk's fine point,
That peers above the darkening wave, where bathes.
The forest elephant.

Mait.—Here we are at home, Halloa! Vardhamana, arise and open the door.

Vardh.—(*Within.*)—Hark, I hear Maitreya's voice: Charudatta is returned; I must let him in. (*Opens the door.*) Sir, I salute you; you also Maitreya. Here are the couches ready spread; please you to repose. (*They enter and sit*).

Mait.—Vardhamana, tell Radanika to bring water for the feet.

Char.—Nay, nay, disturb not those who are asleep.

Vardh.—I will bring water, and Maitreya, here can wash your feet.

Mait.—Do you hear, my friend, the son of a slave? he is to hold the water, and he sets me, who am a Brahman, to wash your feet.

Char.—Do you, Maitreya, hold the water? Vardhamana can perform the rest.

Vardh.—Come then, worthy Maitreya, pour out the water. (*Vardhamana, washes Charudatta's feet, and is going.*)

Char.—Nay, Vardhamana, wash the feet of the Brahman.

Mait.—Never mind; it is of little use; I must soon go tramping over the ground again, like a jackass.

Vardh.—Most worthy Maitreya, you are a Brahman, are you?

Mait.—To be sure I am; like the boa amongst serpents, so am I, a Brahman amongst Brahmans.

Vardh.—I cry you mercy: that being the case, I will wash your feet. (*Does so.*) Now, Maitreya, this gold casket, of which I have had the charge by day, it is your turn to take care of. (*Gives it to him and exit.*

Mait.—So; it is safe through the day. What! have we no thieves in Ujjayin, that no one could have carried off this vile pilferer of my rest: pray let me carry it into the court-yard.

Char.—Impossible, it has been left in trust;

And is not to be parted with to any
But the right owner; Brahman, take heed to it. (*Lies down.*)
Still do I hear the soothing strain.

Mait.—Pray, sir, is it your intention to go to sleep?

Charu.—Assuredly.

I feel the drowsy deity invade
My forehead, and descend upon my eyelids,
Sleep, like decay, viewless and variable,
Grows stronger in its triumph o'er our strength.

Mait.—Very true, so let us go to sleep.

(*They sleep.*)

Enter SARVILAKA (*outside*).

Creeping along the ground, like a snake crawling out of his old skin, I effect with slight and strength a passage for my cowering frame. (*Looking up.*) The sovereign of the skies is in his decline: 'tis well. Night, like a tender mother, shrouds with her protecting darkness those of her children whose prowess assails the dwellings of mankind, and shrinks from an encounter with the servants of the king. I have made a breach in the garden wall, and have got into the midst of the garden. Now for the house. Men call this practice infamous, whose chief success is gained from the sleep of others, and whose booty is won by craft. If not heroism, it is at least independence, and preferable to the homage paid by slaves. As to nocturnal attacks, did not Aswatthaman long ago overpower in a night-onset his slumbering foes? Where shall I make the breach? what part is softened by recent damp? where is it likely that no noise will be made by the falling fragments? where is a wide opening most practicable which will not be afterwards visible? in what part of the wall are the bricks old, and corroded by saline exudations? where can I penetrate without encountering women? and where am I likely to light upon my booty? (*Feels the wall.*) The ground here is softened by continual sprinkling with water and exposure to the sun, and is crusted with salt. Here is a rat hole. The prize is sure this is the first omen of success the sons of Skanda have laid down. Let me see: how shall I proceed? The god of the golden spear teaches four modes of breaching a house: picking out burnt bricks, cutting through unbaked ones, throwing water on a mud-wall, and boring through one of wood. This wall is of baked bricks: they must be picked out, but I must give them a sample of my skill. Shall the breach be the lotus blossom, the full sun or the new moon, the lake, the swastika, or the water-jar? It must be something to astonish the natives. The water-jar looks best in a brick wall;—that shall be the shape. In other walls that I have breached by night, the neighbours have had occasion both to censure and approve my talents. Reverence to the prince Karttikeya, the giver of all good; reverence to the god of the golden spear; to Brahmanya, the celestial champion of the celestials; the son of fire. Reverence to Yogacharya, whose chief scholar I am, and by whom well pleased was the magic unguent conferred upon me, anointed with which, no eye beholds nor weapon harms me. Shame on me! I have forgotten my measuring-line,—never mind, my Brahmanical thread will answer the purpose. This thread is a most useful appendage to a Brahman, especially one of my complexion: it serves to measure the depth and height of walls, and to withdraw ornaments from their position; it opens a latch in a door as well as a key, and is an excellent ligature for the bite of a snake. Let us take measure, and go to work: so, so—(*extracting the bricks*)—one brick alone remains. Ha! hang it; I am bitten by a snake—(*ties the finger with the cord*)—'tis well again,—I must get on. (*Looks in.*) How! a lamp alight! the golden ray streaming through the opening in the wall shows amidst the exterior darkness, like the yellow streak of pure metal on the touchstone. The breach is perfect; now to enter. There is no one. Reverence to Karttikeya. (*Enters.*) Here are two men asleep; let me set the outer door open to get off easily if there should be occasion; how it creeks! it is stiff with age; a little water will be of use. (*Sprinkles the floor.*) Nay, not so, it makes too much noise pattering on the ground. (*Supports the door with his back, and opens it.*) So far, so well. Now are these true sleepers or only counterfeits? (*He tries them.*) They are sound: the breathing is regular and not fluttered; the eye is fast and firmly shut; the body is all relaxed; the joints are loose, and the limbs protrude beyond the limits of the bed. If shamming sleep, they will not bear the gleam of the lamp upon their faces. (*Passes the lamp over their faces.*) All is safe. What have we here? a drum, a tabor, a lute, pipes; and here are books. Why, zounds, I have got into the house of a dancer or a poet. I took it for the dwelling of some man of consequence, or I should have let it alone. Is this poverty, or only the show of poverty? fear of thieves, or dread of the king? Are the effects hid underground? whatever is underground is my poperty. Let us scatter the seed, whose showing leaves nothing undiscernible. (*Throws about seeds.*) The man is an absolute pauper, and so I leave him. (*Going.*)

Mait.—(*Dreaming.*) Master, they are breaking into the house. I see the thief. Here, here! do you take care of the gold casket.

Sar.—How! does he perceive me? does he mock me with his poverty? he dies. (*Approaching.*) Haply he dreams. (*Looking at Maitreya.*) Eh! sure euough, there is in the light of the lamp something like a casket wrapped up in a ragged bathing-gown; that must be mine. No, no; it is cruel to ruin a worthy man, so miserably reduced already. I will even let it alone.

Mait.—(*Dreaming.*) My friend, if you do not take the casket, may you incur the guilt of disappointing a cow, and of deceiving a Brahman.

Sar.—These invocations are irresistible: take it I must. Softly: the light will betray me. I have the fire-flapping insect to put it out. I must cast it into the lamp. (*Takes out the insect.*) Place and time requirring, let this insect fly. It hovers round the wick—with the wind of its wings the flame is extingnished. Shame on this total darkness, or rather shame on the darknes with which I have obscured the lustre of my race! how well it suits that Sarvilaka, a Brahman, the son of a Brahman, learned in the four Vedas, and above receiving donations from others, should now be engaged in such unworthy courses! And why? For the sake of a harlot, for the sake of Madanika. Ah, well! I must even go on, and acknowledge the courtesy of this Brahman.

Mait.—(*Half-awake.*) Eh, my good friend, how cold your hand is!

Sar.—Blockhead! I had forgotten, I have chilled my hand by the water I touched; I will put it to my side. (*Chafes his left hand on his side and takes the casket with it.*)

Mait.—(*Still only half-awake.*) Have you got it?

Sar—The civility of this Brahman is exceeding! I have it.

Mait.—Now, like a pedlar that has sold all his wares, I shall go soundly to sleep. (*Sleeps.*)

Sar.—Sleep, illustrious Brahman! May you sleep a hundred years! Fie on this love! for whose dear sake I thus bring trouble on a Brahman's dwelling—nay, rather call down shame upon myself; and fie! and fie! upon this unmanning poverty, that urges me to acts which I must needs condemn. Now to Vasantasena to redeem my beloved Madanika with this night's booty. I hear footsteps; should it be the watch—what then?—shall I stand here like a post?—no, let Sarvilaka be his own protection. Am I not a cat in climbing, a deer in running, a snake in twisting, a hawk in darting upon the prey, a dog in baying man, whether asleep or awake? In assuming various forms am I not Maya herself, and Saraswati in the gift of tongues? A lamp in the night, a mule in a defile, a horse by land, a boat by water, a snake in motion, and a rock in stability? In hovering about I complete with the king of birds, and in an eye to the ground, and keener than the hare. Am I not like a wolf in seizing, and like a lion in strength?

Enter RADANIKA.

Bless me! what has become of Vardhamana? He was asleep at the hall door, but is there no longer. I must wake Maitreya. (*Approaches.*)

Sar.—(*Going to stab her.*) Ha! a woman! she is safe, and I may depart.

[*Exit.*

Rad.—Oh, dear me! A thief has broken into the house, and there he goes out at the door. Why, Maitreya! Maitreya! up, up I say. A thief has broken into the house, and has just made his escaye?

Mait.—Eh, what do you say, you foolish toad? a thief made his escape?

Rad.—Nay, this is no joke—see here.

Mait.—What say you, hey, the outer door opened! Charudatta, friend, awake! a thief has been in the house and has just made his escape.

Char.—This is not an hour to jest,

Mait.—It is true enough, as you may satisfy yourself.

Char.—Where did he get in?

Mait.—Look here. (*Discovers the breach.*)

Char.—Upon my word, a not unseemly fissure; the bricks are taken out above and below; the head is small, the body large: there is really talent in this thief.

Mait.—The opening must have been made by one of two persons; by a novice, merely to try his hand, or by a stranger to this city; for who in Ujjayin is ignorant of the poverty of our mansion.

Char.—No doubt, by a stranger—one who did not know the condition of my affairs, and forgot that those only sleep soundly who have little to lose. Trusting to the external semblance of this mansion, erected in more prosperous times, he entered full of hope, and has gone away disappointed. What will the poor fellow have to tell his comrades? I have broken into the house of the son of the chief of a corporation, and found nothing.

Mait.—Really, I am very much concerned for the luckless rogue. Ah, ha! thought he, here is a fine house; now for jewels, for caskets. (*Recollecting.*) By the by, where is the casket? oh yes, I remember. Ha, ha! my friend, you are apt to say of me, that blockhead Maitreya! that dunderhead Maitreva! but it was a wise trick of mine to give the casket to you: had I not done so, the villain would have walked off with it.

Char.—Come, come, this jesting is misplaced.

Mait.—Jesting—no, no; blockhead though I be, I know when a joke is out of season.

Char.—When did you give the casket to me?

Mait.—When I called out to you, "How cold your hand is!"

Char.—It must be so. (*Looking about.*)—My good friend, I am much obliged by your kindness.

Mait.—Why: is not the casket stolen?

Char.—It is stolen.

Mait.—Then what have you to thank me for?

Char.—That the poor rogue has not gone away empty-handed.

Mait.—He has carried off what was left in trust.

Char.—How! in trust, alas! (*Faints.*)

Mait.—Revive, revive, sir! though the thief has stolen the deposit, why should it so seriously affect you?

Char.—Alas! my friend, who will believe it stolen?
A general ordeal waits me. In this world
Cold poverty is doomed to wake suspicion.
Alas! till now, my fortune only felt
The emnity of fate; but now its venom
Sheds a foul blight upon my dearer fame.

Mait.—I tell you what. I will maintain that the casket was never entrusted to us. Who gave it, pray? who took it? where are your witnesses?

Char.—Think you I can sanction thus a falsity?
No, no; I will beg alms, and so obtain
The value of the pledge, and quit its owner;

But cannot condescend to shame my soul
By utterance of a lie. [*Exit.*

Rad.—I will go and tell my mistress what has happened.

[*Exit.*

SCENE—ANOTHER ROOM.

Enter the WIFE *of* CHARUDATTA *and* RADANIKA.

Wife.—But indeed is my lord unhurt? is he safe, and his friend Maitreya?

Rad.—Both safe, madam, I assure you, but the ornaments left by the courtesan are stolen.

Wife.—Alas, girl! what say you? My husband's person is unharmed: that glads me. Yet better had his person come to harm than his fair fame incur disparagement. The people of Ujjayin will now be ready to suspect that indigence has impelled him to an unworthy act. Destiny, thou potent deity, thou sportest with the fortunes of mankind, and renderest them as tremulous as the watery drop that quivers on the lotus leaves. This string of jewels was given me in my maternal mansion: it is all that is left to us, and I know my husband, in the loftiness of his spirit, will not accept it from me. Girl, go call the worthy Maitreya hither.

[*Exit.*

RADANIKA *returns with* MAITREYA.

Mait.—Health to you, respected lady.

Wife.—I salute you, sir.—Oblige me by facing the east.

Mait.—You are obeyed.

Wife.—I pray you accept this.

Mait.—Nay, not so.

Wife.—I fasted on the Ratnashashthi, when, as you know, wealth must be given to a Brahman. My Brahman had been provided elsewhere, and I beg therefore that, in his stead, you will accept this string of jewels.

Mait.—Very well; I will go and state the matter to my friend.

Wife.—Thanks, Maitreya; but take heed, do not put me to shame.

SCENE—THE HALL. CHARUDATTA *discovered.*

Char.—Maitreya tarries long; in his distress I hope he does not purpose aught unfitting.

Enter MAITREYA.

Mait.—Here am I, sir, and bring you this. (*Gives the string of jewels.*)

Char.—What is this?

Mait.—The fruit borne by the excellence of a wife worthy of her husband.

Char.—Is this the kindness of the Brahman's wife?

Out on it!—that I should be reduced so low
As, when my own has disappeared, to need
Assistance from a woman's wealth. So true

It is, our very natures are transformed
By opulence: the poor man helpless grows,
And woman wealthy acts with manly vigour.—
'Tis false; I am not poor:—a wife whose love
Outlives my fortune; a true friend who shares
My sorrows and my joy; and honesty
Unwarped by indigence, these still are mine.
Maitreya, hie thee to Vasantasena,
Tell her the casket, heedlessly impledged,
Who lost by me at play, but in its stead
I do beseech her to accept these jewels.

Mait—I will do no such thing. What! are we to part with these gems, the quintessence of the four oceans, for a thing carried off by thieves, and which we have neither eaten nor drank, nor touched a penny for?

Char.—Not so; to me, confiding in my care
And honesty, the casket was entrusted;
And for that faith, which cannot be o'ervalued,
A price of high amount must be repaid.
Touching my breast, I therefore supplicate,
You will not hence, this charge not undertaken.
You, Vardhamana, gather up these bricks
To fill the chasm again; we'll leave no trace
To catch the idle censure of men's tongues.
Come, come, Maitreya, rouse a liberal feeling,
Nor act in this a despicable niggard.

Mait.—How can a pauper be a niggard? he has nothing to part with.

Char.—I am not poor, I tell thee, but retain
Treasures I prize beyond whate'er is lost.
Go then, discharge this office, and meanwhile
I hail the dawn with its accustomed rites. [*Exit.*

END OF THE THIRD ACT.

ACT IV.

VASANTASENA'S HOUSE.

Enter FEMALE ATTENDANT.

I am sent to the lady Vasantasena by her mother: oh, here she is, looking on a picture, and engaged in conversation with Madanika.

Enter VASANTASENA *as described.*

Vas.—But, Madanika is this a good likeness of Charudatta?

Mad.—Very good.

Vas.—How do you know?

Mad.—I conclude so, madam, from the affectionate looks which you bestow upon it.

Vas.—How, wench, do you say this in the language of our profession?

Mad.—Nay, madam, surely even one of us is not incapable of speaking truth.

Vas.—The woman, wench, that admits the love of many men is false to them all.

Mad.—Yet, madam, when the eyes and thoughts are intent but on one object, it is very unnecessary to inquire the cause.

Vas.—But tell me, girl, do I not seem ridiculous to my friends?

Mad.—Nay, not so, madam ; a woman is secure of the sympathy of her companions.

ATTENDANT *advances.*

Att.—Madam, your mother desires you to ascend your litter and repair to the private apartments.

Vas.—To meet my Charudatta.

Att.—The person, madam, who has sent the chariot has sent very costly ornaments.

Vas.—Who is he ?

Att.—Samsthanaka, the Raja's brother-in-law.

Vas.—Begone, let me not hear him named.

Att.—Forgive me, madam ; I but deliver my message.

Vas.—The message is odious.

Att.—What reply am I to convey to your lady mother ?

Vas.—Tell her, if she would not have me dead, she must send me no more such messages.

Att.—I shall obey.

[*Exit.*

The outside of the House.—A GARDEN.

Enter SAEVILAKA (*below*).

Sar.—My course is like the moon's, and with the dawn
Declines its fading beams : my deeds have shamed
The lazy night, have triumphed over sleep,
And mocked the baffled vigilance of the watch.
Yet I am scant secure, and view with terror

Him who appears to track my rapid steps,
Or seems to hasten where I rest my flight.—
Thus guilty conscience makes me fear, for man
Is ever frightened by his own offences.
'Tis for Madanika's dear sake alone
I perpetrate this violence, as I shun
The leader and his train, avoid the mansion
A woman sole inhabits, or I stand
Still as the door-post, while the town-guard passes,
And with a hundred tricks thus make the night
As full of action as the busy day.

Vas.—(*Within.*) Here, girl, take the pieture, lay it on my couch; and here, bring me my fan.

Mad.—I obey. [*Exit Madanika.*

Sar.—This is the dwelling of Vasantasena. (*Enters.*) Where can Madanika be found?

MADANIKA *enters with the fan.*

Sar.—Ah, here she comes, as graceful as the bride
Of love, and soothing to my burning heart
As sandal to the fevered flesh. Madanika!

Mad.—Eh! Sarvilaka? health to you. Whence do you come?

Sar.—I will tell you.

Enter VASANTASENA (*above*).

Vas.—(*Above.*) Madanika tarries long; where can she be? (*Looks from the window.*) How! she is engaged in conversation with a man: her eyes are fixed intently upon him, and seem to quaff overflowing drafts of love; they appear to understand each other. He woos her probably to be his companion: well, be it so; never be genuine affection thwarted. I will wait her leisure.

Mad.—Well, Sarvilaka, proceed. (*He looks cautiously round.*) Why do you thus examine the place? You seem alarmed.

Sar.—I have a secret to entrust you with; are we alone?

Mad.—Quite.

Vas.—A secret! then I must not listen longer.

Sar.—Tell me, Madanika what cost procures
Your manumission of Vasantasena?

Vas.—He names me; the secret then regards me, and I must be a party in it; behind this window I can overhear him unobserved.

Mad.—My lady has often declared, Sarvilaka, that she would liberate us all without price if she were her own mistress; but where is the wealth with which you are to purchase my freedom?

Sar.—To tell you sooth, my poverty and love
Have urged me to an act of violence.

Vas.—How has this act transformed his otherwise goodly appearance!

Mad.—Ah! Sarvilaka, for a transitory enjoyment you have endangered two valuable things.

Sar.—And what are they?

Mad.—Your person and your reputation.

Sar.—Silly girl! fortune favour force.

Mad.—(*Ironically.*)—Your conduct is without blame: the violence you have comitted on my account is no doubt quite proper.

Sar.—It may be venial, for I have not plundered
A lovely woman graced with glittering gems,
The blossoms of a creeper. I have not filched
A Brahman's gold, for the purposes of piety
Collected, nor from the heedless nurse
Have I borne off the innocent babe for hire.
I have well weighed whate'er I have committed.
Apprise your mistress, then, these gems are hers,
That seem as they were made on purpose for her.
If she will yield you up, but let her keep them
Carefully concealed.

Mad.—An ornament that must never be worn is but ill suited to my mistress. But come, let me see these trinkets.

Sar.—Bo hold them.

Mad.—I have certainly seen them before: where did you get them?

Sar.—That concerns not you; ask no questions, but take them.

Mad.—(*Angrily.*) If you can place no confidence in me, why seek to make me yours?

Sar.—I was informed, then, that near the Bazar resided the chief of his tribe, one Charudatta.

VASANTASENA *and* MADANIKA *both faint.*

Sar.—Madanika, revive! what ails the wench
Her limbs are all unstrung, her looks are wild.
Why, girl, is this your love? is then so terrible
The thought to share your destiny with mine?

Mad.—Avoid me, wretch! Yet stay, I dread to ask. Was no one hurt or murdered in that mansion?

Sar.—I touch not one who trembles or who sleeps.
Unharmed by me were all in that abode.

Mad.—In truth?

Sar.—In very truth

Vas.—Do I yet live?

Mad.—This is indeed a blessing.

Sar.—(*With jealous warmth.*)
You seem to take strange interest in this business
'Twas love of you that urged me to the act—
Me, sprung of virtuous and of pure descent.
Spurred by my passion, I have offered you
A life of credit and a faithful heart;
And this is my reward—to be reviled,
And find your cares devoted to another.
In vain the lofty tree of flowering youth
Bears goodly fruit, the prey of harlot birds.
Wealth, manhood, all we value, are consumed
By passion's fierce ungovernable fire.
Ah! what a fool is man, to place his trust
In woman or in fortune, fickle both
As serpent-nymphs! Be woman's love unwoo'd,

For humble love she pays with scorn. Let her
First proffer tenderness, and whilst it lasts
Be kind, but leave her as her fondness cools.
'Tis wisely said, for money woman weeps
And smiles at will, and of his confidence,
The man she trusts not, craftily beguiles.
Let then the youth of merit and of birth
Beware the wanton's charms, that baleful blow
Like flowers on charnal ground; the ocean waves
Are less unsteady, and the varying tints
Of eve less fleeting than a woman's fondness.
Wealth is her aim; as soon as man is drained
Of all his goods, like a squeezed colour bag,
She casts him off. Brief as the lightning's flash
Is woman's love. Nay, she can look devotion
To one man whilst another rules her heart,
And even whilst she helds in fond embrace
One lover, for his rival breathes her sighs.
But why expect what nature has withheld?
The lotus blooms not on the mountain's brow,
Nor bears the mule the burthen of the horse;
The grain of barley buds not into rice,
Nor dwells one virtue in the breast of woman.
Fool that I was, to let that wretch escape;
'Tis not too late, and Charudatta dies. (*Going.*)

Mad.—(*Catching hold of him.*) You have talked a great deal of stuff, and are angry without rhyme or reason.

Sar.—How, without reason?

Mad.—These ornaments are in truth the property of Vasantasena.

Sar.—Indeed!

Mad.—And were left by her in deposit with Charudatta.

Sar.—For what purpose?

Mad.—I will tell you. (*Whispers.*)

Sar.—I am overcome with shame. The friendly branch
That gave me shadow when oppressed with heat,
My heedless hand has shorn of its bright leaves.

Vas.—I am glad that he repents: he has acted without reflection.

Sar.—What is to be done?

Mad.—You are the best judge.

Sar.—Nay, not so.
Nature is woman's teacher, and she learns
More sense than man, the pedant, gleans from books

Mad.—I should advice you then, go and return these ornaments to Charudatta.

Sar.—And what if he deliver me up to justice?

Mad.—There is no heat from the moon.

Sar.—I heed not of his gentleness, and brave
Unshrinkingly the consequence of all
I dare to do—but this, this act I blush for;
And of such petty scoundrels as myself
How must the prince dispose? No—no,
We must devise some other means.

Mad.—I have.

Vas.—What can she suggest?

Mad.—You shall pass yourself off as a messenger from Charudatta, sent to restore these trinkets to my lady.

Sar.—And what results?

Mad.—You will be no thief; Charudatta will sustain no loss, and my lady recover her own property.

Sar.—This is downright robbery, carrying off my booty.

Mad.—If you do not relinquish it, that will be much more like roberry.

Vas.—Well said, Madanika; you advise as a faithful friend.

Sar.—I have gained much by asking your advice.

When there is no moon at night, 'tis difficult
To get a guide that may be safely followed.

Mad.—Stay here, whilst I give notice to my mistress.

Sar.—Be it so.

Mad.—(*Approaches Vasantasena.*) Lady, a Brahman attends you from Charudatta.

Vas.—How do you know his mission?

Mdd.—Do I not know my own affairs?

Vas.—(*Smiling.*) Very true; let him advance, Madanika.

[*She descends, and brings Sarvilaka forward as Vasantasena enters below.*

Sar.—Lady, I salute you ; peace be with you.

Vas.—I salute you. Pray be seated. (*Sits.*)

Sar.—The respected Charudatta informs you, that as his house is very insecure, he is apprehensive this casket may be lost, and therefore begs you will take it back again. (*Gives it to Madanika and is going.*)

Vas.—Stay ; I have a favour to request. Let me trouble you to convey to the worthy sender something from me.

Sar.—(*Aside.*) Who the deuce is to give it to him ? (*Aloud.*) What am I to take ?

Vas.—Madanika.

Sar.—I understand you not.

Vas.—I understand myself.

Sar.—What mean you ?

Vas.—The truth is, it was agreed between Charudatta and me, that the person by whom he should send back these jewels should receive Madanika as a present from me on his account : you are therefore to take this damsel, and thank Charudatta for her. You understand me now.

Sar.—(*Apart.*) She knows the truth ; that is clear. No matter. (*Aloud.*)

May all prosperity bless Charudatta.
'Tis politic in man to nurture merit,
For poverty with worth is richer far,
Than majesty without all real excellence.

Nought is beyond its reach; the radiant moon
Won by its worth a seat on Siva's brow.

Vas.—Who waits? bring forth the litter.

Sar.—It attends. *(The carriage comes on.)*

Vas.—My dear girl, Madanika, ascend the litter; I have given you away: look at me well; do not forget me.

Mad.—(*Weeping.*) I am discarded by my mistress. *(Falls at her feet.)*

Vas.—Nay, wench, rise, it is now my place to stoop to you; go take your seat, and keep me ever in your recollection.

Sar.—Lady, may every good attend you! Madanika, with grateful looks survey your bounteous benefactress; bow your head in gratitude to her to whom you owe the unexpected dignity that waits upon the title and the state of wife.

[*They salute* VASANTASENA *as she departs, and ascend the car.*

(*Behind.*)

Who hears? who hears? the Governor commands. In consequence of a reported prophecy, that the son of a cowherd, named Aryaka, shall ascend the throne, his majesty Palaka has deemed it expedient to apprehend him, and detain him in confinement. Let all men therefore remain quietly in their houses, and entertain no alarm.

Sar.—How! the king has seized my dear friend Aryaka, and I am thinking of a wife!

This world presents two things most dear to
all men,
A friend and mistress; but the friend is prized
Above a hundred beauties. I must hence,
And try to liberate him (*Alights.*)

Mad.—Stay but a while, my dearest lord; consign me first to reputable friends then leave me, if it must be so.

Sar.—You speak my thoughts, love. Hark ye. (*To the servant.*) Know you the residence of Rebhila,
The chief of the musicians.

Serv.—I do, sir.

Sar.—Convey my lady thither.

Serv.—As you command.

Mad.—I obey. Farewell. For my sake, be not rash. [*Exit.*

Sar.—Now then to rouse the friends of Aryaka,
Our kindred and associates—all who deem
The king has wronged their will, and all who
trust
The prowess of their arms. We will redeem
Our chief from bonds, as by his faithful
minister
Udayana was rescued.
This seizure is unjust, it is the deed
Of a most cowardly and treacherous foe;
But we shall soon release him from such grasp
Like the fair moon from Rahu's jaws set free.
[*Exit.*

VASANTASENA'S DWELLING (*inside*).

Enter A FEMALE ATTENDANT, *meeting* VASANTASENA.

Att.—Lady, you are fortunate, a Brahman from Charudatta.

Vas.—This is indeed a lucky day. Receive him with all respect; request him to enter, and call the Chamberlain to attend him.

Att.—As you command.

[*Exit.*

OUTSIDE OF THE HOUSE.

Enter MAITREYA *and* BANDHULA.

Mait.—Here's honour! The sovereign of the Rakshasas, Ravana, travels in the car of Kuvera, obtained by the force of his devotions; but I, who am a poor Brahman, and no saint, yet I am conveyed about by lovely damsels.

Att.—This is the outer door, sir.

Mait.—A very prerty entrance, indeed. The threshold is very neatly coloured, well swept and watered; the floor is beautified with strings of sweet flowers; the top of the gate is lofty and gives one the pleasure of looking up to the clouds, whilst the jasmine fastoon hangs tremblingly down, as if it were now tossing on the trunk of Indra's elephant. Over the door way is a lofty arch of ivory; above it again wave flags dyed with safflower, their fringes curling in the wind, like fingers that beckon me, "come thither." On either side, the capitals of the door-posts support elegant crystal flower-pots, in which young mango-trees are springing up. The door panels are of gold, stuck, like the stout breast of a demon, with studs of adamant. The whole cries "away" to a poor man, whilst its splendour catches the eye of the wisest.

Att.—This leads to the first court. Enter, sir, enter.

(*They enter the first Court.*)

Mait.—Bless me! why here is a line of palaces, as white as the moon, as the conch, as the stalk of the water-lily—the stucco has been laid on here by handfuls; golden steps, embellished with various stones, lead to the upper apartments, whence the crystal windows, festooned with pearls, and bright as the eyes of a moon-faced maid, look down upon Ujjayin. The porter dozes on an easy-chair as stately as a Brahman deep in the Vedas; and the very crows crammed with rice and curds, disdain the fragments of the sacrifice, as if they were no more than scattered plaster. Proceed.

Att.—That is the second court. Enter.

(*They enter the second Court.*)

Mait.—Oh, here are the stables; the carriage oxen are in good case, pampered with javasa I declare; and straw and oil-cakes are ready for them; their horns are bright with grease. Here we have a buffallo snorting indignantly, like a Brahman of high caste whom somebody has affronted; here the ram stands to have his neck well rubbed, like a wrestler after a match; here they dress the manes of the horses; here is a monkey tied as fast as thief; and here the mahauts are plying the elephants with balls of rice and ghee. Proceed.

Att.—This, sir, is the third gateway.

(*They enter the third Court.*)

Mait.—Oh, this is the public court, where the young bucks of Ujjayin assemble; these are their seats, I suppose—the half-read book lies on the gaming table, the men of which are made of jewels. Oh, yonder are some old hangers-on, lounging about with many-coloured pictures in their hands, and skilled in the peace and war of love. What next?

Att.—This is the entrance to the fourth court.

(*They enter the fourth Court.*)

Mait.—Oh, ho! this is a very gay scene: here the drums, whilst beaten by taper-fingers, emit, like clouds, a murmuring tone; there the cymbals beating time, flash as they descend like the unlucky stars that fall from heaven. The flute here breathes the soft hum of the bee, whilst here a damsel holds the vina in her lap, and frets its wires with her finger-nails, like some wild minx that sets her mark on the face of her offending swain: some damsels are singing, like so many bees intoxicated with flowery nectar; others are practising the graceful dance, and others are employed in reading plays and poems. Tho place is hung with water-jars, suspended to catch the cooling breeze. What comes next?

Att.—This is the gate of the fifth court.

(*They enter the fifth Court.*)

Mait.—Ah, how my mouth waters! what a savoury scent of oil and asafoetida! The kitchen sighs softly forth its fragrant and abundant smoke—the odours are delicious—they fill me with rapture. The butcher's boy is washing the skin of an animal just slain, like so much foul linen; the cook is surrounded with dishes; the sweetmeets are mixing; the cakes are baking. (*Apart.*) Oh that I could meet with some one to do me a friendly turn; one who would wash my feet, and say, eat, sir, eat. (*Aloud.*) This is certainly Indra's heaven; the damsels are Apsaras, the Bandhulas are Gandharbas. Pray, why do they call you Bandhulas?

Att.—We inhabit the dwellings of others and eat the bread of the stranger: we are the offspring of parents whom no tie connects: we exercise our indiscribable merits in gaining men's money, and we sport through life as free and unrestrained as the cubs of the elephant.

Mait.—What do we come to next?

Att.—This is the sixth entry.

(*They enter.*)

Mait.—The arched gateway is of gold and many-coloured gems on a ground of shapphire, and looks like the bow of Indra in an azure sky. What is going forward here so busily? It is the jeweller's court: skilful artists are examining pearls, topazes, sapphires, emeralds, rubies, the lapis-lazuly, coral, and other jewels; some set rubies in gold, some work gold ornaments on coloured thread, some string pearls, some grind the lapis-lazule, some pierce shells, and some cut coral. Here we have perfumers drying the saffron bags, shaking the musk bags, expressing the sandal-juice and compounding essences. Whom have we here? fair damsels and their gallants, laughing, talking, chewing musk and betel, and drinking wine, Here are the male and female attendants, and here are miserable hangerson—men that neglected their own families and spent their all upon the harlot, and are now glad to quaff the draining of her wine-cup.

Att.—This is the seventh court. Enter.

(They enter the seventh Court.)

Mait.—This is the aviary—very handsome indeed! The doves bill and coo in comfort; the pampered parrot croaks like a Brahman Pandit, stuffed with curds and rice, chanting a hymn from the Vedas; the Maina chatters as glibly as a housemaid issuing her mistress's command to her fellow-servants, while the koil, crammed with juicy fruit, whines like a water-carrier. The quails fight; the partridges cry; the domestic peacock dances about delighted, and fans the palace with his gem-emblazoned tail, as if to cool its heated walls; the swans, like balls of moonlight, roll about in pairs, and follow each graceful maid, as if to learn to imitate her walk, whilst the long-legged cranes stalk about the court, like eunuchs on guard. I declare the lady lives here amongst the winged race as if she tenanted Indra's garden. Well, where do you go now?

Att.—Enter, sir, the eighth court.

(*They enter.*)

Mait.—Pray, who is that gentleman dressed in silken raiment, glittering with rich ornaments and rolling about as if his limbs were out of joint?

Att.—That, sir, is my lady's brother.

Mait.—Humph—what course of pious austerity in his last life made him Vasantasena's brother? Nay, not so; for after all, though smooth, bright, and fragrant, the Champa tree that grows on funeral ground is not to be approached. And pray, who is, that lady dressed in flowered muslin? a goodly person truly; her feet shining with oil thrust into a pair of slippers: she sits in state, high on a gorgeous throne.

Att.—That is my lady's mother.

Mait.—A portly old hag, indeed: how did she contrive to get in here? Oh, I suppose she was first set up here, as they do with an unwieldey Mahadeva, and then the walls were built round her.

Att.—How now, slave? What! do you make a jest of our lady, affected, too, as she is with a quartan ague?

Mait.—A what? O mighty Fever, be pleased to afflict me with a quartan, if such are its symptoms.

Att.—You will die, slave.

Mait.—No, hussey; better that this bloated porpoise, swelled up with wine and years, die; there will then be a dinner for a thousand jackals. But no matter; what do you know about it? I had heard of Vasantasena's wealth, and I now find it true; it seems to me that the treasures of the three worlds are collected in this mansion. I am in doubt whether to regard it as the dwelling of a courtesan or the palace of Kuvera. Where is your lady?

Att.—She is in the arbour. Enter.

(*They enter the Garden.*)

Mait.—A very lovely scene! the numerous trees are bowed down by delicious fruit, and between them are silken swings constructed for the light form of youthful beauty: the yellow jasmine, the graceful malati, the full-blossomed mallika, and the blue clitoria, spontaneous shed their flowers, and strew the ground with a carpet more lovely than any in the groves Indra; the reservoir glows with the red lotus blossoms like the dawn with the fiery beams of the rising sun: and here the asoka tree, with its rich crimson blossoms, shines like a young warrior bathed with the sanguine shower of the furious fight. Where is your lady?

Att.—Look lower, and you will see her.

Mait.—(*Approaching Vasantasena.*) Health to you, lady?

Vas.—(*Rising.*) Welcome, Maitreya; take a seat.

Mait.—Pray, keep you yours. (*They sit.*)

Vas.—I hope all is well with the son of the Sarthavaha.

Mait.—Is all well with your ladyship?

Vas.—Undoubtedly, Maitreya; the birds of affection gladly nestle in the tree, which, fruitful in excellence, puts forth the flowers of magnanimity and the leaves of merit, and rises with the trunk of modesty from the root of honour.

Mait.—(*Apart.*) Figurative indeed. (*Aloud.*) What else?

Vas.—What brings you hither?

Mait.—I will tell you:—Charudatta presents his respects to you.

Vas.—With respect I receive his commands.

Mait.—He desires me to say, that he has lost your golden casket; it was impledged by him at play, and the keeper of the tables, a servant of the prince, is gone, no one knows whither.

Att.—Lady, you are in luck; the grave Charudatta turned gambler.

Vas.—(*Apart.*) How? the casket has been stolen, and he says it was lost at play. Yet, even in this I love him.

Mait.—As the accident cannot now be helped, he

requests, in lieu of the casket, you will accept this string of diamonds.

Vas.—(*Apart.*) Shall I show him the ornaments? (*considering.*) No, not so.

Mait.—Will you not receive this equivalent?

Vas.—(*Smiling.*) Why not, Maitreya? (*Takes and puts it to her heart.*) But how is this? do drops of nectar fall from the mango-tree after it has shed its blossoms? My good friend, tell that sad gambler, Charudatta, that, I shall call upon him in the evening.

Mait.—(*Apart.*) So, so; she intends to get more out of him, I suppose. (*Aloud.*) I shall so inform him, madam. (*Apart.*) I wish he was rid of this previous acquaintance. [*Exit.*

Vas.—Here, girl, take the jewels and attend me to Charudatta.

Att.—But look, madam, look! a sudden storm is gathering.

Vas.—No matter.

> Let the clouds gather and dark night descend,
> And heavy fall unintermitted showers;
> I heed them not, wench, when I haste to seek
> His presence, whose loved image warms my heart.—
> Take charge of these, and lightly trip along.
> [*Exit.*

END OF THE FOURTH ACT.

ACT V.

CHARUDATTA'S GARDEN.

Enter CHARUDATTA (*looking up*).

A heavy storm impends : the gathering gloom
Delights the peafowl and distracts the swan,
Not yet prepared for periodic flight ;
And these deep shades contract with sad despondence
The heart that pines in absence. Through the air,
A rival Kesava, the purple cloud
Rolls stately on, girt by the golden lightning,
As by his yellow garb, and bearing high
The long white line of storks, the God's pure shell :
From the dark womb, in rapid fall descend
The silvery drops, and glittering in the gleam,
Shot from the lightning, bright and fitful, sparkle
Like a rich fringe rent from the robe of heaven.
The firmament is filled with scattered clouds,
And, as they fly before the wind, their forms,
As in a picture, image various shapes,
The semblances of storks and soaring swan

Of dolphins and the monsters of the deep,
Of dragons vast, and pinnacles, and towers.
The spreading shade, methinks, is like the host
Of Dhritarashtra shouting loud in thunder.
Yon strutting peacock welcomes its advance,
Like proud Duryodhan, vaunting of his might :
From its dread enmity, the Koil flies,
Like luckless Yudhishthira, by the dice
Bereaved of power, and scatter wild the swans'
Like the proscribed and houseless Pandavas,
Wandering from home and every comfort far,
Through paths untrod, till then, and realms unknown.
Maitreya long delays. Will not to-day
Apprise me of the issue of his visit ?

[*Retires.*

Enter MAITREYA.

What a rapacious, mean wretch is this harlot! Scarcely a word did she say, but, without any ceremony, pounced upon the necklace. With all her pomp and parade, she could not say to me, my good friend, Maitreya, take a little refreshment ; not even so much as to offer me a draught of water—her wealth is positively all thrown away upon her. It is very true, there is no lotus that has not a stalk ; no trader that is not a cheat ; there is not a goldsmith that is not a thief ; there never was village meeting without a quarrel; and there never will be a harlot without rapacity: these are things that alway go together. I shall threfore dissuade my worthy friend from his infatuation. Ha! yonder I see him in the garden. Health and prosperity to Charudatta!

Char.—(*Comes forward.*) Welcome, my good friend; Maitreya, sit down.

Mait.—I am seated. (*Sits.*)

Char.—Now, my good friend, your news?

Mait.—It is all over.

Char.—How so? does she refuse the proeffred gems?

Mait.—We have no such luck; she put her soft hands to her forehead, and then laid hold of the necklace.

Char.—Then, why do you complain?

Mait.—Why? reason enough. We have made a pretty job of it; to lose a necklace worth the four seas, for a thing of little value, and one we neither ate, nor drank, and which a thief carried off.

Char.—You reason idly.

> The pledge was here deposited in trust,
> And for that trust a costly price was due.

Mait.—I have another cause of complaint. She made signs to her damsels, and they covered their faces with their veils and made me their merriment. I beg, therefore, that you will desist from such unbecoming intercouse. A courtesan is like a thorn that has run into your foot; you cannot even get rid of it without pain; and it is indisputably true, that wherever a harlot, an elephant, a scribe, a mendicant, a spy, or a jackass, find admission, they are sure to do mischief.

Char.—Enough of this unmerited reviling.

My fallen fortunes are a sure protection.
The fiery steed bounds fleetly o'er the plain
Till fading breath retards his lagging course;
So man's desires first urge his heedless path,
But soon exhausted shrink into his bosom.
Believe me, friend, a female of this order,
A true wealth-hunter, troubles not the poor:
(*Apart.*) She, she, alone, bestows her love on merit.
(*Aloud.*) We are by wealth abandoned, and by her.

Mait.—(*Apart.*) This love is the devil: he turns up his eyes and sighs from the very bottom of his heart. I see plainly my advice to him to conquer his passion only serves to confirm it. (*Aloud.*) She desired me to say, she intends paying you a visit this evening. I suspect she is not satisfied with the necklace, and intends to demand something more valuable.

Char.—Well, let her come; she shall depart contended.

Enter KUMBHILAKA, *Vasantasena's Servant.*

I wish every one to take notice, that the harder it rains, the more thoroughly do I get ducked, and the colder the wind that blows down my back, the more do my limbs shiver. A pretty situation for a man of my talents; for one who can play the flute with seven holes, the vina with seven strings, can sing like a jackass, and who acknowledges no musical superior, except perhaps Tamburu or Narada. Vasantasena sends me to Charudatta's house. (*Advances.*) There is Charudatta in the garden, and that dunderhead Maitreya with him. I must throw out a signal to him. (*Throws a clod of earth at Maitreya.*)

Mait.—Holloa! who pelts me with a pellet, like a kapittha tree in an orchard?

Char.—It was probably thrown down in their sport by the pigeons that tenant the top of the garden wall.

Mait.—Wait a while, you saucy son of a slave, and with this stick I will knock you off the wall, like a ripe mango from the tree.

Char.—Sit down, sit down; fright not the gentle bird, nor chase him from his mate.

Kum.—The blockhead! he sees the pigeons and cannot see me. I must give him another salutation. (*Throws another clod.*)

Mait.—Hey, again! (*Looks up.*) O Kumbhilaka! is it you? Wait a while, and I will come to you. (*Goes to the door.*) Come in; how fares it?

Kum.—I salute you, sir.

Mait.—And what brings you here in such foul weather?

Kum.—She sent me.

Mait.—And who is she?

Kum.—She—she—she.

Mait.—She—she—she! What are you sputtering about, like an old miser when things are dear? Who—who—who?

Kum.—Hoo—hoo—hoo! What are you too-whooing about, like an owl that has been sacred from a sacrifice?

Mait.—Speak out, man, intelligibly.

Kum.—I will; but first I'll give you something to guess.

Mait.—I shall give you a box of the ears, I believe.

Kum.—Never mind that. In which season, pray, does the mango blossom?

Mait.—In the season of Grishma to be sure, you blockhead!

Kum.—Blockhead yourself! it does no such thing.

Mait.—Hey, how is that? I must ask my friend. Stop a moment. (*Goes to Charudatta.*) Pray, sir, in which season does the mango blossom?

Char.—Why, you simpleton, in Vasanta.

Mait.—(*To Kumb.*) Why, you simpleton, the mango blossoms in Vasanta.

Kum.—Very well. Now answer me one more question: Who guards wealthy towns?

Mait.—Why, the town guard, to be sure.

Kum.—No; that is not it.

Mait.—No? Let me see. (*Aside.*) I must consult Charudatta. Pray, sir, who guards wealthy towns?

Char.—The Sena undoubtedly.

Mait.—(*To Kum.*) The Sena undoubtedly.

Kum.—Very well; now put your answers together; quick, quick!

Mait.—Ha, I have it! Vasantasena.

Kum.—She is here.

Mait.—I must apprise my friend. Sir, we have a dun here.

Char.—Here? a dun in my house?

Mait.—I do not know anything about the house, but there is one at the door. Vasantasena is arrived.

Char.—Nay, now you jest?

Mait.—If you do not believe me, ask this fellow. Here, you Kumbhilaka!

Kum.—(*Advancing.*) Sir, I salute you.

Char.—You are welcome; tell me, is Vasantasena here?

Kum.—She is, sir.

Char.—Never be grateful message unrewarded this for your pains. (*Gives him his garment.*)

Kum.—(*Bows.*) I shall inform my mistress.

[*Exit.*

Mait.—Now, I hope you are satisfied. To come out in such weather; you can have no doubt what brings her.

Char.—I do not feel quite confident.

Mait.—Depend upon it, I am right; the casket was worth more than the necklace, and she comes for the difference.

Char.—(*Apart.*) She shall be gratified.

[*They retire.*

(*Outside of the Garden.*)

Enter VASANTASENA *splendidly dressed, attended by the* VITA, *A Female Servant, and one carrying a large umbrella.*

Att.—Lady, upon the mountain's brow, the clouds
Hang dark and drooping, as the aching heart
Of her who sorrows for her absent lord;
Their thunders rouse the peafowl, and the sky
Is agitated by their wings, as fanned
By thousand fans with costly gems inchased.
The chattering frog quaffs the pellucid drops
That cleanse his miry jaws. The peahen shrieks
With transport, and the Nipa freshly blooms.
The moon is blotted by the driving scud,
As is the saintly character by those
Who wear its garb to veil their abject lives;
And like the damsel whose fair fame is lost
In ever-changing loves, the lightning, true
To no one quarter, flits along the skies.

Vas.—You speak it well, my friend: to me it seems—
The jealous night, as with the gloom she wantons,

Looks on me as a rival bride, and dreading
I may disturb her pleasures, stops my path
And bids me angrily my steps retrace.

Att.—Reply with courage, chide her to submission.

Vas.—Reviling is the weakness of our sex,
And but of small avail,—I heed her not.
Let the clouds fall in torrents, thunder roar,
And heaven's red bolt dash fiery to the ground,
The dauntless damsel faithful love inspires,
Treads boldy on, nor dreads the maddening storm.

Vita.—Like an invading prince, who holds his court
Within the city ol his humbled foe,
Yon mighty cloud, advancing with the wind,
With store of arrowy shower, with thundering drums,
And blazing streamers, marches to assail
In his own heavens the monarch of the night.

Vas.— Nay, nay, not so ; I rather read it thus :
The clouds, that like unwieldly elephants
Roll their inflated masses grumbling on,
Or whiten with the migratory troop
Of hovering cranes, teach anguish to the bosom.
The stork's shrill cry sounds like the plaintive tabor
To her who, while she wanders o'er its parchment,

Is lost in musings of her lord's return,
And every tone that hails the rainy season,
Falls on her heart like brine upon a wound.

Vita.—Behold, where yonder ponderous cloud assumes
The stature of the elephant, the storks
Entwine a fillete for his front, and waves
The lightning, like a chouri o'er his head.

Vas.— Observe, my friend, the day is swallowed up
By these deep shades, dark as the dripping leaf
Of the tamala tree, and, like an elephant
That cowering shuns the battle's arrowy sleet,
So shrinks the scattering ant-hill from the shower.
The fickle lightning darts such brilliant rays,
As gleam from golden lamps in temples hung,
Whilst, like the consort of an humble lord,
The timid moonlight peeps amidst the clouds.

Vita.—There, like a string of elephants, the clouds
In regular file, by lightning fillets bound,
Move slowly at their potent god's commands
The heavens let down a silver chain to earth.
The earth, that shines with buds and sheds sweet odours,
Is pierced with showers, like diamond-shafted darts
Launched from the rolling mass of deepest blue,
Which heaves before the breeze and foams with flame ;

Like ocean's dark waves by the tempest driven,
And tossing high their flashing surge to shore.

Vas.—Hailed by the peafowl with their shrillest cries,
By the pleased storks delightedly caressed,
And by the provident swans with anxious eye
Regarded, yonder rests one threatening cloud.
Involving all the atmosphere in gloom.

Vita.—The countenance of heaven is close concealed,
By shades the lightning scant irradiates.
The day and night confusedly intermix,
And all the lotus eyes of either close,
The world is lulled to slumber by the sound
Of falling waters, sheltered by the clouds
That countless crowd the chambers of the sky.

Vas.—The stars are all extinct, as fades the memory
Of kindness in a bad man's heart. The heavens
Are shorn of all their radiance, as the wife
Her glory loses in her husband's absence.
In sooth, I think the firmament dissolves :
Melted by Indra's scorching bolt it falls
In unexhausted torrents. Now the cloud
Ascends—now stoops—now roars aloud in thunder—
Now sheds its streams—now frowns with deeper gloom,
Full of fantastic change, like one new raised
By fortune's fickle favours.

Vita.— Now the sky
With lightning flames, now laughs with whitening storks—

Now glows with Indra's painted bow, that hurls
Its hundred shafts—now rattles with his bolt—
Now loud it chafes with rushing winds, and now
With clustering clouds, that roll their spiry folds
Like sable snakes along—it thickens dark,
As if 'twere clothed with vapours, such as spread
When incense soars in curling wreaths to heaven.

Vas.—Shame on thee, cloud, that seekest to
affright me
With thy loud threats, and with thy watery shafts
Wouldst stay my progress, hastening to my love,
Indra! I voilate no vows to thee,
That thou shouldst thunder angrily reproof;
It ill becomes thee to obstruct my path.
Draw off thy clouds in pity to my passion,
If ever thou wert conscious of affection,
And for Ahalya wore a husband's form.
Or be it so—rage on—still pour thy deluge,
And launch thy hundred-shafted bolt, in vain.
Thou canst not stop the faithful maid that flies
To lose her terrors in a lover's arms.
If the clouds roar—e'en be it so—it is
Their nature—all of man is ever savage.
But gentle lightning, how canst thou not know
The cares that agitate the female bosom?

Vita.—Enough—she now befriends us, like a lamp
That glows in Indra's palace, like a banner,
Whose white folds wave upon a mountain's brow,

Or like the gold cord on Airavat's breast,
She gleams and shows you where your lord resides.

Vas.—Is this the mansion ?

Vita.—It is ; I will announce your coming.

Ho there ! inform the worthy Charudatta,
A lady at his door awaits ; her locks
Are drenched with rain, her gentle nerves are shaken
By angry tempests, and her delicate feet
By cumbering mire and massy anklets wearied,
She pauses to refresh with cooling streams.

Char.—(*To Maitreya.*) Hear you, my friend ?

Mait.—As you command. (*Opens the door.*)
Health to you, my lady.

Vas.—Sir, I salute you. (*To the* Vita.) Here let the umbrella-bearer wait upon you.

Vita.—(*Apart.*) A hint for me, I take it, to withdraw. I shall obey you.

[*Exit.*

Vas.—Now, good Maitreya, where is your gambler

Mait.—(*Apart.*) Gambler indeed ! my friend is much honoured by the appellation. There he sits, madam, in the arbour.

Vas.—In the arbour—is it dry ?

Mait.—Quite ; there is nothing to eat or drink in it : enter, enter.

Vas.—(*To her Servant.*) What shall I say ?

Ser.—Gambler, good evening to you.

Vas.—Shall I be able?

Ser.—Opportunity will give you courage.

Mait.—Enter, lady, enter.

Vas.—(*Enters, and approaching Charudatta throws flowers at him.*) Gambler, good evening to you.

Char.—(*Rising.*) Vasantasena!

Lady, believe me, every day has passed
Most heavily, and sleepless dragged my nights,
But now your charms appear my cares are over,
And this glad evening terminates my sorrows.
Then welcome, welcome to my bower—be
seated.

Mait.—Take a sit, madam. (*They sit.*)

Char.—Maitreya, from the flowers that grace her ear
Surcharged with rain, the drops have trickled
down
And bathed her bosom, like a young prince
installed
The partner of imperial honours. Haste and bring
A vest of finest texture to replace
This chilling robe.

Fem. Att.—Stop, Maitreya, I will assist my mistress if you please. (*Does so.*)

Mait.—(*To Charudatta.*) Now, sir, shall I inquire he object of this visitation?

Char.—Do so.

Aait.—And now, madam, may I ask what

has brought you out, on such a vile, dark, rainy evening?

Att.—Lady, here's a smart Brahman!

Vas.—Nay, an able one, so call him.

Att.—My mistress, sir, wished to be informed of the real value of the necklace that you brought her.

Mait.—There, I said so. (*To Charudatta.*)

Att.—The reason why she wishes to know is that she has pledged it at play, and the keeper of the tables, being a servant of the prince's, is gone on some duty, and is not to be found.

Mait.—Umph, tit for tat.

Att.—Until he can be heard of, and the necklace be redeemed, be pleased to accept in lieu of it this golden casket. (*Gives him the casket stolen by Sarvilaka. Maitreya examines it.*) You examine it very closely; one would suppose you had seen it before.

Mait.—It is very curious: the cunning of the workman beguiles my eyes.

Att.—No, your eyesight is defective, it is the very same.

Mait.—Indeed! my worthy friend, here is the gold casket again that was stolen from our house.

Char.—No, no, it is but a requital
Of our attempt to substitute a change
Of that entrusted to us; that is the truth,
Howe'er the casket may appear the same.

Mait.—It is the same! I swear it, as I am a Brahman.

Char.—I am glad of it.

Mait.—Shall I ask how they came by it?

Char.—Why not?

Mait.—(*Whispers the Attendant.*) Is it so indeed?

Att.—(*Whispers Maitreya.*) It is indeed.

Char.—What is? why leave us out?

Mait.—(*Whispers Charudatta.*) This it is indeed,

Char.—(*To the Attendant.*) Is this indeed, my girl, the golden casket?

Att.—It is the same, sir.

Char.—A pleasing speech with me should never go
Without fit recompence,—accept this ring.

(*Looks at his hand; finds he has no ring; expresses shame.*)

Vas.—How well he merits wealth.

Char.—(*Apart.*) How can that man be said to live, who lives
A pauper, and whose gratitude and wrath
Are barren both. The bird whose wings are clipped—
The leafless tree—the desiccated pool—
The desolate mansion, and the toothless snake—
Are all meet emblems of the hapless wretch
Whose festive hours no fond associates grace,
And brightest moments yield no fruit to others.

Mait.—(*To him.*) Enough, enough, there is no good in fretting.—(*Aloud.*) But, lady, I shall thank you to restore me my bathing-gown, in which the casket was wrapped at the time it was stolen.

Vas.—And now, worthy Charudatta, believe me when the casket was stolen, it was quite unnecessary to send me this equivalent.

Char.—Had I not sent it, lady, who had trusted me?

I and my wealth in most men's eyes are equal,
And poverty will ever be suspected.

Mait.—A word, damsel; do you mean to take up your abode here?

Att.—Fie, Maitreya, how you talk!

Mait.—My good friend, the clouds are collecting again, and the heavy drops drive us from our easy seats.

Char.—'Tis true, they penetrate the yielding clouds

As sink the lotus stalk into its bed
Of plashy mire, and now again they fall
Like tears celestial from the weeping sky
That wails the absent moon.
The clouds, like Baladeva's vesture, dark,
Profusely shed a shower of precious pearls
From Indra's treasury—the drops descend
Rapid and rattling, like the angry shafts
From Arjun's quiver, and of like purity

As are the hearts of holy men.
See, lady, how the firmament, anointed
With unguent of the black tamala's hue,
And fanned by fragrant and refreshing gales,
Is by the lightning tenderly embraced,
As the loved lord whom fearlessly she flies to.

[*Vasantasena's gesticulates affection, and falls into Charudatta's arms.*

Char.—(*Embracing her.*)
Louder and louder still roar on, ye clouds !
To me the sound is music, by your aid
My love is blessed, my heart expands with hope.

Mait.—(*As to the cloud.*) You foul-faced rascal, you are a worthless reprobate, to have so scared her ladyship by your lightnings.

Char.—Reprove it not, for let the rain descend,
The heavens still lour, and wide the lightnings launch
A hundred flames ; they have befriended me,
And given me her for whom I sighed in vain.
Happy, thrice happy, they whose walls enshrine
The fair they worship, and whose arms enfold
Her shivering beauties in their warm embrace.
Look, love, the bow of Indra arches heaven ;
Like outspread arms, extended with fatigue,
It stretches forth ; the yawning sky displays

Its lightning tongue—its chin of clouds hangs
low—
All woo us to repose—let us retire : the drops
Fall musical, and pattering on the leaves
Of the tall palm, or on the pebbly ground,
Or in the brook, emit such harmony
As sweetly wakens from the voice and lute

[*Exit.*

END OF THE FIFTH ACT.

ACT VI.

CHARUDATTA'S HOUSE.

Inside and Outside as before.

Inside.—Enter FEMALE SERVANT.

Hey-day! does not my lady mean to rise this morning? I shall make bold to call her. Madam!

Enter VASANTASENA.

Look, madam, it is day.

Vas.—How! why the morning dawns as darkling as if it still were night.

Ser.—It is morning to us, though it may be night to you, madam.

Vas.—Where is your gambler?

Ser.—Charudatta, madam, having given his orders to Vardhamana, is gone to the old flower garden Puspakaranda.

Vas.—What orders gave he?

Ser.—To get your litter ready.

Vas.—Whither am I to go?

Ser.—Whither Charudatta is gone.

Vas.—Very well, girl, I have scarcely yet beheld him; to-day will gratify me with his sight. What! did I find my way into the inner apartments?

Ser.—Not only that, madam, but into every one's heart.

Vas.—I fear me his family are vexed.

Ser.—They will be vexed then only when—

Vas.—When?

Ser.—When you depart.

Vas.—Then is it my place first to be afflicted. Here, girl, take this necklace to my respected sister, and say from me, I am Charudatta's handmaid and your slave, then be this necklace again the ornament of that neck to which it of right belongs.

Ser.—But, lady, Charudatta will be displeased.

Vas.—Go, do as I bid you; he will not be offended.

Ser.—As you command.

[*Exit, and returns presently.*

Madam, thus says the lady: you are favoured by the son of my lord; it is not proper for me to accept this necklace. Know that the only ornament I value is my husband.

Enter RADANIKA *and* CHARUDATTA'S CHILD.

Rad.—Come along, my child, let us ride in your cart.

Child.—I do not want this cart; it is only of clay—I want one of gold.

Rad.—And where are we to get the gold, my little man? Wait till your father is rich again, and then he will buy you one: now this will do. Come, let us go and see Vasantasena. Lady, I salute you.

Vas.—Welcome Radanika. Whose charming boy is this? although so ill-attired, his lovely face quite fascinates me.

Rad.—This is the Rohasena, the son of Charudatta.

Vas.—(*Stretching out her arms.*) Come here, my little dear, and kiss me. (*Takes him on her lap.*) How like his father!

Rad.—He is like him too in disposition. Charudatta dotes on him.

Vas.—Why does he weep?

Rad.—The child of our neighbour had a golden cart, which this little fellow saw and wanted. I made him this of clay, but he is not pleased with it, and is crying for the other.

Vas.—Alas, alas, this little creature is already mortified by another's prosperity. O fate! thou sportest with the fortunes of kind, like drops of water trembling on the lotus leaf. Don't cry, my good boy, and you shall have a gold cart.

Child.—Radanika, who is this?

Cas.—A handmaid purchased by your father's merits.

Rad.—This is your lady mother, child.

Child.—You tell me untruth, Radanika, how can this be my mother when she wears such fine things?

Vas.—How piteous a speech for so soft a tongue! (*Takes off her ornaments in tears.*) Now I am your mother. Here, take this trinket and go buy a gold cart.

Child.—Away, I will not take it, you cry at parting with it.

Vas.—(*Wiping her eyes.*) I weep no more. Go, love, and play. (*Fills his cart with her jewels.*) There go, get you a golden cart.

[*Exit Radanika with Child.*

Outside.—Enter VARDHAMANA *with the litter.*

Radanika, let the lady know the carriage waits for her at the private door.

Inside.—Enter RADANIKA.

Lady, the covered litter attends you at the back-door.

Vas.—Stay a moment whilst I prepare myself.

Rad.—Stay a moment, Vardhamana, the lady is not quite ready.

Var.—And I have forgotten the cushions of the carriage. Wait till I bring them. These oxen are not steady enough to be left; I will drive back and return presently.

[*Exit with the car.*

Vas.—(*Inside.*) Bring me my things, girl, I can put them on myself. (*Dressing.*)

Outside.—Enter STHAVARAKA, *the Servant of* SAMSTHANAKA *with a carriage.*

I am ordered by the king's brother-in-law, my master, to take this vehicle with all speed to the old flower-garden, Pushpakaranda. Come up, come up, (*Looking.*) Why, the road is blocked with country carts. Holloa there! get out of the way. What says he, whose carriage is it? Samsthanaka's, the king's brother-in-law; quick, quick! clear the road. (*Drives on.*) Who should that be, that looked at me so curiously, and then stole off down another road, like an nnlucky gambler that runs away from the table-keeper? No matter; I must get on. Holloa you! out of the way there! What! Come and give you a turn of the wheel: it sticks, does it! It is very likely that the king's brother-in-law's man shall assist you to atwist of the wheel. Oh, it is a poor miserable rustic, and alone too. Well, I will lend you a hand. This is Charudatta's postern door. I can leave the carriage here in the meantime, so stop there, I will be with you.

[*Exit, leaving the carriage at the door.*

Ser.—(*Inside.*) I hear the wheels: the carriage is returned, madam.

Vas.—Quick, quick! I feel strangely flurried;—open the door.

Ser.—'Tis done.

Vas.—Go you to rest.

Ser.—As you command.

[*Exit.*

Vas.—(*Goes forth and ascends Samsthanaka's carriage.*) My right eye twinkles; never mind, meeting Charudatta will prove it causeless. (*Draws the curtains.*)

Re-enter STHAVARAKA.

I have helped him, and now have a clear road. (*Mounts and proceeds.*) Why, the vehicle is heavier than it was, or it appears so to me, because I am tired with helping yonder cart. No matter, I must proceed ;—come up.

(*Behind the scenes.*)

Who ho, there, guards ! look to it ; be vigilant—sleep not at your posts : the cowherd has burst his bonds, slain his goaler, and broken from his prison ; he is now in flight—seize him ! seize him !

Stha.—Here's a precious uproar ? I had better get clear of it. [*Exit with the car.*

Enter ARYAKA *as in flight.*

I have swam thus far to shore, and from the wave
Of fell captivity, the tyrant Palaka
Had plunged me into, once more have escaped.
Like a tame elephant from his stall broke loose,
I drag along with me my ruptured chain.
Sarvilaka, my friend, to thee I owe
My freedom and my life. Condemned to pine
In the dark dungeon, where the monarch's fears,
Awakened by the sage's prophecies,
Cast me to die, dragged from my humble home. (*Weeps.*)
What crime have I committed, to be sought
Thus like a venomous snake, to be destroyed !
If such my destiny, as is foretold,

In what consists my guilt? be fate accused—
Fate is a power resistless, and a king
Alike demands our homage. Who contends
With force superior? mine is to submit.
Yet for my life I fly—ah! whither now
Shall I find refuge? See, yon door invites me!
Some good man's gate is open, and like me
Its withered fortunes, for the bolt is broken,
And the broad valves are shattered and de-
cayed:
It calls me kinsman, and it proves my friend.

VARDHAMANA *returning with Charudatta's carriage (without).*

Come up, come up!

(ARYAKA *listening.*)

A carriage, and it comes this way.
If it should be a village car, not frighted
With passengers uncourteous, or a vehicle
For women, but its fair load not received,
Or be it travelling from the town, and fit
For decent occupancy—be it but empty
And unattended, and my fate befriends me.

Enter VARDHAMAN *with the carriage.*

What ho! Radanika, I have got the cushions, and the car is ready: so inform the lady Vasantasena; tell her to ascend, that I may set off for Pushparandaka.

Ary.—It is a courtesana's, and travelling outwards;

'Tis fortunate—I mount. (*Advances.*)

Vard.—(*Listening and hearing the ringing of Aryaka's chain.*) I hear the sound of the anklets, she is hear. Get up quick, lady; get up behind; the cattle are impatient, I must not leave them.

ARYAKA *ascends.*

Vard.—The sound has ceased, and the carriage is heavier than it was: her ladyship must be seated, so here goes.

[*Exit with the car.*

Scene—ANOTHER STREET.

Enter VIRAKA, *Captain of the Watch, attended.*

Halloa! Jaya, Jayamana, Chandanaka, Mangala, Pushpabhadra, and the rest, follow quick, and we shall catch the villain, though he has broken his prison and the king's slumbers. Here, fall in; go you to the east gate, you to the west, you to the south, you to the north: on this pile of broken bricks, Chandanaka and I will stop and look about us. What ho, Chandanaka!

Enter CHANDANAKA *attended, in a bustle.*

What ho! Viraka, Visalaya, Bhimangada, Dandakala, Dandasura, quick, quick! never let the king's fortune move off into another family: away with you, search the streets, the roads, the gardens, the houses, the stalls, the markets, and let no suspicious corner pass unexamined:—away! (*Exeunt guard.*) Well, Viraka, what say you? will any one convey this runaway cowboy out of peril? Verily, whoever dares to carry him off whilst Chandanaka lives, had better have had at his birth the Sun in the eighth mansion, the Moon in the fourth, Venus in the sixth, Mars in the fifth, Jupiter in the sixth, and Saturn in the ninth.

Vir.—He must have had assistance, no doubt, valiant Chandanaka; but, by your heart, I swear that he escaped before dawn.

Enter VARDHAMANA *with the car and* ARYAKA *concealed.*

Chan.—What ho, there! see, see, a covered litter passes along the high road; inquire whose it is and whither going.

Vir.—What ho, driver! stop and answer. Whose vehicle is this; who is inside; and where are you going?

Var.—The carriage belongs, sir, to the worthy Charudatta; the lady Vasantasena is inside, and I am carrying her to the old flower-garden to meet Charudatta there.

Chan.—Let him pass.

Vir.—Without inspection?

Chan.—Undoubtedly.

Vir.—On what surety?

Chan.—Charudatta's.

Vir.—Who is Charudatta, or who is Vasantasena, that the carriage is to pass free?

Chan.—Do you not know who they are? If you know not Charudatta and Vasantasena, you know not the moon and moonlight when you see them together in the skies. Who is there that is not acquainted with that moon of mildness, that lotus of merit, that liberator from sorrow, that pearl,—the essence of the four oceans,—Charudatta? Both are of the highest respectability, the boast and pride of the city, the lovely Vasantasena and virtuous Charudatta.

Vir.—Phoo-phoo! I know them well enough, but in the discharge of my duty my own father must be a stranger.

Aryaka.—(*In the car.*)

> Yon Viraka has ever been my foe,
> Chandanaka my friend; the two are ill
> Associated in a common duty.
> One fire the marriage ceremony asks,
> Another serves to light the funeral pile.

Chan.—Well, careful captain, high in the king's confidence, do you then look into the carriage, I will look to the cattle.

Vir.—Nay, you are in command and confidence as well as I am; do you inspect it.

Chan.—What I see is in fact seen by you.

Vir.—Not only by me, but by the king himself.

Chan.—Holloa, you! stop the car.

Ary.—Unfortunately, I am discovered; I have no sword;
Like Bhima then I must employ my hands;
Better to die than be again a captive.
Yet, hold, it is not despair.

(*Chandanaka looks into the car.*)

Ary.—Protection!—I am at your mercy.

Chan.—Fear not, who seeks protection will obtain it.

Ary.—Fortune forsakes, tribe, family, and friends
Discard; and all men scorn the coward slave,
Who fears to grant protection to the wretched.

Chan.—How! Aryaka!
Like the poor bird that, flying from the hawk,
Falls in the fowler's net, art thou my prize,
And, luckless wretch, appliest to me for aid?
He is in Charudatta's car, his crime
Is none; Sarvilaka, to whom I owe
My own life, is his friend; but then—
My duty to the prince. What's to be done?
E'en be it so—I told him not to fear;
The words have passed my lips. I must befriend him,
Come on't what will: the succour once assured,
Must be extended, though the end be ruin.

(*Returning.*)—I have seen—Arya—Arya Vasantasena, and she says right; it is indecorous to detain her on the road when she has an appointment with Charudatta.

Vir.—Excuse me, Chandanaka; I have some doubts in the matter.

Chan.—How so?

Vir.—You seem flurried, and it was with some indistinctness you call out first Arya, then corrected yourself, and said Aryá Vasantasena. I have some strange misgivings.

Chan.—Misgivings, indeed! why, you, know, we of the South are not very nice in our articulation, and are apt to confound sounds. Being accustomed to speak the dialects of a number of barbarous and other outcast tribes, it would be all the same to us, whether it was Arya or Arya, masculine, feminine, or neuter.

Vir.—Ah, well—I shall take a look myself: such are the prince's orders—he knows he can trust me.

Chan.—And am I not trusted by him?

Vir.—True, but I must obey his orders.

Chan.—(*Apart.*) If it is known that the cowherd was seized in Charudatta's carriage, he will be involved in the punishment. I must give my friend here a specimen of Carnatic eloquence. (*Aloud.*) Hark ye, Viraka, I have already inspected the carriage; why are you to inspect it again? who the deuce are you, I should like to know?

Vir.—And who are you, pray?

Chan.—I'll tell you: one entitled to your most profound respect: you should recollect your caste.

Vir.— caste, what is it then?

Chan.—Oh, I do not wish to say.

Vir.—Say, say if you like, and if you don't like it, leave it alone.

Chan.—I do not wish to shame you: let it be; it is not worth while to break a wood apple.

Vir.—Nay, I insist.

[*Chandanaka intimates by signs that Viraka is a Chamar, or worker in leather.*

Vir.—It is false—I deny it.

Chan.—You were wont to carry a dead jackal in your hand, to replace dislocated joints, and to flourish a pair of shears; and you are now a general. A very pretty general!

Vir.—You are a most high and mighty hero, no doubt, far above your real origin.

Chan.—What was my origin?

Vir.—Excuse me.

Chan.—I defy you,—my caste is as pure as the moon.

Vir.—No doubt; vastly pure, when your mother was a tabor, your father a kettle-drum, and your brother a tamborine; but you—you are a general.

Chan.—I a Chamar, I Chandanaka, a Chamar; mighty well, mighty well! look by all means.

Vir.—Ho, driver! Stay till I inspect the car.

Viraka approaches it; Chandanaka seizes him by the hair, drags him back, throws him down and kicks him.

Vir.—(*Rising.*) What do you mean by this treatment of me?—but I will have vengence. If I have not your head severed from your body, and your limbs quartered and exposed in the public place, I am not Viraka. [*Exit.*

Chan.—Away to the palace, or the court. Complain; I care not. Who will heed such a dog as you? (*To Vardhamana.*) Quick, and if any one stops you, say the carriage has been inspected by Viraka and Chandanaka. Lady Vasantasena, I give you this as a passport. (*Gives Aryaka a sword.*)

Ary.—My right arm throbs as I receive the weapon.
Fortune is friendly to me. I am safe.

Chan.—The Arya will remember Chandana.
I ask not this for favour, but in love.

Ary.—Fate has this day made Chandana my friend.
If the saint's prophecy should be fulfilled,
I will remember well how much I owe him.

Chan.—May every deity befriend your cause;
And may your enemies before you fall,
Like Sumbha and Nisumbha by the wrath
Of the resentful goddess. Drive on
[*Exit Vardhamana with Car.*

Chan.—(*Looking after it.*) Ha! yonder I see my friend Sarvilaka follows the carriage. Well, may they prosper. Viraka will now to the prince and tell how he has been handled: I must collect my friends and relatives, and follow him without delay. [*Exit.*

END OF THE SIXTH ACT.

ACT VII.

THE GARDEN PUSHPAKARANDA.

Enter CHARUDATTA *and* MAITREYA.

Mait.—How bravely the old garden looks.

Char.—'Tis true; like wealthy merchants are the trees.
Who spread in clustering flowers the choicest wares;
Amongst them busily the bees are straying
To gather tribute for the royal hive.

Mait.—Here is a fine block of stone; sit down on it.

Char.—(*Seated.*)—Vardhamana tarries long.

Mait.—I told him to make all possible haste.

Char.—Then why so tardy? Or the car rolls heavily;
Or it has broken down upon the way;
Or the old traces have been snapped; or lies
A tree across their path; or have they strayed
Another road, or are the beasts untractable?
Or have—oh, here he comes.

Enter VARDHAMANA *with the Car.*

Come up.

Ary.—(*In the car.*)—
Fled from the monarch's myrmidons, and cramped
By this vile fetter round my foot, I owe

My safety to this vehicle—where, like the cuckoo
Nursed in a stranger nest, I find concealment.
Now, far beyond the city, I am safe.
Shall I alight, and seek to gain a refuge
Amidst the dark recesses of these groves,
Or shall I dare encounter with the owner
Of this befriending car? 'Twere far more grateful
To meet with Charudatta, than to hear
His pity only as I darkling lurk
Among these shades. My new acquired liberty
Will yield him pleasure, and my wasted form
Will grow once more to vigour from the interview.

Var.—This is the place:—what ho! Maitreya.

Mait.—Welcome, Vardhamana; I have been looking out for you.

Var.—Well, here I am; and so is Vasantasena.

Mait.—But, you son of a slave, what has detained you so long?

Var.—Do not be angry, Maitreya. I was obliged to go back to find the cushions which I had at first forgot.

Char.—Well, well,—Maitreya, assist Vasantasena to alight.

Mait.—What! has she got fetters on her feet; that she cannot come down by herself? (*Goes to the Car and looks in.*) Holloa! what have we here? This is not Vasantasená—it is Vasantasena, I suppose.

Char.—Refrain your mirth, my friend; love ill-sustains
The least delay. I help her to alight. (*Rises.*)

Ary.—Here comes the worthy Charudatta;
Cheering his voice, and gentle is his aspect:
I need not fear.

Char.—(*Looking in.*)—How! who is this?
His arms are like the elephant's vast tusks—
His breasts, his shoulders, brawny as the lion's—
His eyes are coppery-red and roll in anger—
How should a person of such goodly presence
Bear fetters on his limbs? Who art thou, say?

Ary.—My name is Aryaka: to tend the herds
The duty I was born to: and to thee
I hither come, a suppliant for protection.

Char.—Art thou that Aryaka, our prince's fears
Dragged from his humble station to a prison?

Ary.—The same.

Char.—Fate, that has brought thee hither, is thy friend.
My life I may resign, but cannot turn
Away from one who sues to me for refuge.
Vardhamana, remove those fetters.

Var.—(*Obeys.*) The chains are off, sir.

Ary.—(*To Char.*) And chains more lasting by this aid imposed.

Mait.—Then now pray take yourself off too. Come, my good friend, now this gentleman is at large, I think we had better get home as quick as we can.

Char.—Fie on thy speech! what need of haste?

Ary.—Excuse me, Charudatta, that I mounted,
Nor sought permission first, into this car,

Char.—You have graced me by such courtsey.

Ary.—Have I your leave to leave you?

Char.—It is yours.

Ary.—I will descend.

Char.—Nay, friend, not so.
Your steps still labour from the weighty bond
So recently removed: besides, the car
Will unsuspected bear you on your way
Beyond our boundaries—pray keep your seat.

Ary.—As you direct.

Char.—Auspicious be your way
To join your friends.

Ary.—I hope I leave one here.

Char.—'Tis one who hopes to be remembered by you
In other times.

Ary.—Can I forget myself?

Char.—The gods protect your path.

Ary.—It is to you
I owe my safety.

Char.—Not so, you owe it
To your bright fortunes.

Ary.--Of the which, indeed,
I hold you as the cause.

Char.—But Palaka
Must still be heeded; and around he sends
A numerous guard, who may detain your steps.
Use no delay; but with all speed depart.

Ary.—To meet again. [*Exit.*

Char.—The deed that I have done will little please
The king, should it be kuown; and kings behold
Their subjects' actions by their spies, 'T were well
To leave this spot at once. Maitreya, cast
The fetters deep into this ancient well. (*His eyes throbbing.*)
'Tis sad to miss a meeting with my love
But that such chance to-day at least is hope-less
My left eye indicates; and without cause
A sudden langour creeps into my heart.
Let us leave this (*Going.*)]Ha, an evil omen!
A heretic approaches us (*Stops.*) Yet—hold—
Let him advance—we'll take another path.
[*Exit*

END OF THE SEVENTH ACT.

ACT VIII.

SCENE THE SAME.

Enter the SRAMANAKA, *or Bauddha mendicant, with a wet garment in his hand.*

SRAMANAKA (*sings*).

Be virtue, friends, your only store,
And restless appetite restrain
Beat meditation's drum, and sore
Your watch against each sense maintain
The thief that still in ambush lies,
To make devotion's wealth his prize.

Cast the five senses all away,
That triumph o'er the virtuous will
The pride of self-importance slay,
And ignorance remorseless kill:
So shall you safe the body guard,
And Heaven shall be your last reward.

Why shave the head and mow the chin
Whilst bristling follies choke the breast?
Apply the knife to parts within,
And heed not how deformed the rest:
The heart of pride and passion weed,
And then the man is pure indeed.

My cloth is heavy with the yet moist dye. I will

enter this garden belonging to the Raja's brother-in-law, and wash it in the pool, and then I shall proceed more lightly. (*Does so.*)

(*Behind.*) What, ho! you rascally Sramanaka, what are you doing there?

(*Sram.*) Alas, alas! here he is, Samsthanaka himself. He has been affronted by one mendicant, and whenever he meets another he sends him off with his nose slit like an ox. Where shall I fly to?—the lord Buddha be my refuge.

Enter SAMSTHANAKA *with the* VITA, *his sword drawn.*

Sams.—Stop, you vile vagabond, or off I take that head of thine, as they snap off the top of a red radish in a dram-shop. (*Beats him.*)

Vita.—Nay, nay, hold! beat not the poor wretch thus clad in the coloured garment of humility. This garden was intended by your excellency to be the seat of delight, and these trees were destined to afford shade and relief to the unsheltered; but now they are disappointed of their objects; they fail their promise, like the no longer hidden villainy of a scoundrel, and are only to be enjoyed at the risk of peril, like a new sovereignty disposed of before it is yet subdued.

Sram.—Mercy, sir; be my protector, my saviour.

Sams.—Hear him, the scoundrel, how he abuses me.

Vita.—How so?

Sams.—He calls me a shaver.

Vita.—Not so, he entreats you humbly.

Sams.—And what are you doing here?

Sram.—I was about to cleanse my garment in this pond.

Sams.—Villain, was the superlative garden given to me by my sister's husband, the Raja, for such a base purpose? Dogs drink here by day, and jackals by night: exalted in rank as I am, I do not bathe here, and shall you presume here to wash your foul and fetid rags;—but I shall make short work with you.

Vita.—In that case I suspect he will not have long followed the profession.

Sams.—How so?

Vita.—Observe: his head shines as if it had only been lately shaven; and his garment has been so little worn that there are no scars on his shoulder. The ochry dye has not yet fully stained the cloth, and the open web, yet fresh and flaccid, hangs loosely over his arms.

Sram.—I do not deny it, worthy sir; it is true I have but lately adopted the profession of a beggar.

Sams.—And why so? why did you not become a beggar as soon as you were born, you scoundrel? (*Beats him.*)

Sram.—Glory to Buddha.

Vita.—Enough, enough! now let him go. (*To the Sram.*) Away with you.

Sams.—Stop, stop! I must first ask leave.

Vita.—From whom?

Sams.—My own mind.

Vita.—Well, he is not gone.

Sams.—My life, my heart, my chick, my child, shall this fellow go or stay? Very well, my mind says:—

Vita.—What?

Sams.—He shall neither go, nor stay, nor move, nor breathe—let him fall down and be put to death.

Sram.—Glory to Buddha! mercy, mercy!

Vita.—Oh, let him go.

Sams.—On one condition.

Vita.—What is that?

Sams.—He shall take all the clay of this pool out without muddying the water; or shall make a pile of clean water and throw the mud aside.

Vita.—Absurd! You might as well ask for skins of stone, and meat from trees. This world is sadly burthened with fools.

[*Sram. gesticulates imprecations.*

Sams.—What does he mean?

Vita.—He blesses you.

Sams.—Speak my blessings.

Sram.—Be as prosperous as you are pious.

[*Exit Sram.*

Vita.—Come. come. to other thoughts direct your mind;
Look round the ground; mark these stately trees,
Which duly, by the king's command attended,
Put forth abundantly their fruits and flowers,

And clasped by twining creepers, they resemble
The manly husband and the tender wife.

Sams.—The ground is quite a picture, strewed with many-tinted flowers; the trees are bowed down with blossoms; the graceful creepers completely surmount even their tops; and the monkeys are sporting about like so many jack-fruits.

Vita.—Here let us take our seat.

Sams.—I am seated. And now, my good friend, trust me, I cannot help thinking of Vasantasena: she holds her place in my heart, and rankles like the abuse of a black guard.

Vita.—(*Aside.*)—To little purpose are these thoughts indulged:

So true it is—
The scorn of woman in ignoble breasts,
But adds fresh fuel to the scorching flame.
The manly heart disdain with scorn repays,
And soon subdues its unrequited passion.

Sams.—What hour is it? That fellow Sthavaraka was ordered to be here early; what can be the reason he does not make his appearance? It is almost noon; I feel hungry, and it is impossible to think of walking at this time of day. The sun is now in mid-heaven, and looks as fierce as an angry ape; and the ground is as dry and shrivelled as Gandhari looked when her hundred sons were slain.

Vita.—'Tis true: the cattle dozing in the shade
Let fall the unchamped fodder from their mouths:

The lively ape with slow and languid pace
Creeps to the pool to slake his parching thirst
In its now tepid waters; not a creature
Is seen upon the public road, nor braves
One solitary passenger the sun.
Perhaps the carriage from the heated track
Has turned aside, and waits a cooler hour.

Sams.—Very likely, I am left here to furnish a lodgment in my brains for the rays of the sun. The birds have all slunk into shelter amongst the branches, and passengers panting and breathing flame, are glad to mount the umbrella even in the shade. That fellow will not be here to-day; come, let us amuse ourselves: I will give you a song.

(*He sings.*)

There, sir, what say you to that?

Vita.—Say? That you are verily a Gandharba.

Sams.—How should I fail being so; I make a practice of taking asafœtida, cummin-seed, orris-root, treacle and ginger; my voice must necessarily be very sweet. I will give you another specimen. (*Sings.*)

There, what think you now?

Vita.—That you are a very Gandharba.

Sams.—I knew you would think so; but I take care to train myself suitably. I always feed upon meat presented to me by some of my slaves, and I have it fried in oil and ghee, and seasoned well with asafœtida and black pepper; that is your only diet for a sweet voice. Oh, that scoundrel, he will never arrive!

Vita.—Have patience: he will soon be here. (*They retire.*)

Enter STHAVARAKA *with the Car in which* VASANTASENA *is.*

Stha.—I am in a terrible fright; it is near noon; my master will be in a violent rage. Come up.

Vas.—(*In the car.*) Alas! alas! that is not Vardhamana's voice. Who can it be? Whose vehicle is this? Has Charudatta sent another car and servant to spare his own? Ha! my right eye throbs, my heart flutters, my sight is dim, everything forebodes misfortunes.

Sams.—Master, the car is here.

Vita.—How do you know?

Sams.—Do you not hear a snorting like an old hog's?

Vita.—You are right; here it is.

Sams.—How, my good fellow, Sthavaraka, are you come at last?

Stha.—Yes, sir.

Sams.—And the car?

Stha.—Here it is, sir.

Sams.—And the oxen?

Stha.—Here they are.

Sams.—And yourself?

Stha.—We are all together, your honour.

Sams.—Then drive in.

Stha.—Which way, sir?

Sams.—Here, where the wall is broken.

Stha.—It is impossible, sir: it will kill the beasts, smash the car, and I shall get my neck broken into the bargain.

Sams.—Do you recollect, sirrah, that I am the the king's brother-in-law: be the cattle killed, I can buy others; let the car smash, I can have another made; and if you break your neck, I must hire another driver.

Stha.—That is very true, your honour; the loss will be mine; I shall not be able to replace myself.

Sams.—I care not; drive in here, over the broken walls,

Stha.—Very well, sir, here goes. Break the car, go to pieces you and your driver; others are to be had, and I must report your fate to your master. (*Drives.*) How, all safe! There, sir, the carriage has come in.

Sams.—You see what a lying rogue you are, and no mischief.

Stha.—Very true, sir.

Sams.—Come, my friend, let us go to the car. You are my ever honoured teacher and master, precede: I know what is due to your dignity, ascend.

Vita.—I comply.

Sams.—Stop! stop! Did you make the carriage,

pray? I am the owner of it, and shall therefore get in the first.

Vita.—I did as you desired.

Sams.—Very possibly; but you erred in not requesting me to precede.

Vita.—Will your excellency be pleased to enter?

Sams.—That is right. I shall ascend. (*Getting up, returns hastily, and lays hold of the Vita in alarm.*) Oh dear! I am a lost man; there's a thief or a she-devil in the carriage! If a devil, we shall be robbed; if a thief, we shall be devoured alive!

Vita.—Fear not; how should a she-devil get into a bullock carriage? It was nothing but the shadow of Sthavaraka, I dare say, which, your eyes having been dazzled with the glare, you saw indistinctly, and mistook for a living figure.

Sams.—My poor Sthavaraka, are you alive?

Stha.—I rather think so, your honour.

Sams.—There certainly is a woman in the car,—look yourself. (*To the Vita.*)

Vita.—A woman! ha, ha!

Afraid to gaze upon the man of birth,
Who prides himself on my companionship,
They walk with downcast eyes, like shrinking cattle
That hang their heads against the driving rain.

Vas.—Alas, that odious wretch, the Raja's brother!
What will become of me—unhappy girl!

A luckless seed my coming hither sows
In the parched soil of my disastrous fate.

Sams.—That vile slave, not to have examined the carriage!—Come, master, look.

Vita.—I am going.

Sams.—Do jackals fly or crows run? Do men eat with their eyes and see with their teeth? So surely will I not stay here.

Vita.—(*Looking in.*) How! can it be?

What brings the doe into the tiger's den?
Or does the cygnet fly the distant mate,
Though bright as autumn's moon, to wed the crow
It is not well; or has your mother's will,
On gain intent, compelled you to come hither
To earn reluctant presents late despised?
You are by nature false, your fickle tribe,
I told you truly, ever are prepared
To yield their blandishments to those they scorn.

Vas.—Believe it not of me—I was deceived,
Mistook the vehicle, and the fatal error
Has brought me hither. Oh, befriend—protect me!

Vas.—I will befriend you, banish every fear,
I will beguile this blockhead. (*Descends.*)
There is indeed a devil in the car.

Sams.—Indeed! how happens it she has not run

off with you? If a thief, how is it she has not eaten you up?

Vita.—Never mind.

Hence to Ujjayin a line of groves affords
Unbroken shade; let us walk there, 'twere better,

Sams.—How so?

Vita.—'Twill yield us healthy exercise, and spare
The jaded cattle.

Sams.—So be it. Come, Sthavaraka, follow us with the carriage.—No, stop; I go on foot only before gods and Brahmans—I cannot walk along the road; I must get into the car, and then as I pass, the citizens will say to each other, There, that is he, his excellency the prince's most noble brother-in-law.

Vita.—(*Apart.*) What is to be done? the case is critical,—

The remedy not obvious; yes, this were best.
(*Aloud to the prince.*) I did but jest.
There is no female fiend.
Vasantasena has come here to meet you.

Vas.—Ah me!

Sams.—Am I not, master, a fine fellow, another Vasudeva?

Vita.—Undoubtedly.

Sams.—It is therefore that this unparalleled goddess waits upon me. I lately displeased her; I will now go and cast myself at her feet.

Vita.—Well devised.

Sams.—I go. *(Kneels to Vasantasena.)* Celestial Mother, listen to my prayers; behold me with those lotus eyes thus lowly at thy feet, and mark my hands up-lifted thus to thy heavenly countenance. Forgive, most graceful nymph, the faults that love, has urged me to commit, and accept me for thy servant and thy slave.

Vas.—Away! your regard in my abhorrence. *(Spurns him with her foot.)*

Sams.—*(Rising in great wrath.)* What! shall this head that bows not to the gods, this head that my mother caressed, be humbled to the ground, to be treated like a dead carcase by the jackals in a thicket? What ho! Sthavaraka, where did you pick up this woman?

Stha.—Why, sir, to tell you the truth, some village carts blocked up the road near Charudatta's garden; I got down to clear the way, and in the meantime left the carriage at his gate; I fancy she then came out of his house and ascended the car, mistaking it for another.

Sams.—A mistake! Oh, then, she did not come here to seek me. Come down, madam, this carriage is mine. You come, I suppose, to meet, that beggar's brat, the son of a higgler, and you take advantage of my cattle,—but turn out directly, I say.

Vas.—That which you make my blame I make my boast;
As for the rest, whatever must be may be.

Sams.—With these fair hands, armed with ten nails, and dexterous in inflicting punishment, I drag you from the carriage by the hair of your head, as Jatayu seized upon the wife of Bali.

Vita.—Forbear, forbear, nor rudely thus invade
These graceful tresses. What destructive hand
Would roughly rend the creeper from the tree,
Or tear the blossom from the slender stem?
Leave her to me, I'll bring her from the car.

(*Goes and hands* Vasantasena *down.*)

Sams.—(*Aside.*) The wrath that her disdainful treatment justly kindled is now more violent than ever: a blow! a kick! to be spurned! I am resolved, —she dies. (*Aloud.*) Master, if you have any relish for a mantle with a broad border and a hundred tassels, or have any curiosity to taste a bit of delicate flesh, now is your time.

Vita.—What mean you?

Sams.—Will you oblige me?

Vita.—In anything not unreasonable.

Sams.—There is no more flavour of unreasonableness than of she-devils in it.

Vita.—Well, speak on.

Sams.—Put Vasantasena to death.

Vita.—(*Stopping his ears.*)

Murder a young and unoffending female,
Of courteous manners and unrivalled beauty,
The pride of all Ujjayin! Where shall I find,

Believe you, a fit raft to waft my soul
Safe o'er the river of futurity?

Sams.—I will have one made for you. Come, come, what have you to fear? In this lowly place, who shall see you?

Vita.—All nature—the surrounding realms of space
The genii of these groves, the moon, the sun,
The winds, the vault of heaven, the firm-set earth,
Hell's awful ruler, and the conscious soul—
These all bear witness to the good or ill
That men pertorm, and these will see the deed.

Sams.—Throw a cloth over her then, hide her.

Vita.—Fool! You are crazed.

Sams.—And you are an old good-for-nothing dastardly jackal. Very well, I shall find some one else. Sthavaraka shall do it. Here, Sthavaraka, my lad, I will give you gold bracelets.

Stha.—Thank your honour, I will wear them.

Sams.—You shall have a gold seat.

Stha.—I will sit upon it.

Sams.—You shall have every dainty dish from my table.

Stha.—I will eat it; never fear me.

Sams.—You shall be head over all my slaves.

Stha.—I shall be a very great man.

Sams.—But attend to what I order.

Stha.—Depend upon me, in everything that ma be done.

Sams.—It may be done well enough.

Stha.—Say on, sir.

Sams.—Kill this Vasantasena.

Stha.—Excuse me, sir, I brought her here.

Sams.—Why, you villain, am I not your master?

Stha.—You are, sir; my body is yours, but not my innocence: I dare not obey you.

Sams.—Of whom are you, my servant, to be afraid?

Stha.—Futurity.

Sams.—And who is Mr. Futurity, pray?

Stha.—The requiter of our good and evil deeds.

Sams.—And what is the return for good?

Stha.—Wealth and power like your honour's.

Sams.—And what for evil?

Stha.—Eating, as I do, the bread of slavery; I will not do, therefore, what ought not to be done,

Sams.—You will not obey me? (*Beats him.*)

Stha.—Beat me if you will, kill me if you will, I cannot do what ought not to be done. Fate has already punished me with servitude for the misdeeds of a former life, and I will not incur the penalty of being born again a slave.

Vas.—Oh, sir, protect me. (*To the Vita.*)

Vita.—Come, come, be pacified. (*To the prince.*)

> Sthavaraka is right; revolving fate
> Has doomed him to a low and servile station,
> From which he wisely hopes a life of virtue
> Hereafter sets him free. Do you too think,

Though degradation wait not close on crime,
And many, obstinately foes to virtue,
Suffer not here the punishment they merit,
Yet destiny not blindly works. Though now
Her will gives servitude to him, to you
A master's sway; yet in a future being,
Your affluence may his portion be assigned,
And yours, to do submissively his bidding.

Sams.—(*Apart.*) The old dastard, and this fool of a slave, are both afraid of futurity; but what shall I fear; I, who am the brother of a prince; and a man of courage as well as rank? (*To Sthavaraka.*) Begone, slave; retire into the garden, and wait apart.

Stha.—I obey, sir. (*To Vasantasena.*) Lady, fear not me. [*Exit.*

Sams.—(*Tightening his girdle.*) Now, Vasantasena, die. (*Goes to seize her; the Vita stops him.*)

Vita. In my presence! (*Throws him down.*)

Sams.—Ah, villain! would you kill your prince? (*Faints.*) Ah, you have so long fed at my cost, do you now become my foe? (*Rising; apart.*) Let me think; this will do. I saw the old scoundrel give a signal. I must get him out of the way and then despatch her. (*Aloud.*) My good friend, how could you so mistake what I said? How could you suppose that I, born of so high a race, should seriously purpose such an unworthy action? I merely used those menaces to terrify her into compliance.

Vita.—Believe me, sir, it is of little import
To boast of noble birth, unless accord
The manners with the rank:—ungrateful thorns
Are most offensive in a goodly soil.

Sams.—The truth of the matter is, that Vasantasena is bashful in your presence: leave us by ourselves a little. That fellow Sthavaraka, too, I am sure, intends to run away; go, bring him back, and I dare say when we are alone a little she will relent.

Vita.—(*Apart.*) It may be true that, valiant in my presence,
Vasantasena may continue still
To drive this fool to madness by denial.
Passion in privacy gains confidence.
I will consent to leave them for a while.
(*Aloud.*) I shall retire and obey your orders.

Vas.—(*Laying hold of his garment.*)
Oh, leave me not! I have no hope but you.

Vita.—You have no cause for terror. Hear me, sir:
I leave Vasantasena as a pledge,
And safe expect her from your hands again.

Sams.—Be assured of it, she shall be so accepted.

Vita.—In truth?

Sams.—In truth.

Vita.—(*Apart.*) He may deceive me. I'll at first retire;
But so, that unobserved I may behold
His acts, and satisfy me of his purpose.

Sams.—He is gone, and now she dies. But hold:—perhaps he juggles with me, the sly old fox, and now lies watch to see what I am doing: he shall meet his match; the deceiver be deceived, (*He gathers flowers and decorates himself.*) Come, Vasantasena, child, why so pettish? come, come.

Vita.—I see his love revives; I now may leave them. (*Departs.*)

Sams.—I will give you gold, I will treat you tenderly, I will lay head and turban at your feet. Oh, if you still disdain me, and will not accept me as your slave, what have I to do longer with mankind?

Vas.—Why should I hesitate? I spurn you;

Nor can you tempt me, abject wretch, with gold.
Though soiled the leaves, the bees fly not the lotus.
Nor shall my heart prove traitor to the homage
It pays to merit, though its lord be poor.
To love such excellence exalts my life,
And sheds a lustre on my humble lot.
And why should I forego it? Can I leave
The mango's stately stem to twine around
The low and worthless dhak?

Sams.—What! dare you compare the beggar Charudatta to a mango-tree, and me to the dhak, not even a kimsuka! Is it thus you treat me and cherish the recollection of Charudatta?

Vas.—How can I cease to think of one who dwells for ever in my heart?

Sams.—We'll soon try that, and cut short your recollections and yourself together. Stop, you inamorata of a beggarly Brahman.

Vas.—Delightful words! proceed, you speak my praise.

Sams.—Let him defend you if he can.

Vas.—Defend me! I were safe if he were here!

Sams.—What, is he Sakra, or the son of Bali—Mahendra, or the son of Rambha—Kalanemi, or Subhandu—Rudra or the son of Drona—Jatayu—Chanakya—Dhundhumara or Trisanku? If he were all these together, he could not aid you. As Sita was slain by Chanakya, as Draupadi by Jatayu, so art thou by me. (*Seizes her.*)

Vas.—Oh, my dear mother! Oh, my loved Charudatta!

Too short and too imperfect are our loves—
Too soon I perish. I will cry for succour—
What! shall Vasantasena's voice be heard
Abroad? Oh, that were infamy! No more
But this. Bless, bless my Charudatta.

Sams.—Still do you repeat that name! Once more, now. (*Seizing her by the throat.*)

Vas.—(*In a struggling tone.*) Bless my Charudatta.

Sams.—Die, harlot, die. (*Srangles her with his hands.*) 'Tis done, she is no more. This bundle of vice, this mansion of cruelty, has met her fate, instead of him whom she came in her love to meet. To what shall I compare the prowess of this arm? Destroyed in the fulness of her hopes, she has fallen like Sita in the Bharata. Deaf to my desires, she perishes in my resentment. The garden is empty; I may drag her away unperceived. My father and my mother, that Draupadi, as well as my brothers, may regret that they did not see the valiant actions of my mother's son. The old jackal will be here again presently. I will withdraw and observe him.

Enter the VITA *and* STHAVARAKA.

Vita.—I have brought back Sthavaraka. Where is he! Here are foot-marks,—these are woman's!

Sams.—(*Advances.*) Welcome, master: you are well returned, Sthavaraka.

Vita.—Now render back my pledge.

Sams.—What was that?

Vita.—Vasantasena.

Sams.—Oh, she is gone.

Vita.—Whether?

Sams.—After you.

Vita.—She came not in that direction.

Sams.—Which way went you?

Vita.—To the east.

Sams.—Ah, that accounts for it; she turned off to the south.

Vita.—I went south too.

Sams.—Then, I suppose, she went north.

Vita.—What mean you? I comprehend you not. Speak out.

Sams.—I swear by your head and my feet, that you may make yourself perfectly easy. Dismiss all alarm; I have killed her.

Vita.—Killed her!

Sams.—What! you do not believe me? Then look here, see this first proof of my prowess. (*Shows the body.*)

Vita.—Alas, I die! (*Faints.*)

Sams.—Hey-dey! is it all over with him?

Stha.—Revive, sir; it is I who am to blame: my inconsiderately bringing her hither has caused her death.

Vita.—(*Reviving.*) Alas Vasantasena,

> The stream of tenderness is now dried up,
> And beauty flies us for her native sphere.
> Adorned with every grace, of lovely aspect,
> Radiant with playfulness, alas! poor wench,
> River of gentle feeling, isle of mirth.
> And friendly refuge for all such as I am;
> Alas! love's richest store, a mart exhaustless
> Of exquisite delights, is here broke open,
> This crime will amply be avenged. A deed
> Done by such hands, in such a place committed,
> Will bring down infamy upon the state,
> And drive our guardian goddess from our city.

Let me reflect ;—this villain may involve
Me in the crime—I will depart from hence.

[*The prince lays hold of him.*

Detain me not ; I have already been
Too long your follower and friend.

Sams.—Very likely, indeed. You have murdered Vasantasena, and seek to accuse me of the crime. Do you imagine I am without friends ?

Vita.—You are a wretch.

Sams.—Come, come, I will give you money, a hundred suvarnas, clothes a turban. The consequence of abuse is common to all men.

Vita.—Keep your gifts.

Stha.—Shame ! shame !

Vita.—Restrain your mirth. Let there be hate between us.

That friendship that confers alone disgrace
Is not for me ; it must no more unite us.
I cast it from me, as a snapped.
And stringless bow.

Sams.—Come, good master, be appeased. Let us go bathe.

Vita.—Whilst you were free from crime you might exact
My duty, but obedience to you now
Would but proclaim myself alike unworthy.
I cannot wait on guilt, nor, though I know
My innocence, have courage to encounter
Those speaking glances every female eye

Will cast abhorrent upon one who holds
Communion with a woman's murderer.
Poor, poor Vasantasena! may thy virtues,
Win thee in after-life a happier portion;
And may the days of shame, and death
of violence
That thou hast suffered in existence past,
Ensure thee honoured birth, the world's
regard,
And wealth and happiness, in that to come.
(Going.)

Sams.—Where would you fly? In this, my garden, you have murdered a female; come along with me, and defend yourself before my brother-in-law. *(Seizes him.)*

Vita.—Away, fool. *(Draws his sword.)*

Sams.—*(Falls back.)* Oh, very well, if you are afraid; you may depart.

Vita.—I am in danger here; yes, I will join
Sarvilaka aud Chandana, and with them seek
The band that Arya has assembled. [*Exit.*

Sams.—Go, fool, to death. Well, Sthavaraka, my lad, what think you of this business?

Stha.—That it is most horrible.

Sams.—How, slave, do you condemn me? With all my heart, be it so. Here, take these. *(Gives him his ornaments.)* I make you a present of them, that when I am full dressed, you may be suitably equipped to attend me; it is my command.

Stha.—These are too costly,—what am I with them sir?

Sams.—Take them, take them, and away with you. Conduct the carriage to the porch of my palace, and there wait my coming.

Stha.—I obey, sir. [*Exit.*

Sams.—My worthy preceptor has taken himself off in alarm. As to the slave, as soon as I return I will put him in confinement; so my secret is safe, and I may depart without apprehension. Hold! let me be sure,—is she dead, or must I kill her again? no, she is safe. I will cover the body with my mantle. Stop! it bears my name, and will discover me. Well thought of,—the wind has scattered about a quantity of dry leaves; I will cover her over with them. (*Collects the leaves and piles them over* Vasantasena.) Now to the court, where I will enter an accusation against Charudatta for having murdered Vasantasena for her wealth. Ingeniously devised! Charudatta will be ruined; the virtuous city cannot tolerate even the death of an animal. Now to my work. (*Going.*) Here comes that rascally mendicant again, and by the very road I was about to take; he owes me a grudge for threatening to slit his nose, and should he see me here, he will out of revenge come forward and tax me with this murder. How shall I avoid him? I can leap the broken wall here. Thus I fly, as the monkey Mahendra leaped through heaven, over earth and hell, from Hanumat Peak to Lanka. (*Jumps down*).

Enter the SRAMANAKA *or Mendicant, as before.*

I have washed my mantle, and will hang it on these boughs to dry. No, here are a number of monkeys; I'll spread it on the ground. No, there is too much dust. Ha! yonder the wind has blown together a pile of dry leaves; that will answer exactly; I'll spread it upon them. (*Spreads his wrapper. Over Vasantasena and sits down.*) Glory to Buddha! (*Repeats the moral stanzas as above.*) But enough of this. I covet not the other world, until in this I may make some return for the lady Vasantasena's charity. On the day she liberated me from the gamester's clutches she made me her slave for ever. Holloa! something sighed amidst yon leaves! or perhaps it was only their crackling, scorched by the sun, and moistened by my damp garment. Bless me, they spread out like the wings of a bird. (*One of Vasantasena's hands appears.*) A woman's hand, as I live, with rich ornaments—and another; surely I have seen that hand before. It is, it is—it is the hand that once was stretched forth to save me. What should this mean! (*Throws off the wrapper and leaves, and sees Vasantasena.*) It is the lady Vasantasena; the devoted worshipper of Buddha. (*Vasantasena expresses by signs the want of water.*) She wants water: the pool is far away; what's to be done? Ha!

my wet garment. (*Applies it to her face and mouth and fans her.*)

Vas.—(*Reviving.*) Thanks, thanks, my friend; who art thou?

Sram.—Do you not recollect me, lady? You once redeemed me with ten suvarnas.

Vas.—I remember you; aught else I have forgotten. I have suffered since.

Sram.—How, lady?

Vas.—As my fate deserved.

Sram.—Rise, lady, rise; drag yourself to this tree: here, hold by this creeper. (*Bends it down to her*;) she lays hold of it and rises. In a neighbouring convent dwells a holy sister; rest a while with her, lady, and recover your spirits: gently, lady, gently. (*They proceed.*) Stand aside, good friends, stand aside; make way for a young female and a poor beggar. It is my duty to restrain the hands and mouth, and keep the passions in subjection. What should such a man care for kingdoms? His is the world to come. [*Exit.*

END OF THE EIGHTH ACT.

ACT IX.

THE HALL OF JUSTICE.

(Exterior and Interior.)

Enter OFFICER.

I am commanded to prepare the benches in this hall for the judges. (*Arranges them.*) All is ready for their reception, the floor is swept, and the seats are placed, and I have only now to inform them all is ready. (*Going.*) Ha! here comes the king's brother-in-law, a worthless fellow; I will get out of his way. (*Retires.*)

Enter SAMSTHANAKA *splendidly dressed.*

I have bathed in limpid water and reposed in a shady grove, passing my time like a celestial chorister of elegant form, amidst an attendant train of lovely damsels, now tying my hair, then twisting it into a braid, then opening it in flowing tresses, and again gathering it into a graceful knot. Oh! I am a most accomplished and astonishing young prince, and yet I feel a vacancy, an interior chasm; such as is sought for by the fatal worm that works its darkling way through the human entrails. How shall I fill it up?—on whom shall I satiate my craving? Ha! I recollect; it is designed for the miserable Charudatta. So be it. I will repair to the court, and cause an accusation to be registered against him, of the death of Vasantasena, asserting that he has robbed and murdered her. The court is open, I see. (*Enters.*) How! the seats are ready for the arrival of the judges. I shall wait their coming on this grass plot.

Doorkeeper.—Here comes the Court; I must attend.

Enter the JUDGE, *with the* PROVOST *and* RECORDER *and others.*

Crier.—Hear, all men, the judge's commands.

Judge.—Amidst the conflicting details of parties engaged in legal controversy, it is difficult for the judge to ascertain what is really in their hearts. Men accuse others of secret crimes, and even though the charge be disproved, they acknowledge not their fault, but, blinded by passion, persevere; and whilst their friends conceal their errors, and their foes exaggerate them, the character of the prince is assailed. Reproach indeed is easy, discrimination of but rare occurrence, and the quality of a judge is readily the subject of censure. A judge should be learned, sagacious, eloquent, dispassionate, impartial; he should pronounce judgment only after due deliberation and inquiry; he should be a guardian to the weak, a terror to the wicked; his heart should covet nothing, his mind be intent on nothing but equity and truth, and he should keep aloof the anger of the king.

Provost and Rec.—The character of your worship

is as free from censure, as the moon is from the imputation of obscurity.

Judge.—Officers, lead the way to the seat of judgment.

Off.—As your worship commands. (*They sit.*)

Judge.—Now go forth, and see who comes to demand justice.

Off.—By command of his honour the judge, I ask, who waits to demand justice?

Sams.—(*Advancing.*) Oh, oh! the judges are seated. I demand justice; I, a man of rank, a Vasudeva, and brother-in-law of the Raja;—I have a plaint to enter.

Off.—Have the goodness to wait a moment, your excellency, I apprize the Court. (*Returns.*) So please your worship, the first plaintiff is his Majesty's brother-in-law.

Judge.—The Raja's brother-in-law to proffer a plaint? An eclipse of the rising sun foreruns the downfall of some illustrious character: but there are other matters before us. Return and tell him his cause cannot come on to-day.

(*Officer returns to Samsthanaka.*)

Off.—I am desired to inform your honour that your cause cannot be tried to-day.

Sams.—How! not to-day? Then I shall apply to the King, my sister's husband. I shall apply to my sister, and to my mother, and have this judge dismissed, and another appointed immediately. (*Going.*)

Off.—Stay one moment, your honour, and I will carry your message to the Court. (*Goes to the judge.*) Please your worship, his excellency is very angry; and declares if you do not try his suit to-day, he will complain to the royal family, and procure your worship's dismissal.

Judge.—The blockhead has it in his power, it is true. Well, call him hither: his plaint shall be heard.

Off.—(*To Sams.*) Will your excellency be pleased to enter; your plaint will be heard.

Sams.—Oh, oh! first it could not be tried; now it will be heard; very well; the judges fear me: they will do what I desire. (*Enters.*) I am well pleased, gentlemen; you may therefore be so too, for it is in my hands to distribute or withhold satisfaction.

Judge.—(*Apart.*) Very like the language of a complainant this! (*Aloud.*) Be seated.

Sams.—Assuredly. This place is mine, and I shall sit where I please. (*To the Provost.*) I will sit here; no (*to the Recorder*), I will sit here; no, no (*puts his hands on the judge's head, and then sits down by his side*), I will even sit here.

Judge.—Your excellency has a complaint?

Sams.—To be sure I have.

Judge.—Prefer it.

Sams.—I will, in good time, but remember, I am born in a distinguished family. My father is the

Raja's father-in-law; the Raja is my father's son-in-law; I am the Raja's brother-in-law: and the Raja is my sister's husband.

Judge.—We know all this; but why dwell on family honours? Personal excellence is more important; there are always thorn-bushes in the fairest forests: declare therefore your suit.

Sams.—This it is; but it involves no fault of mine. My noble brother-in-law, in his good pleasure, presented me, for my ease and recreation, the best of the royal gardens, the ancient Pushpakarandaka. It is my practice to visit it daily, and see it well swept and weeded, and kept in order; and having, as my wont, gone this day thither, what should I behold, but—I could scarcely believe my eyes—the dead body of a female!

Judge.—Did you know the person?

Sams.—Alas! too well. She was once our city's greatest pride. Her rich attire must have tempted some execrable wretch to beguile her into the lonely garden; and there, for the sake of her jewels, was the lovely Vasantasena strangled by his hands, not by me. (*Stops himself.*)

Judge.—What neglect in the police! You heard the plaint, gentlemen; let it be recorded, including the words "not by me."

Rec.—(*Writes it.*) It is done.

Sams.—(*Apart.*) Vile carelessness! My heedlessness has plunged me into peril, like a man crossing a narrow bridge precipitately, who tumbles into the stream: it cannot now be helped. (*Aloud.*) Well, sagacious administrators of justice, you make a mighty fuss about a trifle. I was going to observe, not by me was the deed beheld. (*Puts his foot on the record, and wipes out the last part.*)

Judge.—How, then, do you know the truth of what you have stated, that for the sake of her ornaments she was strangled by some person's hands?

Sams.—I conclude so, for the neck was bare and swollen, and her dress rifled of its ornaments.

Prov.—The case is likely enough.

Sams.—(*Apart.*) Good; I am alive again.

Prov.—Whom else do we require in this suit?

Judge.—The case is two fold, and must be investigated both in relation to assertion and facts; the verbal investigation relates to plaintiff and and respondent, that of facts depends upon the judge.

Prov.—The cause then requires the evidence of Vasantasena's mother.

Judge.—Undoubtedly. Officers, go and civilly call Vasantasena's mother into court.

Off.—(*Exit Officer, and returns with the old woman.*) Come along, dame.

Moth.—My daughter is gone to a friend's house. This old fellow comes and says to me: "Come along; his honour the judge has sent for you." I am ready to faint, and my heart flutters so.—Very well, sir, very well, sir, lead me to the court.

Off.—Here we are ;—enter. (*They enter.*)

Moth.—Health and happiness to your worships !

Judge.—You are welcome ;—sit down. (*She sits.*)

Sams.—Oh, old procuress, you are there, are you ?

Judge.—You are the mother of Vasantasena ?

Moth.—I am.

Judge.—Where is your daughter ?

Moth.—At a friend's house.

Judge.—The name of that friend ?

Moth.—(*Apart.*) Oh dear me, this is very awkward. (*Aloud.*) Surely, your worship, this is not a fit question for your worship to ask.

Judge.—No hesitation ;—the law asks the question.

Prov. and Rec.—Speak out ; the law asks the question ; there is no impropriety in answering.

Moth.—Why then, gentlemen, to say the truth, she is at the house of a very nice gentleman :—the son of Sagaradatta, grandson of the Provost Vinyadatta, whose own name is Charudatta ; he lives near the Exchange : my daughter is with him.

Sams.—You hear, judges ;—let this be registered. I accuse Charudatta.

Prov.—Charudatta, her friend ! he cannot be criminal.

Judge.—The cause, however, requires his presence.

Prov.—Certainly.

Judge.—(*To the Scribe.*) Dhanadatta, write down that Vasantasena last went to Charudatta's residence: this is the first step. Let me consider; how can Charudatta be summoned hither? However, the law must be enforced. Officer, repair to Charudatta, and say to him, the magistrate, with all due respect, requests to see him at his perfect convenience.

(*Officer goes out, and re-enters with Charudatta.*)

Off.— This way, sir.

Char.—The prince well knows my rank and character,
And yet thus calls me to his public court.
Haply he may have heard my car conveyed
The fugitive he feared beyond his reach,
Borne to his ear by some unfriendly spy.
Or haply—but away with fancies; soon
I learn the truth, arrived at the tribunal.

Off.— This way, this way, sir.

Char.—What should this mean? his harshest note,—you crow
Responsive utters to his fellow's call,
With croak repeated. Ha! my left eye throbs;
What new misfortunes threaten?

Off.— Proceed, sir, never fear.

Char.—Facing the sun, on yonder blighted tree,
The bird of evil augury is perched;
Ha! on my path, the black snake sleeping lies.
Roused from his slumber, he unfolds in wrath
His spiry length, and threatening beats the ground

With bulk inflated; as he turns on me
His angry eyes, and from between his fangs
Protrudes his hissing tongue. I slip, yet here
No plashy mire betrays my heedless feet.—
Still throbs my left eye, and my left arm
trembles;
And still that bird in flight sinistral cries,
To warn me of impending ill. Yes, death—
Terrible death awaits me. Be it so—
It is not mine to murmur against destiny,
Nor doubt that righteous which the gods
ordain.

Off.— This is the court, sir, enter.

Char.—(*Entering and looking round.*)

The prospect is but little pleasing.
The court looks like a sea;—its councillors
Are deep engulphed in thought; its tossing
waves.
Are wrangling advocates; its brood of
monsters
Are these wild animals—death's ministers—
Attorney's skim like wily snakes the surface—
Spies are the shell-fish cowering 'midst its
weeds,
And vile informers, like the hovering curlew,
Hang fluttering o'er, then pounce upon their
prey
The beach that should be justice, is unsafe,

Rough, rude, and broken by oppression's
storms.

[*As he advances he knocks his head against the door-frame.*

More inauspicious omens! they attend
Each step I take; fate multiplies its favours.

Judge.—Charudatta approaches. Observe him;—that face and form never gave shelter to causeless crime. Appearance is a test of character; and not only in man, but in elephants, horses and kine, the disposition never deviates from the perfect shape.

Char.—Hail to the court; prosperity attend
The delegated ministers of justice.

Judge.—Sir, you are welcome; officer bring a seat.

Off.—It is here; be seated, sir. (*To Charudatta; he sits.*)

Sams.—So, Mr. Woman-killer, you are here: very decorous this, indeed, to treat such a fellow with so much civility; but never mind.

Judge.—Worthy Charudatta, allow me to ask if any intimacy or connexion has ever subsisted between you and this woman's daughter?

Char.—What woman?

Judge.—This. (*Showing Vasantasena's mother.*)

Char.—(*Rising.*) Lady, I salute you.

Moth.—Son, long may you live. (*Apart.*) This is Charudatta, then; really my daughter has made a good choice.

Judge.—Tell us, Charudatta, were you ever acquainted with that courtezan? (*Charudatta ashamed, hesitates.*)

Sams.—Ah! he pretends to be vastily modest, or very much alarmed; it is merely a pretext to evade confessing his vicious courses: but that he murdered the woman for her wealth, the prince shall soon make manifest.

Prov.—Away with this hesitation, Charudatta: there is a charge against you.

Char.—Well, sirs, what shall I say? What if she were a friend of mine? be youth accused, not habit.

Judge.—Let me beg,—no evasion, banish all reserve, speak the truth and act ingenuously: remember it is the law that calls upon you.

Char.—First tell me who is my accuser?

Sams.—I am—I.

Char.—Thou! a mighty matter truly.

Sams.—Indeed, you woman-killer! What! are you to murder such a woman as Vasantasena, and rob her of her jewels, and to think it will not be known?

Char.—Thou art crazed.

Judge.—Enough of this; declare the truth: was the courtezan your friend?

Char.—She was, she was.

Judge.—And where is Vasantasena now?

Char.—Gone.

Prov.—Gone! how, whither, and how attended?

Char.—(*Apart.*) Shall I say she went privately (*Aloud.*) She went to her own dwelling: what more can I say?

Sams.—What more? Why, did you not accompany her to my princely garden; and did you not there, for the sake of her jewels, strangle her, with your own hands? How then can you say she is gone home?

Char.—Foul calumniator.

> No rain from heaven upon thy face descends,
> Dark as the joy's unmoistened wing in showers.
> These falsehoods parch thy lips, as wintry winds
> Despoil the shrivelled lotus of its beauty.

Judge.—(*Apart.*) I see it were as easy to weigh Himalaya, ford the ocean, or grasp the wind, as fix a stain on Charudatta's reputation. (*Aloud.*) It cannot be, that this worthy man is guilty.

Sams.—What have you to do with his defence?—let the case be tried.

Judge.—Away, fool, is it not thus?—if you expound the Vedas will not your tongue be cut out? if you gaze upon the mid-day sun, will you not lose your eye-sight? if you plunge your hand into flame, will it not be burnt? and think you that if you revile Charudatta, the earth will not open and swallow you? This is Charudatta—how can such a man have committed such a crime? He has exhausted in lavish munificence the ocean of his disregarded wealth, and is it impossible that he, who was the best among the best, and who has ever shown the most princely liberality, should have been guilty of a deed most hateful to a noble mind, for the sake of plunder?

Sams.—I say again, it is not your province to undertake his defence; you are to try the cause.

Moth.—I say the accusation is false. When in his distress my daughter entrusted a casket of jewels to his care, and it was stolen from him, even then he replaced it with a necklace of still greater value; and can he now, for the sake of wealth, have turned murderer? Oh, never! Alas! would that my daughter were here! (*Weeps.*)

Judge.—Inform us, Charudatta, how did she leave you—on foot or in a carriage?

Char.—I did not see her depart, and know not.

Enter VIRAKA *in haste.*

Now go I to the court, to tell them how I have been maltreated, kicked, and abused for keeping a good look-out after the run-away. Hail to your worships!

Judge.—Ha! here is Viraka, the Captain of the watch: what brings you hither, Viraka?

Vir.—Hear me, your honour. Whilst engaged last night in quest of Aryaka, who had broke loose, we stopped a covered carriage: the captain, Chandanaka, looked into it, and I was going to do so too, when he prevented me, pulled me back, and cuffed and kicked me. I beg your honours will take proper notice of this business.

Judge.—We will. Whose was the carriage, do you know?

Vir.—The driver said it belonged to this gentleman, Charudatta; and that it carried Vasantasena to meet him in Pushpakarandaka.

Sams.—You hear, sirs!

Judge.—Truly this spotless moon is threatened by the demon of eclipse; the limpid stream is sullied by the falling of the banks. We will enquire into your compliant, Viraka; in the meantime mount one of the messenger's horses at the gate; go to Pushpakarandaka with all speed, and bring us word whether the body of a murdered woman lies there.

Vir.—I shall. (*Goes out and presently returns.*) I have been to the garden, and have ascertained that a female body has been carried off by the beasts of prey.

Judge.—How know you it was a female?

Vir.—By the remaius of the hair, and the marks of the hands and feet.

Judge.—How difficult it is to discover the truth: the more one investigates, the greater is the perplexity. The points of law are sufficiently clear here, but the understanding still labours like a cow in a quagmire.

Char.—(*Apart.*) When first the flower unfolds,
as flock the bees

To drink the honeyed dew, so mischiefs crowd
The entrance opened by man's falling fortune.

Judge.—Come, Charudatta, speak the truth.

Char.—The wretch that sickens at another's merits
The mind, by passion blinded, bent to ruin
The object of its malice, do not claim
Reply, nor any heed to what they utter,
Which from their very nature must be falsehood.
For me—you know me—would I pluck a flower,
I draw the tender creeper gently to me,
Nor rudely rob it of its clustering beauty.
How think you then?—could I with violent hands
Tear from their lovely seat those jetty locks,
More glossy than the black bee's wing, or how
So wrong my nature, and betray my love,
As with remorseless heart to blast in death
The weeping charms that vainly sued for mercy?

Sams.—I tell you, judges, you will be held as the defendant's friends and abettors, if you allow him longer to remain seated in your presence.

Judge.—Officer, remove him from his seat. (*Officer obeys.*)

Char.—Ministers of justice, yet reflect. (*Sits on the ground*).

Sams.—(*Apart.*) Ha, ha! my deeds are now safely deposited on another's head; I will go and sit near Charudatta. (*Does so.*) Come, Charudatta, look at me; confess; say honestly, "I killed Vasantasena."

Char.—Vile wretch, away! Alas! my humble friend,
My good Maitreya, what will be thy grief;
To hear of my disgrace? and thine, dear wife,
The daughter of a pure and pious race?
Alas! my boy, amidst thy youthful sports
How little think'st thou of thy father's shame!
Where can Maitreya tarry? I had sent him
To seek Vasantasena, and restore
The costly gems her lavish love bestowed
Upon my child—where can he thus delay?

Outside—Enter MAITREYA *with* VASANTASENA'S *Jewels.*

I am to return these trinkets to Vasantasena; the child took them to his mother; I must restore them, and, on no account, consent to take them back them back again. Ha! Rebhila; how now Rebhila, what is the matter? You seem agitated, what has chanced? (*Listening.*) Hey! what say you, my dear friend? summoned to the court? this is very alarming. Let me think:—I must go to him, and see what it means; I can go to Vasantasena afterwards. Oh, here is the court. (*Enters.*) Salutation to your worships! where is my friend?

Judge.—There.

Mait.—My dear friend, all happiness—

Char.—Will be hereafter.

Mait.—Patience.

Char.—That I have.

Mait.—But why so downcast? what are you brought here for?

Char.—I am a murderer—reckless of futurity—

Repaying woman's tender love with blood—
What else, let him declare.

Mait.—What!

Char.—*(Whispers him.)* Even so.

Mait.—Who says so?

Char.—*To the Raja's brother-in-law.*)

Yon miserable man, the instrument
That destiny employs to work my fall.

Mait.—Why not say she is gone home?

Char.—It recks not what I say; my humble state.
Is not to be believed.

Mait.—How, sirs! what is all this? Can he who has beautified our city with its chief ornaments, who has filled Ujjayin with gardens, and gates, and convents, and temples, and wells, and fountains,—can he, an utter reprobate, for the object of a few beggarly ornaments, have done such an iniquitous act? *(In anger.)* And you—you wretch, you king's brother-in-law, Samsthanaka,—you who stop at nothing, and are a stuffed vessel of everything offensive to mankind,—you monkey, tricked out with golden toys: say again before me, that my friend, who never plucked a flower roughly in his life, who never pulled more than one at a time, and always left the young buds untouched;—say that he has been guilty of a crime detestable in both worlds, and I will break thy head into a thousand pieces with this staff, as knotty and crooked as thy own heart.

Sams.—Hear him, my masters. What has this crow-foot-pated hypocritical fellow to do with the cause between me and Charudatta, that he has to break my head. Attempt it, if you dare, you hypocritical scoundrel. (*Mait. strikes him; a struggle ensues, in which Vasantasena's jewels fall from his girdle. Samsthanaka picks them up.*) See here, sirs! here,—here are the poor wench's jewels, for the sake of which yon villain murdered her.

[*The judges hang down their heads.*

Char.—(*To Mait.*) In an ill hour these jewels spring to light.
Such is my fate, their fall will lead to mine.

Mait.—Why not explain?

Char.—The regal eye is feeble to discern
The truth amidst perplexity and doubt.
I can but urge—I have not done the deed,
And poverty like mine must hope to gain
Unwilling credence; shameful death awaits me.

Judge.—Alas! Mars is obstructed and Jupiter

obscured, and a new planet like a comet wanders in their orbits.

Prov.—Come hither, lady *(to Vasantasena's mother)*; look at this casket; was it your daughter's?

Moth.—It is very like, but not the same.

Sams.—Oh, you old baggage! your eyes tell one story and your tongue another.

Moth.—Away, slanderer!

Prov.—Be careful of what you say: is it your daughter's, or is it not?

Moth.—Why, your worship, the skill of the workman, makes it difficult to trust one's eyes; but this is not my daughter's.

Judge.—Do you know these ornaments?

Moth.—Have I not said? They may be different, though like: I cannot say more; they may be imitations made by some skilful artist.

Judge.—It is true. Provost, examine them: they may be different, though like; the dexterity of the artists is no doubt very great, and they readily fabricate imitations of ornaments they have once seen, in such a manner, that the difference shall scarcely be discernible.

Prov.—Are these ornaments your property, Charudatta?

Char.—They are not.

Prov.—Whose then?

Char.—This lady's daughter's.

Prov.—How come they out of the owner's possession?

Char.—She parted with them.

Prov.—Consider, Charudatta, you must speak the truth. Truth alone is internal satisfaction; not to declare the truth is a crime, the truth is readily told; seek not to conceal it by a lie.

Char.—I do not know the ornaments; but this I know, they are now brought from my house.

Sams.—You killed her in my garden first, and so obtained them; this prevarication is only to hide the truth.

Judge.—Charudatta, own the truth, or it must be my pleasure that heavy lashes fall upon that delicate frame.

Char.—Sprung from a race incapable of crime,
I have not shamed my sires—if you confound
The innocent with the guilty, I must suffer.
(*Apart.*) If I have lost indeed Vasantasena,
Life is a burden to me. (*Aloud.*) What avails it
To proffer further plea? be it acknowledged.
I have abandoned virtue, and deserved
Abhorrence here and punishment hereafter.
Let me be called a murderer, or what else
It pleases him (*to Sams.*) to declare.

Sams.—She is killed: say at once, *I* killed her.

Char.—You have said.

Sams.—You hear him: he confesses it; all doubt

is removed by his own words: let him be punished. Poor Charudatta!

Judge.—Officer, obey the prince—secure the malefactor.

Moth.—Yet, good gentlemen, hear me. I am sure the charge is false. If my dear daughter be slain, let him live, who is my life. Who are the parties in this cause? I make no complaint, and why then is he to be detained? Oh! set him at liberty.

Sams.—Silence, you old fool! what have you to do with him?

Judge.—Withdraw, lady. Officer, lead her forth.

Moth.—My son, my dear son! (*Is forced out.*)

Sams.—I have done the business worthy of myself, and shall now depart. [*Exit.*

Judge.—Charudatta, the business of proof it was ours to effect, the sentence rests with the prince. Officer, apprize the royal Palaka, that the convicted culprit being a Brahman, he cannot according to Manu be put to death, but he may be banished the kingdom with his property untouched.

Off.—I obey. (*Goes out and returns.*) I have been, and the king thus commands. Let the ornaments of Vasantasena be suspended to the neck of the criminal; let him be conducted by beat of drum to the southern cemetery, and there let him be impaled; that, by the severity of this punishment, men may be in future deterred from the commission of such atrocious acts.

Char.—Unjust and inconsiderate monarch.

'Tis thus that evil councillors impel
The heedless prince into the scorching flames
Of fierce iniquity and foul disgrace;
And countless victims perish by the guilt
Of treacherous ministers, who thus involve
Both prince and people in promiscuous ruin.
My friend Maitreya, I bequeath to you
My helpless family; befriend my wife,
And be a second parent to my child.

Mait.—Alas! when the root is destroyed, how can the tree remain?

Char.—Not so; a father lives beyond his death
And in his son survives; 'tis meet my boy
Enjoy that friendship which thou show'dst his sire.

Mait.—You have ever been most dear to me, most excellent Charudatta; I cannot cherish life deprived of you.

Char.—Bring my boy to me.

Mait.—That shall be done.

Judge.—Officer, lead him forth. Who waits there Let the Chandalas be called.

[*Exit with Court.*

Off.—This way.

Char.—Alas, my friend!

Had due investigation been allowed me,
Or any test proposed—water or poison,

The scales or scorching fire, and I had failed
The proof, then might the law have been fulfilled,
And I deservedly received my doom.
But this will be avenged; and for the sentence
That dooms a Brahman's death on the mere charge
Of a malicious foe, the bitter portion
That waits for thee, and all thy line, O king,
Is hell. Proceed—I am prepared.

[*Exeunt.*

END OF THE NINTH ACT.

ACT X.

THE ROAD TO THE PALACE OF EXECUTION.

Enter CHARUDATTA *with two* CHANDALAS *as Executioners.*

1st Chan.—Out of the way, sirs! out of the way! room for Charudatta. Adorned with the Karavira garland, and attended by his dexterous executioners, he approaches his end like a lamp ill-fed with oil.

Char.—Sepulchral blossoms decorate my limbs,
Covered with dust, and watered by my tears,
And round me harshly croak the carrion birds,
Impatient to enjoy their promised prey.

2nd Chan.—Out of the way, sirs! what do you stare at? a good man whose head is to be chopped off by the axe of destiny? a tree that gave shelter to gentle birds to be cut down? Come on, Charudatta.

Char.—Who can foresee the strange vicissitudes
Of man's sad destiny?—I little thought
That such a fate would ever be my portion,
Nor could have credited I should live to be
Dragged like a beast to public sacrifice,
Stained with the ruddy sandal spots and smeared
With meal—a victim to the sable goddess.
Yet as I pass along, my fellow-citizens

Console me with their tears, and execrate
The cruel sentence that awards my death.
Unable to preserve my life, they pray
That heaven await me, and reward my sufferings.

1st Chan.—Stand out of the way—what crowd you to see? There are four things not to be looked at: Indra carried forth, the birth of a calf, the transit of a star, and the misfortune of a good man. Look, brother Ahinta; the whole city is under sentence!—What! does the sky weep, or the thunder bolt fall without cloud;

2nd Chan.—No brother Goha, not so; the shower falls from yonder cloud of women; yet though all the people weep, yet such is the throng, that their tears cannot lay the dust.

Char.—From every window lovely faces shed
The kindly drops, and bathe me with their tears.

1st Chan.—Here stop! strike the drum, and cry the sentence.—Hear ye, hear ye! This is Charudatta, son of Sagaradatta, son of Provost Vinayadatta, by whom the courtezan Vasantasena has been robbed and murdered; he has been convicted and condemned, and we are ordered by king Palaka to put him to death: so will his Majesty ever punish those that commit such crimes as both worlds abhor.

Char.—Dreadful reverse—to hear such wretches herald

My death, and blacken thus with lies my fame:
Not so, my sires—from them the frequent shout
Has filled the sacred temple, where the crowd.
Of holy Brahmans to the gods proclaimed
The costly rite accomplished: and shall I,
Alas! Vasantasena, who have drunk
Thy nectared tones from lips whose ruby glow
Disgraced the coral, and displayed the charms
Of teeth more pearly than the moon's chaste light,
Profane my ears with such envenomed draughts
Of infamy whilst yet my soul is free?

[*Puts his hands to his ears.*

1st Chan.—Stand apart there—make way!

Char.—My friends avoid me as I pass, and, hiding
Their faces with their raiment, turn away.
Whilst fortune smiles each stranger is a friend,
But friends are strangers in adversity.

1st Chan.—The road is now tolerably clear,—bring along the culprit.

(*Behind.*) Father! father!
My friend! my friend!

Char.—My worthy friends, grant me this one indulgence,

1st Chan.—What! will you take anything of us?

Char.—Disdain not my request. Though basely born,
You are not cruel, and a gentle nature
Ranks you above your sovereign. I implore you,
By all your future hopes, oh once permit me
To view my son, ere I depart to death!

1st Chan.—Let him come.—Men, stand back, and let the child approach; here, this way.

Enter MAITREYA *with* ROHASENA.

Mait.—Here we have him, boy, once more; your dear father, who is going to be murdered.

Boy.—Father! father!

Char.—Come hither, my dear child. (*Embraces him and takes his hands.*)

These little hands will ill-suffice to sprinkle
The last sad drops upon my funeral pyre.
Scant will my spirit sip thy love, and then
A long and painful thirst in heaven succeeds
What sad memorial shall I leave thee, boy,
To speak to thee hereafter of thy father?
This sacred string, whilst yet 'tis mine, I give thee.
The Brahman's proudest decoration, boy,
Is not of gold nor gems; but this by which

He ministers to sages and to gods.
This grace my child when I shall be no more.
(Takes off his Brahmanical cord and puts it round his son's neck.)

1st Chan.—Come, you Charudatta, come along.

2nd Chan.—More respect, my master; recollect, by night or day, in adversity or prosperity, fate holds it course, and puts men to trial. Come, sir; compliants are unavailing; and it is not to be expected that men will honour the moon when Rahu has hold of him.

Roha.—Where do you lead my father, vile Chandala?

Chan.—I go to death, my child; the fatal chaplet
Of Karavira hangs around my neck;
The stake upon my shoulder rests, my heart
Is burdened with despair, as, like a victim
Dressed for the sacrifice, I meet my fate.

1st Chan.—Hark ye, my boy; they who are born Chandalas are not the only ones; they who oppress the virtuous are Chandalas two.

Roha.—Why, then, want to kill my father?

1st Chan.—The king orders us; it is his fault, not ours.

Roha.—Take and kill me; let my father go.

1st Chan.—My brave little fellow, long life to you!

Char.—*(Embracing him.)*

This is the truest wealth, love equal smiles
On poor and rich; the bosom's precious balm

Is not the fragrant herb, nor costly unguent—
But nature's breath, affection's holy perfume.

Mait.—Come now, my good fellows, let my worthy friend escape: you only want a body,—mine is at your disposal.

Char.—Forbear, forbear!

1st Chan.—Come on! stand off! what do you throng to see? a good man who has lost his all and fallen into despair, like a gold bucket whose rope breaks and it tumbles into the well.

2nd Chan.—Here stop: beat the drum, and proclaim the sentence. (*As before.*)

Char.—This is the heaviest pang of all; to think
Such bitter fruit attends my closing life.
And oh! what anguish, love, to hear the calumny,
Thus noised abroad, that thou wast slain by me! [*Exeunt.*

SCENE II.—A ROOM IN THE PALACE.

STHAVARAKA *discovered above, bound, listening to the drum and proclamation.*

How! the innocent Charudatta to be executed, and I in chains still! I may be heard. What ho there! friends, hear me:—it was I, sinner that I am, who drove Vasantasena to the royal garden. There my master met us, and finding her deaf to his wishes, with his own hands strangled her. He is the murderer, not this worthy man.—They cannot hear me: I am too far off. Cannot I leap down?—it shall be so; better any chance than that Charudatta should suffer. I can get out of this window and spring from the balcony: better I perish than Charudatta, and if I die, heaven is my reward. (*Jumps down.*) I am not hurt, and fotunately my chain has snapped. Now, whence comes the cry of the Chandalas:—ha! yonder,—I will overtake them. What ho there, stop!

[*Exit.*

Scene III.

Enter Charudatta *as before—to them* Sthavaraka.

Stha.—What ho, stop!

1st Chan.—Who calls to us to stop?

Stha.—Hear me; Charudatta is innocent. I took Vasantasena to the garden, where my master strangled her with his own hands.

Char.—Who comes rejoicing thus my latest hours,
To snatch me from the galling bands of fate?
Like the full cloud, distent with friendly showers,
That timely hangs to save the dropping grain?
Heard you the words?—my fame again is clear.
My death I heeded not, I feared disgrace.
Death without shame is welcome as the babe
Now-born. I perish now by hate

I ne'er provoked; by ignorance and malice—
I fall the mark of arrows dipped in venom,
And aimed at me by infamy and guilt.

1st Chan.—Hark ye, Sthavaraka,—do you speak the truth?

Stha.—I do; and would have ere now proclaimed it: for fear of that I was chained, and shut up in one of the rooms of the palace.

Enter SAMSTHANAKA *(above).*

I have had a most sumptuous regale in the palace here: rice, with acid sauce, and meat, and fish, and vegetables, and sweetmeats. What sounds were those I heard? The Chandala's voice, as harsh as a cracked bell, and the beat of the death-drum; the beggar Charudatta is going to execution. The destruction of an enemy is a banquet to the heart. I have heard, too, that whoever looks upon the death of an adversary will never have had eyes in his next birth. I will ascend the terrace of my palace and contemplate my triumph. (*Ascends.*) What a crowd has collected to see the execution of this miserable wretch! If so many flock to see him, what a concourse there would be to behold a great man like myself put to death! He is dressed like a young steer. They are taking him to the south. What brings them this way, and why ceases the noise? (*Looks into the chamber.*) Hey! where is the slave Sthavaraka? He has made his escape!—all my schemes will be ruined! I must seek him. (*Descends.*)

Stha.—Here comes my master.

1st Chan.—Out of the way there! make room! Here he comes, like a mad ox, butting with the sharp horn of arrogance.

Sam.—Room, room here! My boy Sthavaraka, come you along with me.

Stha.—What, sir! are you not satisfied with having murdered Vasantasena, that you now endeavour to compass the death of the excellent Charudatta?

Sam.—I,—I,—a vessel of rich jewels, I murder a woman!

Crowd.—Yes, yes, you murdered her; not Charudatta.

Sam.—Who says so?

Crowd.—This honest man.

Sam.—Sthavaraka, my servant. (*Apart.*) He is the only witness of my guilt. I have ill-secured him. It shall be so. (*Aloud.*) Hear ye, my masters: this is my slave; he is a thief, and for theft I punished and confined him; he owes me a grudge for this, and has made up this story to be revenged. Confess (*to Sthavaraka*), is it not so? (*Approaches and in an under-tone.*) Take this (*offers him a bracelet*); it is yours;—recall your words.

Stha.—(*Takes the bracelet and holds it up.*) See here, my friends, he bribes me, even now, to silence!

Sams.—(*Snatches the bracelet.*) This is it; the very ornament I punished him for stealing; look here,

Chandalas: for pilfering from my treasury, which was under his charge, I had him whipped; if you doubt me, look at his back.

1st Chan.—It is very true; and a scorched slave will set anything on fire.

Stha.—Alas! this is the curse of slavery, to be disbelieved even when we speak the truth. Worthy Charudatta, I can do no more. (*Falls at his feet.*)

Char.—Rise, thou who feelest for a good man's fall,
And com'st a virtuous friend to the afflicted.
Grieve not thy cares are vain. Whilst destiny
Forbids my liberation, all attempts
Like thine will profit nothing.

1st Chan.—As your honour has already chastised this slave, you should let him go.

Sams.—Come, come. What is this delay, why do you not despatch this fellow?

1st Chan.—If you are in such haste, sir, you had better do it yourself.

Roha.—Kill me and let my father live.

Sams.—Kill both; father and son perish together.

Char.—All answers to his wish. Return, my child,
Go to thy mother, and with her repair
To some asylum, where thy father's fate
Shall leave no stain on thee. My friend conduct them
Hence without delay.

Mait.—Think not, my dear friend, that I intend to survive you.

Char.—My good Maitreya, the vital spirit owes not
Obedience to our mortal will : beware
How you presume to cast that life away .
It is not thine to give or to abandon.

Mait.—*(Apart.)* It may not be right, but I cannot bear to live when he is gone. I will go to the Brahman's wife, and then follow my friend. *(Aloud.)* Well, I obey ; this task is easy. *(Falls at his feet, and rising, takes the child in his arms.)*

Sams.—Holloa ! did I not order you to put the boy to death along with his father? *(Charudatta expresses alarm.)*

1st Chan.—We have no such orders from the Raja,—away, boy, away. *(Forces off Maitreya and Rohasena.)* This is the third station, beat the drum, and proclaim the sentence. *(As before.)*

Sams.—*(Apart.)* The people seem to disbelieve the charge. *(Aloud.)* Why, Charudatta, the townsmen doubt all this ; be honest ; say at once, "I killed Vasantasena." *(Charudatta continues silent.)* Ho ! Chandala, this vile sinner is dumb ; make him speak : lay your cane across his back.

2nd Chan.—Speak Charudatta. *(Strikes him.)*

Char.—Strike ! I fear not blows ; in sorrow plunged,
Think you such lesser ills can shake my bosom ?

Alone I feel the flame of men's reports,
The foul assertion that I slew my love.

Sams.—Confess, confess!

Char.—My friends and fellow-citizens, ye know me.

Sams.—She is murdered.

Char.—Be it so.

1st Chan.—Come; the execution is your duty.

2nd Chan.—No, it is yours.

1st Chan.—Let us reckon. *(They count.)* Now, if it be my turn, I shall delay it as long as I can.

2d. Chan.—Why?

1st. Chan.—I will tell you:—my father, when about to depart to heaven, said to me, "Son, whenever you have a culprit to execute, proceed deliberately; never do your work in a hurry; for, perhaps some, worthy character may purchase the criminal's liberation; perhaps a son may be born to the Raja, and a general pardon be proclaimed; perhaps an elephant may break loose and the prisoner escape in the confusion; or, perhaps, a change of rulers may take place, and every one in bondage be set at large."

Sams.—*(Apart.)* A change of rulers!

1st. Chan.—Come, let us finish our reckoning.

Sams.—Be quick, be quick! get rid of your prisoner. *(Retires.)*

1st. Chan.—Worthy Charudatta, we but discharge our duty; the king is culpable, not we, who must obey his orders; consider—have you anything to say?

Char.—If virtue yet prevail, may she who dwells
Amongst the blest above, or breathes on earth,
Clear my fair fame from the disastrous spots
Unfriendly fate and man's accusing tongue
Have fixed upon me—whither do you lead me

1st. Chan.—Behold the place, the southern cemetry, where criminals quickly get rid of life. See, where jackals feast upon one-half of the mangled body, whilst the other yet grins ghastly on the pointed stake!

Char.—Alas, my fate! (*Sits down.*)

Sams.—I shall not go till I have seen his death. How—sitting!

1st. Chan.—What! are you afraid, Charudatta?

Char.—(*Rising.*) Of infamy I am, but not of death.

1st, Chan.—Worthy sir, in heaven itself the sun and moon are not free from change and suffering: how should we, poor weak mortals, hope to escape them in this lower world: one man rises but to fall, another falls to rise again; and the vesture of the carcase is at one time laid aside, and at another resumed: think of these things, and be firm. This is the fourth station: proclaim the sentence. (*Proclamation as before.*)

Enter the SRAMANAKA *and* VASANTASENA.

Sram.—Bless me, what shall I do? Thus leading

Vasantasena, am I acting conformably to the laws of my order? Lady, whither shall I conduct you?

Vas.—To the house of Charudatta, my good friend;

His sight will bring me back to life, as the bright moon
Revives the leaflets of the drooping flower.

Sram.—Let us get into the high road: here it is. Hey! what noise is this?

Vas.—And what a crowd is here!—inquire the cause;

For all Ujjayin is gathered on one spot,
And earth is off its balance with the load.

1st. Chan.—This is the last station proclaim the sentence. (*Proclamation as before.*) Now, Charudatta' forgive us; all will soon be over

Char.—The gods are mighty.

Sram.—Lady! lady! they say here you have been murdered by Charudatta, and they therefore going to put him to death.

Vas. Unhappy wretch! that I should be the cause
Of so much danger to my Charudatta.
Quick! lead me to him.

Sram.—Quick, lady; worthy servant of Buddha, hasten to save Charudatta. Room, good friends; make way.

Vas.— Room! room! (*Pressing through the crowd.*)

1st. Chan.—Remember, worthy Charudatta, we but obey the king's commands; the sin is his, not ours.

Char.—Enough! perform your office.

1st Chan.—(*Draws his sword.*) Stand straight, your face upwards, and one blow sends you to heaven. (*Charudatta obeys, the Chandala goes to strike, and drops his sword.*) How? I held the hilt firmly in my grasp! yet the sword, as unerring as a thunder-bolt, has fallen on the ground! Charudatta will escape; it is a sure sign. Goddess of the Sahya hills, be pleased to hear me! If Charudatta be yet set free, the greatest favour will be conferred upon the whole Chandala race.

2nd Chan.—Come, let us do as we are ordered.

1st Chan.—Be it so. (*They are leading Charudatta to the stake, when Vasantasena rushes through the crowd.*)

Vas.—Forbear, forbear! in me behold the wretch
For whom he dies!

1st Chan.—Hey! who is this that with dishevelled locks and uplifted arms calls us to forbear?

Vas.—Is it not true, dear, dearest Charudatta? *Throws herself on his bosom.*)

Sram.—Is it not true, respected Charudatta? (*Falls at his feet.*)

1st Chan.—Vasantasena! The innocent must not perish by our hands.

Sram.—He lives! Charudatta lives!

1st Chan.—May he live a hundred years!

Vas.—I revive.

1st Chan.—Away! bear the news to the king; he is at the public place of sacrifice (*Some go out.*)

Sams.—(*Seeing Vasantasena,*) Alive still! Who has done this? I am not safe here, and must fly.

[*Exit.*

1st Chan.—(*To the other.*) Hark ye, brother, we were ordered to put to death the murderer of Vasantasena: we had better therefore secure the Raja's brother-in-law,

2nd Chan.—Agreed; let's follow him. [*Exeunt.*

Char.—Who thus, like showers to dying grain, has come
To snatch me from the uplifted sword and face
Of present death? Vasantasena,
Can this be she? or has another form
Like hers from heaven descended to my succour?

Am I awake, or do my senses wander—
Is my Vasantasena still alive?
Speeds she from spheres divine, in earthly charms
Arrayed again, to save the life she loved,
Or comes some goddess in her beauteous likeness?

Vas.—(*Falls at his feet.*)
You see herself, the guilty cause that brought
This sad reverse upon thy honoured course.

Char.—(*Taking her up and looking at her.*)
My love, Vasantasena, is it thou?

Vas.—That ill-starred wretch.

Char.—Vasantasena—can it—can it be?
And why these starting tears?—away with grief!
Didst thou not come, and like the wondrous power
That brings back life to its deserted source,
Redeem triumphant from the grasp of death
This frame to be henceforward all thine own
Such is the source of love omnipotent,
Who calls the very dead to life again!
Behold, my sweet, these emblems, that so late
Denoted shame and death, shall now proclaim
A different tale, and speak our nuptial joy—
This crimson vesture be the bridegroom's garb,
This garland be the bride's delightful present,
And this brisk drum shall change its mournful sounds
To cheerful tones of marriage celebration.

Vas.—Ingenious ever is my lord's device.

Char.—Thy plotted death, dear girl, was my sad doing.
The Raja's brother has been long my foe;
And in his hate, which future doom will punish,
He sought, and partly worked his will, my fall.

Vas.—Forbear, not utter such ill-omened words.
By him, and him alone, my death was purposed.

Char.—And who is this?

Vas.—To him I owe my life:
His seasonable aid preserved me.

Char.—Who art thou, friend?

Sram.—Your honour does not recollect me. I was employed as your personal servant: afterwards becoming connected with gamblers, and unfortunate, I should have been reduced to slavery, had not this lady redeemed me. I have since then adopted the life of a mendicant; and coming in my wanderings to the Raja's garden, was fortunately enabled to assist my former benefactress.

(Behind.) Victory to Vrishabhaketu, the despoiler of Daksha's sacrifice! glory to the six-faced scatterer of armies, the foe of Krauncha! Victory to Aryaka, the subjugator of his adversaries, and triumphant monarch of the wide-spread, mountain bannered earth!

Enter SARVILAKA.

This hand has slain the king, and on the throne
Of Palaka ascends our valiant chief,
Resistless Aryaka, in haste anointed.
Now to obey his first commands, and raise
The worthy Charudatta far above
Calamity and fear. All is achieved—

Of valour and of conduct destitute
The foe has fallen—the citizens behold
Well pleased the change, and thus has noble
daring
Wrested an empire from its ancient lords,
And won a sway as absolute on earth
As that which Indra proudly holds in heaven.
This is the spot ;—he must be near at hand
By this assemblage of the people. Well
begins
The reign of Aryaka, if his first cares
Reap the rich fruit of Charudatta's life.
Give way, and let me pass; 'tis he—he lives —
Vasantasena too !—my monarch's wish
Is all accomplished. Long this generous
Brahman,
Has mourned his sullied brightness like the
moon
That labours in eclipse, but now he bounds
Again to honour and to happiness,
Borne safely o'er a boundless sea of troubles
By firm affection's bark, and favouring fate.
How shall I, sinner as I am, approach
Such lofty merit ; yet the honest purpose
Is everywhere a passport. Charudatta,
Hail, most worthy sir !

[*Joins his hands and raises them to his forehead.*

Char.—Who thus addresses me ?

Sar.—In me behold
The plunderer, that desperate forced his way
By night into your mansion, and bore off
The pledge intrusted to your care : I come
To own my fault and throw me on your mercy.

Char.—Not so, my friend, you may demand my thanks. (*Embraces him.*)

Sar.—And further I inform you, that the king,
The unjust Palaka, has fallen a victim,
Here in the place of sacrifice, to one
Who has avenged has wrongs and thine ; to Aryaka,
Who ready homage pays to birth and virtue.

Char.—How say you ?

Sar.—That the fugitive,
Whom late your car conveyed in safety hence,
Has now returned, and in the place of offering
Slain Palaka as a victim.

Char.—I rejoice
In his success—it was to you he owed
Escape from his confinement.

Sar.—But to you
Escape from death ; and to requite his debt
He gives to your authority in Ujjayin,
Along the Vena's borders, Kusavati—
A proof of his esteem and gratitude.

(*Without.*) Bring him along ! bring him along !

the Raja's villainous brother-in-law (*Samsthanaka, his arms tied behind him, dragged on by the mob.*)

Sams.—Alas, alas! how am I maltreated, bound and dragged along as if I were a restive ass, or a dog, or any brute beast. I am beset by the enemies of the state; whom can I fly to for protection?—yes, I will have recourse to him. (*Approaches Charudatta.*) Preserve me. (*Falls at his feet.*)

Mob.—Let him alone, Charudatta; leave him to us; we'll dispatch him.

Sams.—Oh, pray Charudatta!—I am helpless, I have no hope but you.

Char.—Banish your terror:—they that sue for mercy
Have nothing from their foes to dread.

Sar.—Hence with the wretch!
Drag him from Charudatta. Worthy sir,
Why spare this villain? Bind him, do you hear,
And cast him to the dogs; saw him asunder;
Or hoist him on the stake: dispatch, away

Char.—Hold, hold! may I be heard?

Sar.—Assuredly.

Sams.—Most excellent Charudatta, I have flown to you for refuge; oh, protect me! spare me now, I will never seek your harm any more.

Mob.—Kill him, kill him! why should such a wretch be suffered to live? (*Vasantasena takes the garland off Charudatta's neck, and throws it round Samsthánakd's.)*

Sams.—Gentle daughter of a courtezan, have pity upon me: I will never kill you again, never, never!

Sar.—Give your commands, sirs, that he may be removed, and how we shall dispose of him.

Char.—Will you obey in what I shall enjoin?

Sar.—Be sure of it.

Char.—In truth?

Sar.—In very truth.

Char.—Then for the prisoner—

Sar.—Kill him.

Char.—Set him free.

Sar.—Why so?

Char.—An humbled foe, who prostrate at your feet
Solicits quarter, must not feel your sword.

Sar.—Admit the law, then give him to the dogs.

Char.—Not so!
His punishment be mercy.

Sar.—You move my wonder, but shall be obeyed.
What is your pleasure?

Char.—Loose him, and let him go.

Sar.—He is at liberty. *(Unties him.)*

Sams.—Huzza! I am again alive.

(Without.) Alas, alas! the noble wife of Charudatta, with her child vainly clinging to her raiment, eseks to enter the fatal fire, in spite of the entreaties of the weeping crowd.

Enter CHANDANAKA.

Sar.—How now, Chandanaka, what has chanced?

Chan.—Does not your excellency see yon crowd collected on the south of the royal palace? There the wife of Lharudatta is about to commit herself to the flames; I delayed the deed by assuring her that Charudatta was safe; but who in the agonies of despair is susceptible of consolation or confidence?

Char.—Alas! my love, what frantic thought is this!

Although thy widowed virtues might disdain
The abject earth, yet, when to heaven transported,
What happiness canst thou enjoy, whilst yet
The husband's presence fails his faithful bride. (*Faints.*)

Sar.—Out on this folly! we sould fly to save
The dame, and he is senseless—all conspires
To snatch from our exertions this reward.

Vas.—Dear Charudatta, rouse thy fainting soul;
Haste to preserve her; want not firmness now,
Or all is unavailing.

Char.—Where is she?
Speak love! where art thou?—answer to my call.

Chan.—This way, this way! [*Exeunt.*

SCENE—*The* WIFE *of* CHARUDATTA, ROHASENA *holding her garment,* MAITREYA *and*

RADANIKA—*The fire kindled.*

Wife.—Loose me, my child! oppose not my desires,
I cannot live and hear my lord defamed.

Roha.—Hold! my dear mother; think of me your child;
How shall I learn to live, deprived of you?

Mait.—Lady, forbear! your purpose is a crime:—our holy laws declare it sinful for a Brahman's wife to mount a separate pile.

Wife.—Better I sin than hear my husband's shame—
Remove my boy; he keeps me from the flames.

Rad.—Nay, madam; I would rather give him help.

Mait.—Excuse me: if you determine to perish, you must give me precedence; it is a Brahman's duty to consecrate a funeral fire.

Wife.—What! neither listen to me! My dear child,
Remain to offer to your helpless parents
The sacred rites they claim from filial duty.
Alas! you know no more a father's care.

Char.—(*Coming forward and takes his Child in arms.*)
His father still will guard him.

Wife.—His voice! his form!—it is my lord, my love.

Roha.—My father holds me in his arms again. Now, mother, you are happy.

Char.—(*Embraces his Wife.*)

My dearest love, what frenzy drove thy mind
To seek destruction whilst thy lord survived?
Whilst yet the sun rides bright along the sky
The lotus closes not its amorous leaves.

Wife.—True, my loved lord; but then his glowing kisses
Give her glad consciousness her love is present.

Mait.—And do these eyes really see my dear friend once more? The wonderful effect of a virtuous wife! Her purpose of entering the fire has reunited her with her lord. Long life to Charudatta.

Char.—My dear, my faithful friend. (*Embraces him.*)

Rad.—Sir, I salute you. (*Falls at his feet.*)

Char.—Rise, good Radanika. (*Puts his hand upon her shoulder.*)

Wife.—*To Vasantasena.*) Welcome, happy sister!

Vas.—I now indeed am happy. (*They embrace.*)

Sar.—You are fortunate in your friends.

Char.—To you I owe them.

Sar.—Lady Vasantasena, with your worth
The king is well acquainted, and requests
To hold you as his kinswoman.

Vas.—Sir, I am grateful. (*Sarvalika throws a veil over her.*)

Sar.—What shall we do for this good mendicant?

Sar.—Speak, Sramanaka, your wishes.

Sram.—To follow still the path I have selected,
For all I see is full of care and change.

Char.—Since such is his resolve, let him be made
Chief of the monasteries of the Bauddhas.

Sar.—It shall be so.

Sram.—It likes me well.

Sar.—Sthavaraka remains to be rewarded.

Char.—Let him be made a free man;—slave no more.
For these Chandalas let them be appointed
Heads of their tribe; and to Chandanaka
The power the Raja's brother-in-law abused
To his own purposes, be now assigned.

Sar.—As you direc: is there ought else? command.

Char.—Nought but this.
Since Aryaka enjoys the sovereign sway,
And holds me as his friend;—since all my foes
Are now destroyed, save one poor wretch released,
To learn repentance for his former faults,
Since my fair fame again is clear, and this
Dear girl, my wife, and all I cherish most,
Are mine once more, I have no further suit
That asks for your indulgence, and no wish
That is not gratified. Fate views the world
A scene of mutual and perpetual struggle.
And sports with life as if it were the wheel
That draws the limpid waters from the well.

For some are raised to affluence, some depressed
In want, and some are borne a while aloft,
And some hurled down to wretchedness and woe.
Then let us all thus limit our desires.
Full-uddered be the kine: the soil be fertile;
May copious showers descend, and balmy gales
Breathe health and happiness on all mankind;
From pain be every living creature free,
And reverence on the pious Brahman wait:
And may all monarchs, prosperous and just,
Humble their foes and guard the world in peace.

[*Exeunt omnes.*

FINISH.